Psychology of Personality: Islamic Perspectives

In the name of Allah,
The Most Gracious, Most Merciful.

Psychology of Personality

ISLAMIC PERSPECTIVES

Amber Haque & Yasien Mohamed

ISBN: 978-1-7372816-2-7 (Paperback)
ISBN: 978-1-7372816-3-42 (E-book)

First printing edition 2009 by Cengage Learning Asia.

Current print by International Association of Islamic Psychology
Publishing
Seattle, Washington,
98102.

Cover design and typesetting done by Raabia Haque.

Contents

Foreword to
Psychology of Personality:
Islamic Perspectives

ABDALLAH ROTHMAN

Our experience of this world is inevitably through the lens of our individual perspective. We are all trying to make sense of who we are, what this life is about, and how we fit within it. This is the condition of the human being and it spans across culture, nationality, geography, ethnicity, and religion. The age-old search for the meaning of life takes many shapes and forms and results in a multitude of answers and postulations about who we really are and what we are here for. Still, at the heart of that multiplicity of perspectives and determinations lies a common yearning for identity.

We are now living in a time when the search for meaning and defining of human purpose has brought forth new frontiers in open interpretations of the self where the individual has full rein to author his or her own identity. We often hear phrases such as 'identity politics' or 'fluid identity' discussed, as postmodernism has created an open playing field for the self to literally define the "self". This phenomenon of self-authorship is no doubt, in part, a reaction to rigidly defined dogmatic assertions of fate and determinism which suffocate peoples' inherent inclination toward freedom. Such restrictions on individual expression are often imposed by social institutions, including organized religion.

While human beings throughout time have certainly used religion as a mechanism for control, dominance, and the wielding of power over individual freedom and identity, the intellectual and spiritual teachings of those very religions contain knowledge and guidance that provide pathways to the liberation and self-knowledge that people seek. Additional to the resistance to the oppressive force of religion's history, many reject the idea of predetermined notions of self and human nature as defined by cosmological paradigms. However, the role of natural disposition in theological frameworks is often misunderstood as a limitation on individual identity whereas it has the potential to offer a path to liberation of the self.

At the same time that religious definitions of the self get a bad rap for sealing the fate of the person based on unseen spiritual factors, the secular psychological treatment of the study of personality similarly ties one's personal disposition to predetermined biological factors. The 'Big Five' personality traits theory promoted in modern psychology positions genetics and heredity as well as environmental factors as determining one's personal disposition. While it is helpful to understand who we are based on our individual characteristics, traits and tendencies, these theories and tools are most useful when they are seen as insights to fuel self-awareness rather than set in stone inevitabilities that fuel a sense of fatalism.

There would seem to be a polarity between a model of personality that measures who we are based on materialist biological factors and a spiritual orientation that posits a soul that transcends biological determinants. However, the two do not have to be mutually exclusive. Indeed Islam embraces both paradigms, a physical and spiritual reality of the human condition. From an Islamic perspective of personality, we do have innate tendencies that we come with when born into this world, and which get manifested in DNA. And at the same time, we have the potential to transcend those tendencies and achieve a balanced personality based on the natural disposition of the human soul (*fiṭrah*). This is essentially the reason for the following of the Prophetic tradition (sunnah), to emulate the character of the Prophet Muhammad (peace be upon him) as the living example of the perfected personality. Thus, within Islam we have a Prophetic personality model in the form of the perfected person (al-Insān al-Kāmil).

Islam gives us a framework for understanding not only what we are meant to strive for in terms of the perfect personality, but a map of how the structure of the soul works in alignment with God's creation, and God's interaction with human beings. Islam also gives us practical steps on how to go through that process of perfecting the personality. Part of that process allows for the freedoms that people so rightfully yearn for. The soul at peace (*nafs al-muṭma'innah*) is one that has found true freedom, the freedom that comes from realizing and surrendering to one's true nature, as a servant of God.

The intricacies and layers to this discussion of the Islamic perspective of the psychology of personality are explored in depth in the chapters of this book, with great mastery over the intellectual tradition that informs such ideas. This book is a timeless and monumental volume that should be, and I believe will now have the opportunity to become, a classic in the growing literature on Islamic psychology. The only reason it is not already a classic is due to the fact that it has been out of print for so long. At the time during my doctoral study there were very few resources for me to draw on, as the literature in English on Islamic psychology was very limited. I searched far and wide to obtain a copy of *Psychology of Personality: Islamic Perspectives*, and luckily found one copy in a random library in Texas, which I was able to have shipped to me on loan to use for my research. Almost all of the chapters in that book were foundational to my own research on the dynamics of the person and the model of the soul in the development of Islamic psychology.

Some of the most influential thinkers in the field of Islamic psychology in the 20th century are represented in this incredible compilation of essays. Names like Muhammad Najati, Malik Badri, Sayed Naquib Al-Attas, and Laleh Bakhtiar make this a thought leadership publication, as well as the editors, Amber Haque and Yasien Mohamed, who are pioneers of the field in their own right. This is a true gem of a book and one that we could not see relegated to the dusty, hidden shelves of the literary abandoned. One of the aims of the International Association of Islamic Psychology (IAIP) is to disseminate research and publications on the development of Islamic psychology theory and practice. We are dedicated to preserving the classical and recent past intellectual legacy of IP in order for current and future generations of researchers and practitioners to continue building on such foundational works, furthering the legacy and development of the Islamic perspective of psychology. We are therefore thrilled to be able to bring this classic edited volume back into circulation, as it is just as relevant and important as it was when it was originally published, and we trust will be for generations to come.

I would personally like to thank Dr Amber Haque and Dr Yasien Mohamed for allowing us to publish their book with this reprint edition and for their generosity and good will in agreeing to donate the proceeds to further the development of the field. All profits earned from sales of this book will go toward the IAIP Fazal Haque Scholarship for Graduate Studies in Islamic Psychology. This fund was set up by Dr Haque in honor of his late father with the intention of supporting upcoming scholars in the field of IP, to encourage the development of high-quality research and scholarship. We are proud to be able to facilitate this noble effort in honor of this noble man. May God accept our intentions, may this be a lasting legacy of charity (*sadaqah jariyah*) for Syed Fazal Haque, and may it bring blessings and goodness to all who benefit from it. Amin.

Abdallah Rothman

Executive Director, International Association of Psychology

Psychology of Personality: Islamic Perspectives

AMBER HAQUE

Personality is a common word whose pervasiveness should not mislead one into ignoring its profundity and significance. Psychologists believe that the study of personality is crucial to an understanding of human beings and that major social problems are substantially caused by humans themselves. Thus, in order to understand human nature and alleviate problematic conditions in societies, a comprehensive study of personality is crucial. No wonder that "personality" is then both the subject matter and indeed the signifier for a branch within the discipline of psychology that is studied and taught in academic institutions around the world.

What is personality? How does it develop? What changes it and why do people have different personalities? These are important questions that need to be asked. But before we venture into these questions, it should be pointed out that the concept of personality is part of the Western lexicon, which carries implications to be considered later. Gordon Allport, a Harvard professor, first introduced the term into psychology in the 1930s. In contrast, the classical writings of Islamic scholars use terms like *"nafs"*, *"qalb"*, *"rūḥ"* or psyche to signify human personality. However, academics are still grappling with the concept of "human nature" which, while controversial at best in most Western writings, we feel is also critically related with the study of personality. It is certainly a paradox that despite immense progress in science and technology, man has yet to come to grips with an understanding of his own nature.

Numerous schools of psychology, including a dozen newer systems that dominate today, explain human behaviors differently.[1] There are many contending theories on almost every aspect of psychology, including personality, that take diametrically opposite positions. This of course, tells us how little agreement, if any, scholars have been able to achieve over the concept and theory of personality. It seems the systems keep on adding and changing due to an increase in new knowledge and experience of these scientists, yet no system is comprehensive enough to explain most facets and aspects of personality in a manner agreeable to Western psychologists. The present situation can simply be characterized as chaotic and revolutionary. Our contention is that if a correct perception and conceptualization of human nature is lacking, any attempt at explaining human personality will be flawed, inaccurate, and perhaps misleading. A theory is as good as the premises and assumptions on which it is based.[2]

Despite most Western academics' contention that psychology is a science, and its study must entail scientific endeavor, their contributions are largely based on human speculation, especially in the area of personality, which, importantly, is least amenable to scientific research. The problems inherent in the definitions offered by mainstream, usually Western, psychologists derive from neglecting the metaphysical aspects that are instrumental in shaping personality. The view of life prevalent in much of the contemporary world repudiates religious and transcendental concepts and insists on the physical and concrete matters in explaining most phenomena, including human nature and personality. The advent of the modern social sciences is partly a result of the struggle between some quarters of the scientific community against the domination of the Church over Western society. While the Church pleaded on deriving truth from divine scriptures, many social scientists emphasized objectivity and experimentation; the eventual success in secularizing the social sciences was itself accompanied by parallel attempts to exclude religious dogmas from the public domain to the private sphere. Ironically, perhaps, this movement was greatly influenced by Kant, who despite acknowledging the power of reasoning, argued that it is limited in comprehending empirical phenomena.[3]

ORIGINS OF WESTERN PSYCHOLOGY

The popular term psychology, which has attained currency in the secular West, is itself derived from the Greek word "psyche" meaning soul. It was only in 1879 when Wilhelm Wundt (1832-1920) established the first psychology lab in Leipzig, Germany, that psychology started distancing itself from philosophy and later called itself a "science". Wundt and other psychologists of his time who were greatly influenced by the scientific approach studied those aspects of human behavior that are affected by some outside stimulus and can be manipulated and controlled by the experimenter. As a consequence, experimental psychology, which became the dominant trend, did not have any room for a complex topic like personality, as it was not compatible with either the subject matter or methods of the new science of psychology. Further key figures include William James (1842-1910), who founded the school of functionalism, which stressed the value of ever-changing conscious experiences and John

Watson (1878-1958), who also emphasized the study of observable behavior. Watson's influence upon psychology was felt well into the 20th century and was largely headed by B.F. Skinner whose demise in 1991 led to a significant weakening of the influence of behaviorism and the rise of cognitive psychology.[4]

In its formative years, the field of psychology was greatly influenced by Darwin's theory of evolution. Scientific psychologists believed that just as the structure of organic bodies evolve over a period of time, so does human behavior. In turn, human behavior should be analyzed as a continuation of animal behavior. Scientists who subscribe to the evolutionary view of human nature theorize that it is not very different from animal nature, and this is because their focus is on the instinctive aspect and not on the spiritual aspect of personality. The materialistic view of personality, which focuses on the material gain of individuals in everything they do, is paralleled and perhaps most powerfully articulated in Karl Marx's writings. This materialistic view is premised on the idea that human beings are in a continuous struggle for the fulfillment of their economic needs, that economics is the sole or certainly most important influence on shaping society and the individual, and that ultimately there are no substantial religious motivations and influences on human beings' behavior. Marx's dismissal of religion as the "opiate of the masses" speaks much of this perspective's unwillingness and failure to come to grips with the importance of metaphysics.

PROBLEMS OF WESTERN PERSPECTIVES ON PSYCHOLOGY

Largely due to the influences mentioned above, many psychologists started to imitate the methods found among the natural sciences and ignored everything that could not be observed and studied objectively. In addition, they sought to project a dominant paradigm as is found in the physical sciences, and ignore the fact that psychology is dictated by multiple paradigms existing simultaneously. Some modern western theorists are extremely critical of this stance of modern, scientific psychology. Jordan (1995) for example, writes: "There can be no doubt about it, contemporary American scientific psychology is the sterilest of the sterile. Years of arduous labor and the assiduous enterprise of hundreds of professors and thousands of students has yielded precisely nothing...The canard that "psychology is a science" has long outlived its explanatory—away usefulness: the unpleasant and discouraging facts must be faced honestly".[5] Norager criticizes psychology by saying that experimental psychology and behaviorism have lived up to the standards of science, but as soon as psychology extends beyond these two positivistic realms, the "repressed past of philosophy and metaphysics immediately returns."[6] Cyril Burt, a British psychologist, also made an apt remark that "psychology lost it soul, then its mind, and finally its consciousness, as if it were preparing itself for an ultimate demise."[7]

Scientific theories themselves differ in their precision and rigor. In the natural sciences like physics or chemistry, the theories are highly developed, the terms used are precisely defined and there exists a consistency among words, signs, and symbols, as well as the events the theories attempt to explain. In psychology, developed theories do exist in psychophysics, cognition, and learning, but in the area of personality, some theories are not at all scientific; instead, they are based on the theorists' personal or clinical experiences. However, it would be wrong to assume that theories lacking in scientific rigor are not useful at all. According to the principle of falsifiability in the philosophy of science, a theory, in order to be scientific, must generate predictions that run the risk of being disconfirmed.[8] Many personality theories fail this principle and hence are not scientific, however, their usefulness cannot be totally denied.

The overbearing conviction of scientists that objective observation alone can yield accurate knowledge led the positivists to eradicate metaphysics from science. The effect of this doctrine went outside the realm of natural science and influenced almost every part of human inquiry under the verification principle, according to which only empirically verifiable assertions could count as knowledge. Thus, to say that "God exists" or "I believe in a supernatural being" is a metaphysical statement, which is meaningless for any science. This is not an atheistic position however: it is simply outside the realm of science according to the logical positivists. Any transcendental expression for science thus became of no literal significance for the scientists. The appeal of positivism was very strong, and science became successful in terms of its material achievements. It then became blasphemous to challenge the scientific methods, so much so that liberal Christian theologians started to examine the New Testament in this "scientific" spirit and reinterpret religion devoid of its supernatural element.[9] However, the neglect of metaphysics in psychology is artificial, because unlike in the natural sciences, the activities of psychologists as scientists and practitioners are influenced by their own personalities including religious beliefs or non-beliefs, and by unobservable factors. It should be noted that despite the neglect of transcendental elements in Western psychology, increased efforts are being made by Western psychologists in the area of psychology and religion. However, the thrust is on understanding religion from a psychological perspective and not so much on considering the innate spiritual nature of man or his relationship with God.[10] Clearly, contemporary psychology contains a bias towards spirituality that reflects the social and geographical (i.e., European and American) origins of its preeminent scholars, and this "Western"-centric perspective needs to be ameliorated by the perspectives of Muslim scholars, for the benefit of the discipline itself, but also for the betterment of society and individuals.

DEFINING PERSONALITY

There is no commonly agreed upon definition of personality in modern-day psychology. Personality psychologists define it differently based on their theoretical orientations and by analyzing only certain aspects of personality. The problem of defining personality emerges from the fact that we are dealing with numerous issues, as personality comprises many dimensions and causative factors. It is as if each theory is a part of the grand puzzle that personality psychologists are trying to solve. Nonetheless, it can be said that most personality theorists attempt to explain at least three questions: what all human beings have in common, what some have in common, and what makes human beings different from one another. These questions generally pertain to uniqueness and differences among human beings and the crucial question of their nature.

The term personality is derived from its Latin root word *persona* referring to a mask. Based on this derivative, personality would mean the outer characteristics of a person. However, most of us would agree that personality is certainly more than the external behaviors of a person. Generally, it is regarded as the characteristics which are enduring and unique to the person. The term personality also refers to other characteristics of the person that cannot be observed. The debate on the issue of what causes us to be different surrounds nature-nurture, freewill-determinism, optimism-pessimism, past-present, uniqueness-universality, and equilibrium-growth.[11]

Allport's definition is generally regarded as quite lucid, and it is quoted in most modern texts on human personality. According to Allport, personality is "the dynamic organization within the individual of those psychophysical systems that determine his characteristic behavior and thought".[12] Allport asserts that personality is the collection of inner qualities that generally remain stable over time but that can also undergo change. This change can be predictable given that the basic nature of all humans remains the same. For Allport, personality is the product of mind and physical endowment, and although it has some typical characteristics it is still distinctive from person to person. Note that this definition ignores the metaphysical determinants of personality that are crucial from an Islamic perspective.

Personality consists of overt as well as covert behaviors. Although overt behaviors can be studied by objective methods, covert behaviors like thoughts and feelings are only intrinsic to the individual and cannot be studied objectively. Often, instincts, and the unconscious realm are seldom amenable to the person himself, making it harder for the theorist to study and describe such phenomena. In discussing personality, we generally refer to the individual differences and the psychological makeup of the individual, i.e., what psychological components does one consist of, how they function, and what influences them. Although these questions seem simple, they often end up in endless philosophical debates providing no conclusive answers unless the questions are examined from a transcendental point of view as given in the Qur'ān.

Although Western and Eastern religious traditions do have their own transcendental perspectives on personality, it is our attempt to provide the Islamic perspective (and not to undermine the perspective of any other religion). Also, at no stage should the Islamic/Qur'ānic metaphysical framework and clinical psychological models be compromised in a process of synthesis.

PERSONALITY FROM AN ISLAMIC PERSPECTIVE

The topic of personality, or in classical terms, *"nafs"* which roughly signifies "self", is extremely important for the students of psychology because this is where students learn what factors influence our behaviors and thinking processes. Muslim students of psychology must review the concept of personality in accordance with the Qur'ānic reality, which is an exposition of cosmic reality. Both the Qur'ān and *Hadīth* shed sufficient light on the topic of human nature, and we should attempt to explore what they have to say about it. For a Muslim, it is important to regard the unobservable and intangible as more valuable than the physical and the concrete that can be observed by the external sense organs because for the Muslim, matter is secondary to the spirit. Knowledge in Islam is based upon the unity of truth, which devolves from the unity of God. Since God is truth and the revelation is His word, the revelation is equivalent to truth also.

In addition, whatever theory of knowledge comes from human beings may or may not be true but whatever is described in the revelation, as the word of God is the absolute truth. The Qur'ān is a description of how the cosmos really works including the nature of human beings (41:53). Rahman points out that when God creates something, he puts into it its nature and the law that governs it, whereby it falls into a pattern and becomes a part of the total cosmos.[13] All creations of the universe follow the laws ingrained within them and hence are "Muslims", submitting to the Will of God. Man is also deeply ingrained with God's laws and given a choice (91:7-10) to follow or not to follow the commands of God. This refers to the primordial covenant given by humans to God (7:172-73) and in order to be true Muslims, they must behave according to the prescriptions given in the Qur'ān.

In Islam, faith is not blind and does not stand above reason, to the extent that Qur'ānic injunctions always invite man to reflect on all what it says (2:164, 10:101, 12:105, 16:5-6, 32:7, 34:9, 35:27-28, 36:77, 45:13, 77:20-24, 88:17-20). In Islam, man possesses a dual nature, as he is both body and soul. However, the body is not as important as the soul because the latter consists of the inner structure of the personality. Among other things, God has bestowed upon man a limited knowledge of the soul or spirit (17:85), and it is through this knowledge that man can arrive at knowledge of God and of all things in the cosmos, including himself.[14] While some Muslim scholars point out that given the nature of this verse, one should avoid delving deep into the meanings of soul and spirit, others argue that this verse was addressed to the Jews who asked Muhammad about the spirit or soul. They explain further that this verse does not categorically say that a Muslim cannot obtain the true knowledge about the nature of the soul, nor does it mean that knowledge on which Islamic law is silent is totally impossible to obtain.[15] The seat of knowledge in man comes from the metaphysical elements referred to in the Qur'ān as heart (*qalb*), soul (*al-nafs*), spirit (*rūḥ*), and intellect (*al-ᶜaql*). Knowledge and *rūḥ* are inherent in the nature of man, and are collectively known as *al-fiṭrah*, which directs man's behavior throughout his life. The Qur'ān alludes to the different ways of gaining knowledge, i.e., inference or deduction, observation, and direct experience.[16]

Muslims believe that God created humanity as His vicegerent on earth (2:30), and men and women can only become that by understanding themselves first and by achieving a personality prescribed by the Qur'ān and *Sunnah*. A Muslim is duty-bound to unravel the mysteries of his nature not only through speculation and science but also through the divine words and attain wisdom by reflecting on the verses of the Qur'ān. Reflecting on the signs of God is also scientific as it is based on observations by the five senses as well as cognitive abilities. This scientific understanding must ultimately transform one's moral nature, without which reflection may not only be futile but also dangerous (30:7). There is a well-known Ṣūfī saying attributed to the Prophet Muhammad stating that "Whoever knows himself knows his Lord". Islam proclaims that man is created in the best of molds, but without true faith and right deeds he is worse than the lowly beasts (95:4-5). The Qur'ān also warns that those who forget God will be made to forget their own souls (59:19), which is true for individuals as well as societies. "Remembrance" ensures a cementing of personality as all facets of life become integrated, as opposed to "forgetfulness", which results in secularization at the macro-level and fragmented or disintegrated personalities.[17]

The collection of articles in this book presents the problems and issues associated with the concept of personality from the two basic sources of knowledge, i.e. the Qur'ān and the Ḥadīth.[18] It is an attempt to articulate an Islamic concept of personality. Western sources of knowledge have been kept to the barest minimum. The articles are written by scholars who have derived their ideas primarily from the Qur'ān, *Ḥadīth* and the works of early Muslim scholars.[19] A few articles were published earlier and may not fit into conventional psychology literature, but they are included here for the first time because of their relevance to formulating an Islamic perspective. The remaining articles were specially written for this volume.

OVERVIEW OF THE CHAPTERS

The contributions have been arranged into three parts, moving from a discussion of cosmic anthropology and the innate disposition, or *fiṭrah,* of humans to an examination in Part II of key concepts of the soul, spirit, heart, and *ᶜaql*. Part III then is concerned with motivation and personality types.

PART I

In Part One on the cosmic anthropology and the innate disposition of man, we assert that the gift of the soul from God to man has shaped certain innate predispositions in him, and his behavior is the outcome of an interaction between his nature *(fiṭrah)* and the surrounding environment. In his "Definition of *fiṭrah*", Yasien Mohamed examines the concept of *fiṭrah* in its linguistic, religious, dualistic and pre-existential dimensions. The term *fiṭrah* is mentioned in an authentic Prophetic tradition that every new-born is in a state of *fiṭrah,* which is a state of faith and original purity and goodness, and that it is the social environment, starting with the parents, that is the cause of the person deviating from this pure state. The author refers to the classical scholars such as Ibn Taymiyyah and Isfahānī, as well as modern scholars, to support the view that *fiṭrah* is a positive concept, and that it is an innate and natural disposition of man to believe and worship God.[20]

In the second contribution by Yasien Mohamed, the classical concept of man and his relation to the universe is discussed by considering the views of the Ikhwān al-Safā, Miskawayh, Isfahānī and Ghazālī on man as a microcosm of the cosmos, i.e., as a small universe in himself. Although they approach this notion in different ways, they insisted on an affinity between man and nature and the existence of common elements between them. Man's evolution, his status in relation to the animal world and angels, and his purpose in the creation are also covered. Implicit in this analogy of man as a small world is the belief that since contemplation of cosmic reality reveals some reflections of the divine, a reflection on the self as a "small universe" would also lead to a comprehensive knowledge and reverence of God.

Malik Badri presents an Islamic critique of secular psychology's explanation of human nature in Chapter Three. The author discusses the inability of the psychoanalytic, behavioral and neuropsychiatric schools to successfully deal with inner cognitive thought and feelings. Importantly, Badri argues this failure is a logical outcome of psychologists' constant attempt to claim psychology to be a "science", thus neglecting people's consciousness, mental processes, soul, and their spiritual essence. He points out that there has been a research shift so that inner cognitive processes are now studied in cognitive psychology, and that psychology has regained its "mind". Yet, modern cognitive psychology falls short of the spiritual vision of humankind as it is still obsessed with the scientific model, limiting itself to the trio of psychological, biological, and socio-cultural aspects while ignoring the spiritual component despite mounting scientific evidence to the contrary of its role in human lives. He opines that real progress in psychology will be achieved only when the concept of soul is brought back into psychology's fold, otherwise psychology will remain "ambiguous, inefficient, and at a loss". Badri quotes the works of John Eccles, who won the Nobel Prize for his research on the human nervous system, and who asserts that the nervous system can only be fully explained by the existence of a realizing soul or in the words of Eccles, a "self-conscious mind". Badri mentions another scientist, Joseph Pearce, who recently showed that the human heart is governed by a higher order of energy (soul): his research indicates that recipients of donor organs demonstrate changes in their behavior which are in accord with the behavior of the late donors. Badri further sheds light on the structure and other aspects of language that determine the way people visualize the world. Discussing the progress in cognitive psychology, Badri points out that if the spiritual/faith factor were added, the discipline would have a greater chance of contributing to healing and purifying human souls.

Shifting from a critique of secular psychology's notion of human nature, the chapter by Mustapha Achoui seeks to advance an understanding of human nature from an Islamic perspective in contrast to the perspective found in non-religious approaches to psychology. He first stresses the need for the discipline of psychology to recognize three dimensions of humans, spiritual, physiological and behavioral. Then Achoui examines in the form of questions, differences between the perspectives of the current dominant paradigms of psychology and Islamic beliefs. Some of the questions raised in this paper are: is man free or is he a determined being; is he absolutely good or absolutely evil in nature; does the individual have a distinctive personality or is there a universality in human nature and personality? The reader is left with a better understanding of both similarities and crucial differences.

The next chapter by Mahmoud Dhaouadi raises awareness of the connection between psychology and sociology in his discussion of Ibn Khaldūn. Dhaouadi examines an aspect of Ibn Khaldūn's thought that is often ignored or not recognized: despite Ibn Khaldūn's positivistic approach to the study of man, society and culture, Ibn Khaldūn has much to say about the importance of personality in shaping societies in his voluminous work, the *Muqqadimah*. He identifies three types of human nature that are discussed by Ibn Khaldūn and notes which kind of personalities led to the rise of the Arab-Muslim civilization and which led to its decline and disintegration. Special emphasis is given to Ibn Khaldūn's interest in the nature of the Bedouin Muslims and their association, in Ibn Khaldūn's mind, with the *fiṭrah*. The chapter ends with the author's view that while humans inherit a human nature of good standing, it is by no means fixed and changes due to external influences.

PART II

The first two chapters of Part II discuss concepts of the soul. Fazlur Rahman's essay introduces the definition of soul as given by Aristotle and two early Muslim philosophers, al-Fārābī and Ibn Sīnā, who were heirs to the philosophic tradition of later Hellenism. These philosophers contended mainly over the question whether the soul is an "entelechy" of the human body. Mulla Ṣadrā, while accepting Aristotle's idea of the soul as an entelechy of the body, rejects Ibn Sīnā's views in various contexts. For Mulla Ṣadrā, the soul and body relationship is unlike any ordinary physical form to its matter; rather "the soul works on its matters through the intermediary of other lower forms or powers" such as, for example, the powers of appetite, nutrition and digestion, and not physical organs like the hands, liver or stomach. Mulla Ṣadrā also emphasized that the soul first emerges as vegetative, then perceptive and locomotive, then transports itself to a potential intellect and finally to a pure intellect. However, the soul is bodily in its origin but spiritual in its survival—the soul actually needs the body as a tool for achieving the existential perfection. For Ṣadrā, the soul at its highest stage of development comprehends everything and resembles God in His absolute simplicity. Ṣadrā rejects the idea of transmigration of souls as well as the view that after death, individual souls dissolve themselves in the ocean of Eternal Being.

In his "Nature of Man and the Psychology of the Human Soul", Syed Naquib al-Attas provides a classical perspective of human nature based on a dualistic dimension of body and soul; the latter is the permanent essence of human beings, which it is their duty to know so that they can find themselves and know their Creator. The author provides a detailed description of the psychology of learning, covering the internal and external senses, the faculties of the soul, and the process of abstraction of sensibles to intelligibles, which is an epistemological process from completion to perfection. Special attention is given to the nature and function of the intellect, which is able to arrive at knowledge of the highest level. Syed Naquib Al-Attas formulates his argument with reference to the ideas of al-Ghazāli and Ibn Sinā, but he has given his own interpretations and explanations in many places. In order to fully comprehend this and the following chapter, readers should have some preliminary knowledge about the concepts of soul and spirit and be familiar with the writings of various early scholars. Since Syed al-Attas' chapter integrates many aspects of human nature and personality that are covered in more detail by several authors in subsequent chapters, the reader is advised to refer to it upon completion of the book for a clearer understanding.

Turning from a conceptual analysis of the soul in the two chapters mentioned above, the remaining chapters in part II focus on the issues of self-consciousness and self-guidance and the role of the human heart in personality transformation. In the Islamic tradition, the concept of heart (*qalb*) is an extremely important dimension of human personality. A detailed analysis of this phenomenon is covered in chapter four by Manzurul Huq. He points out that although psychology lost the importance of all mental constructs with the advent of behaviorism, the recent influence of cognitive psychology is bringing them back into the fold of Western psychology. The author contends that although current scientific methodologies in psychology can act as tools to seek certain aspects of human personality, they are unable to unfold the spiritual basis of human existence and thus cannot give knowledge and direction to guide the real human self. The chapter asserts that the human heart (*qalb*) rather than the brain is the main controller of most major responses. Personality, in fact, depends on the state and condition of the human heart, which carries a transcendental element. Islam refers to this heart as the spiritual heart that rules over the entire body through the physiological medium of the cone-shaped physical heart. Behaviors are but outer manifestations of the psycho-spiritual conditions of the human heart. Concepts like "intellect" and "will" as two distinct qualities of the heart leading to the perception of ultimate reality are described from an Islamic perspective. Special sections explain how *ᶜaql* and *shayṭāniyyah* work through *shahwa* and *ghaḍab* for constructive and destructive purposes and how animal or demonic characteristics dominate personality. The concluding section covers aspects on how *tawḥīd* energizes the heart and subordinates lusts and passions to intellect and revelation, and activates latent divine qualities for growth and maturation.

Similarly, Absar Ahmad also emphasizes that the heart is the main faculty by means of which an individual grasps the truth of ultimate moral and metaphysical varieties. These functions can be disturbed—a condition which the Qur'ān refers to as diseases of the heart—due to a number of reasons. The author explains the nature and etiology of the "diseases of heart" in the light of Qur'ānic knowledge. He notes human tendencies towards placidity, complacency and self-satisfaction, and the more dangerous capacity of self-deception that can lead to the destruction of the inner vision and spiritual vigor and to a "diseased" heart. The author points out that it is not so much the strength of Satan but a failure of oneself that leads to one's destruction. He exhorts that one should be heedful to one's deeds, motives and the inner reality, and not get carried away by the call of some psychologists who enjoin the pursuit of pleasure as the path to real happiness.

In the Muslim world, philosophy has traditionally included the science of ethics, economics, and politics. Traditional psychology is grounded in the science of ethics and can be referred to as psychoethics. One can easily see the importance of psychoethics which Islam propagates in order to evaluate and enhance one's personality. Laleh Bakhtiar explains in her contribution that the nature and the self are both reflections of God's self-disclosure as "Creator." The connection between nature and self is characterized as "nature in its mode of operation." The Divine Guidance has established a means of communication between Creator and the self through signs that are both external and internal to human beings. Understanding of the internal signs can be gained through knowledge, particularly of medicine and philosophy. The author refers to the covenant that humans made with God, and contends that without self-consciousness, communication of the Divine regulations remains indirect, preconscious, or even unconscious. She explains the Divine Guidance as *takwin* or universal guidance, which is part of our *fiṭrah*. However, *tashrī͑* or acquired guidance, which is rational, is sought through the revelations, and she points out that the self is free to follow or neglect *tashrī͑* guidance. A relationship with the Creator can be established through *͑ibādah* (knowledge and actions). Psychoethics is primarily concerned with *amr bi l-ma'rūf wa nahy an al-munkar* as well as the inward struggle of the self or *jihad al akbar*. She explains that in the Islamic tradition the key to knowledge of God is knowledge of one's self, both inwardly and outwardly.

PART III

Part three deals with motivation and personality types from an Islamic perspective. While Western theories emphasize instinct, drive and cognition as tools for human motivation, the Islamic understanding bases its motivational theory on man's relationship with God. In other words, for a Muslim scientist, motivation has both psychological and spiritual dimensions. In chapter eleven, Shafiq Falah Alawneh writes about human motivation from an Islamic Perspective. The author discusses the importance of understanding motivation as a guide for explaining human behavior, and he reviews various conceptions of motivation available within the different schools of psychology. Motivation in Islam, he notes, derives from knowledge both about humanity's origins, and God's and man's relationship with each other and the world around man. Free will and knowledge are important components of human motivations. It is a profound psychological state that influences all forms of motivations. The chapter concludes by identifying the implications of motivation for education and learning.

In chapter twelve, Muhammad Uthman Najati discusses the significance of drives in motivating human personality. While modern psychology had taken a negative and mechanistic approach towards drives, as is the case with Freud, Najati notes more positive interpretations articulated by Maslow and others. In turn, Najati offers an original interpretation based on Qur'ānic references that affirms the role of drives as a means towards bringing the heart closer to God.

Rashid Hamid in chapter thirteen presents what he calls "fundamental and essential constructs" included in the Islamic concept of personality. He sketches the universal characteristics that are displayed by all humans as well as the unique qualities that are specific to an individual. Islam provides man with a divinely ordained culture to promote self-development. Various *sūrah* are quoted in this chapter to elaborate the concept of Islamic personality. He notes that if inner growth is to be realized, God's words must be heeded, and psychology must undergo its own *"tajdīd"* leading to its purification.

Finally, one of the fundamental arguments of Saiyad Fareed Ahmad's study is that most of the problems of Muslims are rooted in their personalities, and any attempt at Islamization and resurgence should of necessity begin with the Muslim personality. As such he discusses some of the characteristics, unique features, qualities and traits of the Islamic personality, and follows this with a discussion of the sequences that are involved in the formation and transformation of an Islamic personality.

CONCLUSION

This volume addresses perspectives on the Islamic theory of personality and encourages recalling the holistic picture of man's nature from the Islamic paradigm. It is hoped that the essays will encourage a process of research to be initiated collectively by Muslim scholars of revealed knowledge and Muslim social scientists who are interested in redefining their discipline based on the knowledge and veracity of their belief system. This process would entail not only drawing upon the transcendental realm of knowledge but also the inclusion of Islamic ethics in the field of psychology, since the practice of psychology includes psychodiagnostics and various forms of therapies in working with different personality types. Unless Muslim psychologists and personality researchers live up to this ideal, they will be deluding themselves and their students with a psychology that is immersed in a materialistic and man-made framework alien to Islam, and which has repeatedly failed in the past to solve human problems. Not that we reject the dominant psychological paradigm entirely. However, we believe a deeper appreciation and comprehension of Islamic sources is even more essential in order to develop a true, and thus, relevant framework for personality psychology.

NOTES

1. See for instance, Noel W. Smith, *Current systems in psychology: history, theory, research, and applications* (Plattsburg: New York, 2001), p. 430. See also a book review of this text by A. Haque, American Journal of Islamic Social Sciences. 18:4 (2001), pp. 143-149.
2. Our intent is not to create a new school but to extend an invitation to all interested scholars to join hands in finding out the intricacies and complexities of human nature and what really ails modern man. It is true, however, that we are attempting to examine personality from a perspective which is broader than what is considered "observable" by modern psychological scientists. The history of sciences reveals that progress consists in confronting problems from various angles. To deny differences in outlook in resolving mysteries is certainly a sign of a non-scientific mind.
3. See his *A Critique of Pure Reason.*
4. For an interesting reading of books related to origins of western psychology, see S.N. Chapman and W.A. Conroy, *Biographical Dictionary of Psychology* (New York: Routledge, 1997) and W.R. Street, A chronology of noteworthy events in American Psychology (Washington DC: American Psychological Association, 1994).
5. N. Jordan. "Themes in speculative psychology", in David Cohen, ed., Psychologists on Psychology (New York: Routledge, 1995), p. 3.
6. T. Norager. "Metapsychology and discourse: A note on some neglected issues in the psychology of religion", The International Journal for the Psychology of Religion, 6 (1998), pp. 139-149.
7. M. B. Badri, *Contemplation*: *An Islamic psychospiritual study* (London: International Institute of Islamic Thought, 2000), p. 7. As early as 1929, Edwin Boring in his presidential address to the American Psychological Association (APA) said, "…Certainly psychology has not been above personal bias. It is true that when psychologists battle, they may hurl Freudian explanations of each other at each other. They may rise with scientific magnanimity against opponents and suggest that falsification is involuntary and unconscious, or that stupidity is inherited and therefore not a matter of individual responsibility. All this is, perhaps, delightfully

scientific, and yet there nevertheless remains in such controversy a seeming lack of objectivity..." "The scientific eye sees dimly when it turns through half a circle to look behind itself. The scientist, it seems to me, is limited by certain paradoxes of human nature and the psychologist shares these limitations with other scientists." See E.G. Boring. Psychological Review, 36 (1929), pp. 97-121. Al-Ghazal[3] also wrote on the dangers of accepting philosophic writings of his time, however; his remarks are very relevant in the case of modern psychology as well: "We approve these works; we give them our confidence; and we finish by accepting the errors which they contain, because of the good opinion of them with which they have inspired us at the outset. Thus, by insensible degrees, we are led astray. In view of this danger the reading of such writings so full of vain and delusive utopias should be forbidden, just as the slippery banks of a river are forbidden to one who knows not how to swim. The perusal of these false teachings must be prevented just as one prevents children from touching serpents..." See, *The Confessions of Al Ghazāli*, tr. Claud Field, (Lahore: Ashraf Publishers 1978), p. 44.

8. Karl Popper, *Conjectures and refutations*. (New York: Basic, 1963).

9. D. Stanseby, *Science, Reason, and Religion*, (London: Routledge, 1985), p. 36.

10. A good example of this is Carl Jung's conception of religion as a therapeutic tool for psychological healing (See his Religion and Psychology). Also, for a recent literature review on the relationship of psychology and religion, see A. Haque, "Psychology and religion: Indicators of integration", North American Journal of Psychology, 3, 1 (2001), pp. 61-76, and "Interface of psychology and religion: trends and developments", Counseling Psychology Quarterly, 14, 3 (2001), pp. 241-253. Also see, K. Loewenthal. Psychology of religion: A short introduction. (Oxford: One World Press: London, 2000).

11. D. Schultz and S. E. Schultz, *Theories of Personality*, 7th edition. (Pacific Grove: Brooks/Cole Publishing, 2001).

12. G. Allport. *Pattern and Growth in Personality* (New York: Holt, 1961), p. 28.

13. F. Rahman. *Major themes of the Qur'ān* (Kuala Lumpur: Islamic Book Trust, 1989).

14. Two eminent neurologists from the University of Pennsylvania have found in their latest research that the human brain is genetically wired for religious beliefs. They call this area of scientific study "neuro-theology". See S. Begley, "Searching for God within", Newsweek, p. 54, Feb 5 (2001). and V. Rause, "Searching for the divine", Reader's Digest, p. 22-27, March (2002).

15. Shah WaliAllah's *Hujjatul Balighah* (The conclusive argument from God), Book I, p. 54. Translation by M.K. Hermansen, (Leiden: E.J. Brill, 1996).

16. S.M.N. al-Attas, *The meaning and experience of happiness in Islam* (Kuala Lumpur: Institute for Islamic Thought and Civilization, 1993).

17. A recent book by M.B. Badri entitled *Contemplation: An Islamic Psychospiritual Study* (London: International Institute of Islamic Thought, 2000) highlights these points succinctly. Also see a book review of this text by A. Haque, American Journal of Islamic Social Sciences, 19:1 (2001).
18. *"Ḥadīth"* refers to narrations from and about the Prophet (pbuh), his family and his companions.
19. Written accounts of works on human nature by Muslim scholars can be traced back to 800AD and then onwards until 1100 C.E. There are several reasons why such materials got lost in the Islamic legacy; but a key factor was the influence of the West on Muslim minds. Recent written accounts on human nature from Islamic perspective in English language are quite rare. For a list of references from the 1980s and 90s, see A. Haque, "Psychology and Religion: Their Relationship and Integration from an Islamic Perspective", American Journal of Islamic Social Sciences, 15,4, (1998), p.115.
20. For a detailed explanation of fiṭrah, see Y. Mohamed, *Human Nature in Islam* (Kuala Lumpur: A.S. Noordeen, 1998). This book developed from his master's thesis under the supervision of Dr. Hofmeyer at the University of Western Cape and the late Prof. Ismail Faruqi.

Part I

Cosmic Anthropology
and the Innate Disposition of Man

Human Natural Disposition (*Fiṭrah*)

YASIEN MOHAMED

n this essay, I shall attempt to explain the meanings of *fiṭrah* (human natural disposition) from classical and modern Islamic perspectives. I shall examine four dimensions of *fiṭrah*, the linguistic, religious, pre-existential and dualistic dimensions. There are at least four interpretations of *fiṭrah*, but I have chosen for discussion the "positive" interpretation, that man is innately good, and the "dualistic" view, that man is innately good and evil. The other two interpretations, namely, the "neutral" view by Ibn ᶜAbd al-Barr (d. 362/972) that man is neither innately good nor innately evil, and the "predestinarian" view held by ᶜAbd al-Qādir al-Jailāni (d. s561/1165), that good and evil have been predetermined from birth, will not be discussed in this chapter.[1]

Classical scholars base their interpretation on the positive view of *fiṭrah*, which accords with the literal meaning of the term. As mentioned, I shall discuss three dimensions of the positive view of *fiṭrah*: the linguistic, the religious, the pre-existential and the dualistic dimensions. For the religious dimension, I shall refer to the views of al-Nawawī (d. 672/1273), Al-Jurjāni (d. 816/1413) and Ibn Taymiyyah (d. 728/1328); for the pre-existential dimension, I shall discuss the views of Sahl al-Tustarī (d. 238/896), al-Rāghib al-Isfahānī (d. 433/1040) and Ibn ᶜArabī (d. 638/1240); and for the dualistic dimension, I shall deal with the views of Ibn Khaldūn (d. 808/1406), Sayyid Quṭb (d.1966) and ᶜAli Sharīᶜatī (d.1977).

THE LINGUISTIC DIMENSION

The term *fiṭrah* is synonymous with *tabᶜ* which signifies inborn disposition or nature. The word *tabᶜ* is synonymous with *sajiyyah, jibillah, khaliqah, tabīᶜah* and *mizāj*. All these words refer to the innate natural disposition which is unchangeable and present in all humans. The linguistic meaning of *fiṭrah,* therefore, does not refer to man's outward behaviour, but to his innate nature, which exists in all humans, and which is unalterable. So, it is the native constitution with which a child is created in his mother's womb and therefore, the state in which the child is born. The literal meaning of *fiṭrah*[2] as natural creation is suggested in the following *Ḥadīth* (Tradition) or saying of the Prophet Muhammad:

> Every child is born in a state of *fiṭrah* (natural disposition). Then his parents make him a Jew, Christian or Magian, just as an animal is born intact. Do you observe any among them that are maimed (at birth)?[3]

THE RELIGIOUS DIMENSION

In this section, I shall discuss the religious meaning of the term *fiṭrah,* and I refer to it as religious because it is discussed by classical Muslim scholars who clearly associate it with *tawḥīd* (Oneness of God) and the religion of Islam itself.

Al-Jurjāni states that *fiṭrah* is the child's natural constitution created in his mother's womb. This natural constitution enables the child to accept the religion of truth, the way of Islam. So *fiṭrah* refers to Islam and being born a Muslim. It means that man is born with the innate faculty to know God. This relation between the human natural disposition and religion (*dīn*) is confirmed in *sūrah* 30:

> *So, set your face towards religion uprightly. It is the original nature according to which Allah fashioned mankind. There is no altering Allah's creation. That is the true religion: but most men do not know (Q. 30:30).*[4]

The fact that Abū Hurayrah used to cite this verse after the above *Ḥadīth* suggests that they both refer to the same *fiṭrah*. The verse refers to *fiṭrah* as something good because the right religion is described as God's *fiṭrah*. Thus, according to Abū Hurayrah, *fiṭrah* is associated with the religion of Islam. Islam teaches that God is one, and so His *fiṭrah* or nature will be characterised by oneness (*tawḥīd*). That is to say, God is unique in His essence and in all His attributes. As it is this divine *fiṭrah* which is engraved on every human soul, every person is born with this natural inclination towards *tawḥīd*. So, man is born with the innate inclination to recognize one God, to have faith in him and to worship Him. If the mission of the prophets is to remind man of God's oneness, then it is also their mission to remind him of his *fiṭrah*.

According to al-Nawawī (d. 676/1277), *fiṭrah* is an unconscious state of belief, which a person acquires at a conscious level through a process of socialisation, depending on his family upbringing and societal influence. If a child were to die before attaining the age of discretion, he would be of the inmates of Paradise. This applies to the children of polytheists as well.[5] This view is supported by the following *Ḥadīth*:[6]

> It is related that the Prophet, may God bless and grant him peace, said that he saw a vision of an old man surrounded by children in front of a large tree. He was told in the vision that the man was Abraham, and the children were those who died before the age of discretion. At this, some Muslims asked, "Messenger of God, what about the children of polytheists?" The Prophet, may God bless and grant him peace, replied, "The children of the Polytheists too".

It is clear from the above Tradition, that all children who were with Abraham; even those from polytheistic parents, were assigned to Paradise. This is because all children who are still of the age of innocence, are pure, and not responsible for their actions until they have reached the age of discretion or sexual maturity (*bulūgh*). However, Islamic law requires that if the children have non-Muslim parents, then they follow the religion of their parents in this world.[7]

According to the Qur'ān (see above), the right religion is the one that teaches the oneness of God, and it is this religion that is in harmony with the innate human nature which is inclined towards this divine monotheism. So, for man to know himself and to realize his innate nature, he must follow this true religion (*dīn ḥanīf*). This religion is Islam, in the wide sense of its belief and submission to God, as confirmed by the verse, *"The true religion with Allah is Islam"* (Q. 3:10).

The term *dīn*, which comes from *dāna* (to be indebted), also signifies indebtedness, and in the religious context it means indebtedness to God who created him and to whom he must ultimately return. To express his gratitude to God, man must submit to Him in worship in accordance with Islam, and by so doing, man will realize his *fiṭrah*. Man's submission to God is termed *ᶜibādah* (worship). This is a conscious submission to the will of God; it is man's fulfilment of the purpose of his creation as God states, *"I have not created the jinn and mankind except to worship Me"* (Q. 51:56). Al-Attas eloquently explains the relation between *fiṭrah* and *dīn* in the following passage:

> This natural tendency in man to serve and worship God is also referred to as *dīn*, with its connotation as *custom*, *habit* and *disposition*. However, here in a religious context it has a more specific signification of the natural state of being called *fiṭrah*. In fact, *dīn* does also mean *fiṭrah*.[8]

According to Ibn Taymiyyah, *fiṭrah* means that every child is born with innate goodness and that is the social environment that causes him to deviate from this original state. Furthermore, that *fiṭrah* is not merely a dormant potential, but an active state of man's inherent inclination to love and know God. Man in this world merely makes a conscious attempt to awaken this given active inclination into conscious reality. Also, the central *Ḥadīth* suggests that *fiṭrah* is a good state, and this good state is the state of Islam, whereas other religious forms such as Christianity, Judaism and Magianism, are the diversions from this original state due to incorrect socialisation. *Fiṭrah* is therefore associated with Islam as submission to God in the wide sense of the meaning.[9]

To conclude this section, the child remains in a state of original purity or *fiṭrah* irrespective of the incorrect socialisation and un-Islamic education he is exposed to. However, when he has reached the age of discretion and sexual maturity (*bulūgh*), he can always *choose* Islam. It is this capacity to make choices that makes man different from the animal. He can be true to his *fiṭrah* and please God, or untrue to it and displease God. There is no compulsion in religion, according to the Qur'ān. So, one who follows the wrong way does not do so because of innate sin, but because he acquires after birth a lower soul (*nafs*) that tempts him to do evil and makes him susceptible to the negative influences of the social environment. I have discussed the religious dimension of *fiṭrah*, which is, according to the classical scholars, essentially a positive view of innate human nature, and which is immutable and incorruptible. A later scholar, Ibn Khaldūn, however, considered *fiṭrah* to be capable of being corrupted.

THE PRE-EXISTENTIAL DIMENSION

In the foregoing section, I have discussed the concept of *fiṭrah* as a pure state in which a person is born on earth. This is man's "existential" state; it is his innate human nature during his earthly existence. In this section I shall discuss the "pre-existential" *fiṭrah*, which means a *fiṭrah* that existed before the creation of man. Classical Muslim philosophers and Ṣūfīs accept the positive meaning attached to the natural earthly *fiṭrah* but tend to place it in a metaphysical context; that is, the context of the "pre-existential" *fiṭrah*. Basically, this concept means that God created *fiṭrah* so that man could come to acknowledge Him as the one God who has power over all things. This is in consonance with man's acknowledgement of God before his earthly existence, when he was still in a pre-existential state of involuntary submission before God, which is confirmed in *sūrah* 7:

> *And [remember] when your Lord brought forth from the loins of the Children of Adam their prosperity and made them testify concerning themselves. [He said: "Am I not your Lord?" They said: "Yes, we testify" [This] lest you should say on the Day of Resurrection: "We were in fact unaware of this" (Q. 7:172).*

I turn now to the view of three classical thinkers who cite this verse in support of their notion of pre-existential *fiṭrah*. According to Tustarī, man sealed a covenant with God long before his entry into this world, when he was still a speck endowed with intellect, and he acknowledged God's supremacy by his affirmative answer to the question, "Am I not your Lord?" The true test of man's faithfulness to the covenant with his Lord is his phenomenal existence in this world. Tustarī states: "The self-consciousness of man derives from the moment of affirmation of Divine Lordship (*rubūbiyyah*) with their first profession of faith".[10] This is man's involuntary submission to God; it is man's pre-existential state, and it is also the state in which he is born on earth. Man's submission in this world, however, is a voluntary submission according to Islam, which complements his innate nature. The pre-existential *fiṭrah* bears testimony against those polytheists and unbelievers who plead ignorance on the Day of Judgement as suggested in *sūrah* 7. Pre-existential *fiṭrah* is man's primordial perfection and the earthly *fiṭrah* is in harmony with this perfect state. The role of prophets is to remind man of the oneness of God (*tawḥīd*), his original nature, and his primordial *fiṭrah*. According to this view of Tustarī, *fiṭrah* may therefore be defined as man's original state in pre-existence, which he still possesses in his earthly career. In his original state, man is a microcosm of the Universal Man (*al-insān al-kamil*) who is a manifestation of divine light in pre-existence. Man in this world is potentially a microcosm of this Universal Man, of this "Light of Muhammad (*nūr-al muhammadī*)". Man's perfection and knowledge of God depends on his faithfulness to the pre-existential covenant, to his *fiṭrah*, by emulating Prophet Muhammad, the primal manifestation of divine names.[11]

Isfahānī does not discuss the Ṣūfī notion of the "universal man", but he is in harmony with the view that *fiṭrah* constitutes the innate knowledge of God. This innate knowledge is not only a condition of man's birth, but a state of man's pre-existence when the whole of mankind had been created with this native knowledge and sense of submission to God which is affirmed by verse 172, *sūrah* 7.[12] Isfahānī also refers to it as man's "general knowledge" (*maʿrifah ʿamiyyā*), which is embedded in the human *fiṭrah*. It enables man to know God through a process of recollecting what is already embedded within his *fiṭrah*. So, nothing can remove this innate knowledge, it can only be retrieved. That is why it is also said: "He who knows his soul, knows his Lord".[13]

The famous Ṣūfī, Ibn ʿArabī supports the pre-existential view of *fiṭrah*; that innate nature unconsciously acknowledges God's existence, oneness and transcendence. Also, that it was affirmed in man's primordial covenant (*mithāq*) with God; an event when God brought forth Adam's offspring and called upon them to testify to His supremacy as suggested in *surah* 7, verse 172. In this covenant lies man's acknowledgement of God's existence (*wujūd*) and his affirmation of his servitude to God alone (*ʿubūdiyyah*). God created man's *fiṭrah* according to this attestation. Thus, the inborn *fiṭrah* mentioned in the *Ḥadīth* suggests that man was originally created pure to submit to God, and not to associate partners with Him, and that it is man's duty in this world to continue in this pure state.

Man's primordial purity should be seen in the context of his primordial existence, not his existential existence, which is subject to material limitations. Man's material nature is the locus of his forgetfulness, but his faithful believing parents will teach him the oneness of God, otherwise man will follow any other religion that his parents adhere to.[14] Just as the slave must affirm the mastership of his master, man, as God's slave, must affirm the mastership of God. Man's servitude to God has to be attested, not only through the verbal affirmation, but also through acts of obedience to the will of God.[15]

THE DUALISTIC DIMENSION

The dualistic dimension of human nature implies that there are two equal tendencies of good and evil within human nature. It does not preclude the positive view of *fiṭrah*, nor does it exclude the possibility of innate good and evil. In its recognition of *fiṭrah* as innate goodness, it also acknowledges a dualistic conception of human nature, which is distinct from *fiṭrah*. This duality of good and evil within the human soul, is dynamic: it is capable of transformation to a higher level in harmony with *fiṭrah*, or degradation to an animal level, with a capacity to corrupt, or even obliterate, the pure innate *fiṭrah*.

Fiṭrah, as a concept, became a useful intellectual tool for the analysis of human nature and its spiritual transformation in classical religious and Ṣūfī thought. However, later scholars, although still believing in it, found the dualistic conception of human nature more useful in explaining the dynamic, dialectical relation between human nature and society. One such scholar is Ibn Khaldūn (d. 1406).

Ibn Khaldūn supported the classical view that *fiṭrah* constitutes innate goodness and that Islam is in harmony with this pure, innate nature. Man deviates from this original good human nature by deviation from Islam. In contrast to the classical perspective noted above, Ibn Khaldūn believed in the corruptibility of *fiṭrah*. He believed that this *fiṭrah* can be corrupted or destroyed by man's corruption of his dualistic human nature. Bad social influences can cause the evil aspect of human nature to predominate, and good Islamic social values can lead to the good aspect of human nature to predominate.

Ibn Khaldūn employs the concept of *fiṭrah* to explain the rise and fall of civilisations. To him, the rise of early Arab-Muslim civilisation was not only due to their strong sense of *ᶜaṣâbiyyah* (group feeling) and Islamic belief, but also to their innate, primitive goodness (*fiṭrah*). This pure, primitive state is best exemplified in the Bedouins, and its corruption is exemplified by the sedentary lifestyle. Religion alone can maintain a healthy dual human nature and bring it closest to its original good state.[16]

There are three levels of human nature for Ibn Khaldūn: *fiṭrah*, dualistic human nature and aggressive human nature. By the aggressive human nature is meant the animalistic side of human nature, which is prone to injustice and destruction. This is the lowest, most depraved level of human nature. When dominant, it weakens the social solidarity of *ᶜaṣâbiyyah* and religious values, and consequently, the human personality of the collectivity becomes so far removed from the original, good primitive state, that the society finally collapses.[17]

Ibn Khaldūn supports the duality of human nature by the following two verses:

"And guided him onto the two highways" (Q. 90:10).

"And the soul and Him who fashioned it well, inspiring it to profligacy and piety. Prosperous shall be he who purifies it and ruined he who corrupts it" (Q. 91-7-10).

Dhāoudī explains it as such: "Thus, human nature has equal inclinations toward doing good and evil. With this even emphasis on good and evil elements, the Qur'ānic perspective appears to give humans a fundamental dialectic characteristic.[18] Man, according to Ibn Khaldūn, is therefore a dynamic creature, constantly in a state of tension and conflict between two opposing forces within his nature. These conflicting forces are the animal and human forces; the former pertains to physical senses and desire for food, and the latter to human reason. Because of this dichotomous nature, man can do wrong and deviate from his original *fiṭrah*, or he can do good and conform to his original *fiṭrah*. As he becomes materialistic and behaves like an animal, his *fiṭrah* will be corrupted. Because of his dialectical human nature, he swings from good and evil, in accordance with the good and evil influences of the external environment. If the external environment is dominated by a sedentary lifestyle; a way of life that deviates from the natural, primitive way of life, and a life that is devoid of Islamic values, then man's human nature will be transformed into an animal and aggressive nature. When this happens, man's *fiṭrah* becomes not only corrupted, but also loses its duality, its good aspect. Dhāoudī states:

Man's animal state appears to mean the lowest level human nature can fall into. With it, not only man's *fiṭrah* state is lost but also its duality.

> Once animality has taken over, the whole direction of man's behaviour changes: that is a clear sign that social solidarity (*ᶜaṣâbiyyah*) and the religious value system have reached a point of no return in weakness and disintegration. ...As such, the disfiguring effect of the materialistic sedentirizing cultural process is not only confined to the macroscopic (societal) structural levels of societies and civilizations, but it undermines the microscopic level (personality of the individual) by setting out a denaturalizing (anti-*fiṭrah*) process on a large social scale.[19]

Thus, for Ibn Khaldūn, man's human nature, in its natural, innate form, is both his *fiṭrah* and his dualistic nature. The good aspect of human nature is predominant, but by no means fixed; it is dynamic and can therefore change according to external influences. Negative external influences can have a negative effect upon man, feeding into his animal nature, which has a decisive influence in corrupting man's *fiṭrah*. In the absence of this aggressive nature, man will retain his *fiṭrah*, and the good aspect of his dual nature will be predominant and in a state of balance.[20]

Ibn Khaldūn is an early precursor of Sayyid Quṭb, who also held the view that man is born innately good, with a pure *fiṭrah*. In this sense, their view is in harmony with the positive view of *fiṭrah*. However, unlike Ibn Khaldūn who held that *fiṭrah* is corruptible to the extent that innate evil predominates over it, Quṭb, like the early classical scholars held that it is incorruptible. The worst that can happen is that man can deviate from it, but not corrupt it as it is part of the creation of God, for which there is no change.

Thus, in commenting on *sūrah* 30, verse 30, noted above, Quṭb states:

> This (verse) indicates the connection between the nature (*fiṭrah*) of the human soul and the nature of this religion; both are the makings of God, both correspond to the existing law, and both correspond to each other in nature and in direction. The same God who created the human heart, also revealed this religion in order to control this heart, purify it of disease and strengthen it against all forms of deviation. He is surely all-knowing of who he has created, He is the Kind, the Aware. *Fiṭrah* and religion are both fixed: "There is no change in Allah's creation". So, if the human souls deviate from *fiṭrah* they cannot return to this original pure state without this [pure] religion which corresponds with this *fiṭrah*. [That is, there is no correspondence between] ... the *fiṭrah* of existence.[21]

From the above passage, we understand that *Quṭb* appears to make a distinction between the original innate *fiṭrah*, which is fixed and unchanging like the pure religion itself, and the nature of the human soul, which changes and deviates from this *fiṭrah*. The problem is that he uses the term *fiṭrah* for both the nature of the soul and the nature of the innate disposition of man. Nevertheless, since *fiṭrah* is fixed and not changing, it cannot be the corruptible aspect of human nature, and in this respect, he differs from Ibn Khaldūn who asserts the innately pure *fiṭrah* but makes provision for its later corruptibility. In Ibn Khaldūn theory, it is the negative aspect of the human soul that leads to the corruptibility of *fiṭrah.* In Quṭb's, this negative aspect causes the soul to deviate from *fiṭrah.* The potential corruptibility of *fiṭrah* in Ibn Khaldūn's suggests that evil can penetrate it, giving *fiṭrah* its dualistic dimension. No such dualistic dimension to *fiṭrah* is discernible in Quṭb's, who situates the arena of introverted struggle in the human soul.

Like Ibn Khaldūn, Quṭb also conceived of a dialectical relationship between human nature and society, and the struggle between good and evil that this relationship entails, both within human nature (or the human soul) and within society. The arena for this dialectical struggle is the human soul as described in *sūrah* 91, verses 7-10. Man, according to Quṭb, has both the constituents of clay and spirit, representing good and evil, guidance and going astray, respectively. Man's conscious faculty enables him to distinguish between good and evil, making him responsible for his actions. The one who uses this faculty to follow his good innate tendency will be successful, and the one who uses it to follow his evil innate tendency will be at a loss. The external influences of divine guidance or Satanic instigation complement the innate tendencies for good and evil respectively. Man can choose between these two alternatives as suggested by the verse: *"We have guided him on the path, either as thankful or thankless"* (Q. 76:3).[22] Because of Quṭb's response to the political challenges of his time, his conception of the dualistic dimension of human nature is reflected in objective reality, in the duality of good and evil in society. The evil is represented by polytheism (*shirk*) and the "System of Ignorance"[23] (*al-nizam al-jāhilī*), and the good is represented by oneness (*tawḥīd*) and the "System of Islam" (*nizam al-islamī*). Man's struggle is therefore both between the good and evil within his human nature and the good and evil outside himself in objective reality. The clay aspect of his nature tends towards the "System of Islam". Man must therefore choose between these two systems.[24]

ᶜAli Sharīᶜatī, the Paris graduate of sociology who inspired the youth in pre-revolutionary Iran, holds a view of human nature which accords with the view of Sayyid Quṭb and Ibn Khaldūn. To him, human nature is dualistic, and it has a dialectical relationship with society, which is also torn between the forces of good and evil, of *tawḥīd* and of *shirk.* The whole of history is a struggle between opposite forces, truth and falsehood, monotheism and polytheism, oppressed and oppressor. *Tawḥīd,* which represents the world as an empire, and *shirk,* which represents the world as a feudal system, are the ultimate thesis and antithesis of all existence. His extroverted reality of historical dualism has an introverted reality reflected in the dualism of human nature. He also uses the Qur'ānic analogy of clay and matter to support his dualistic view of human nature, but extends this polarisation further, making it a precursory phase in his dialectic of the ultimate triumph of *tawḥīd*. The lowliest part of man, clay, is combined in man with the loftiest part, spirit, making man a dual creature with two opposing forces, one that is inclined to descend to mud, and the other that is inclined to ascend to the spirit. Man's free will, which enables him to choose between these two forces, together with his dual constitution, makes of man a dialectical creature: that is, always in motion and in a state of struggle. Sharī'atī employs the Qur'ānic anecdote of Cain and Abel as a metaphorical framework to portray these two antithetical forces that are engaged in struggle throughout history.[25] Note his comprehensive definition of primal man in the following passage:

> Man is a theomorphic being in exile, the combination of the two opposites, the dialectical composed of the opposition of God-Satan and spirit-clay. He is a free-will, capable of fashioning his own destiny, responsible, committed; he accepts the unique trust of God, and receives the prostration of the angels, he is God's vicegerent on earth, but also rebels against Him…He is in constant struggle within himself, striving to rise from clay to God, to ascend, so that this animal made of mud and sediment can take on the characteristics of God.[26]

Dualism is not confined to human nature, but also to 'Ali Sharī'atī's conception of God and the Qur'ān. One dimension of the Qur'ān and God pertains to otherworldly guidance and God's mercy, and the other dimension pertains to worldly guidance and God's justice respectively.[27] Another difference is that his dualistic human nature is not only confined to the human soul, but even extends to the human *fiṭrah*. That is, unlike Ibn Khaldūn and Sayyid Quṭb who considered *fiṭrah* to be pure, Sharī'atī considered it to be innately good and evil.

> The human situation, to use the terminology of existentialism, or the primordial disposition of man (*fiṭrah*)-both terms signifying the dual and contradictory nature of man-can be deduced from the Qur'ān as follows: man is a free and responsible will occupying a station intermediate between two opposing poles—God and Satan. The combination of these two opposites, the thesis and the antithesis, which exist both in man's nature and in his fate, create motion in him, a dialectic, ineluctable and evolutionary movement, and a constant struggle between the two opposing poles in man's essence and in his life. The opposing, contradictory compound—God and Satan, or spirit and clay – that comprises man makes him a dialectic reality.[28]

In sum, I have attempted an exposition of the classical conception of *fiṭrah* (innate human disposition), which connotes man's innate goodness and a natural tendency to submit to God. I have discussed four dimensions of *fiṭrah*, namely, the linguistic, the religious, the pre-existential and the dualistic. All three scholars, Ibn Khaldūn, Sayyid Quṭb and ᶜAli Sharīᶜatī, share the view of the duality of human nature and its dialectical relation with society. They all connect it to the duality of the human soul. Both Ibn Khaldūn and Quṭb not only acknowledged the original purity of the human *fiṭrah,* but they shifted their attention to the duality of the human soul to explain man's dialectical relation and struggle with society. However, because of the animal part of human nature, Ibn Khaldūn made provision for the corruption of *fiṭrah* to the extent that it becomes dualistic. External influences brought about by a sedentary lifestyle leads to a corrupted *fiṭrah.*

As noted, ᶜAli Sharīᶜatī, unlike the other two scholars, also identified duality with the innate *fiṭrah,* whereas for Quṭb, this innate nature remains pure; for Ibn Khaldūn it is also pure, but not immutable. However, for ᶜAli Sharīᶜatī, this dualistic human nature, which is made up of conflicting tendencies for good and evil, is intrinsic to the nature of *fiṭrah* in as much as it is to the human soul. Sharīᶜatī is the only one who explicitly mentions the term *fiṭrah* as an innate state constituting both good and evil.

NOTES

1. See Yasien Mohamed, *Fiṭrah: The Islamic Concept of Human Nature* (London: 1996) pp. 35-81, where the author discusses all four interpretations of *fiṭrah* in detail and argues in favour of the positive interpretation. Refer to this source for an exposition of the neutral and predestinarian views of *fiṭrah.*
2. Edward W Lane, *Arabic-English Lexicon,* 1-2, (Cambridge: 1984) p. 1823; al-Rāghib al-Isfahānī *Kitāb al-Dharīᶜah ilā makārim al-sharīᶜah,* Ed. Abū l-Yazīd al-ᶜAjamī, (Cairo:
1987), p, 113; al-Rā\ghib al-Isfahānī (n.d.), *Mucjam mufradāt alfāz} al-Qur'ān,* ed. Nadīm Marcashlī, Beirut, p. 310.
3. Hanīf, I. M., *Muslim bi sharH al-Nawawī,* Book of Qadar, 16, (Cairo: 1930), p. 207.
4. Majid Fakhry, *The Qur'ān: A Modern English Version* (London: 1997). [Also, for subsequent translations]
5. Ibn Taymiyyah, *Darcu tacarud al-ᶜaql wa l-naql,* vol. 8, ed. M.R.Sa'im, (Riyadh: 1981), p. 382f.
6. Ibn Manzur, *Lisān al-ᶜArab al-Muhīt,* ed. ᶜAbdullah al-ᶜalāyalī, (Beirut: 1988), p. 1109; al-Qurtubi, Muhammad al Ansari, *al-jamiᶜu al-ahkām al-Qur'ān,* (Cairo, 1967), p. 30.
7. Ibn Taymiyyah, *Darᶜu taᶜarud al-ᶜaql wa l-naql,* p. 383.
8. al-Attas, S.M.N., Islam, Secularism and the Philosophy of the Future, (London: 1985).

9.   Ibn Taymiyyah, *Darᶜu taᶜarud al-ᶜaql wa l-naql*, p. 385.

10. Gerhard Böwering, *The Mystical Vision of Existence in Classical Islam*, (Berlin/ New York: 1980), p. 57; Mohamed, *Fiṭrah:* The Islamic concept of human nature, p. 46.

11. Gerhard Böwering, *The Mystical Vision of Existence*, p. 157; Mohamed, *Fiṭrah: The Islamic Concept of Human Nature*, p. 47

12. al-Rāghib al-Isfahānī, *Kitāb al-Dharīᶜah ilā makārim al-sharīᶜah*, p. 226f; Mohamed, *Fiṭrah: The Islamic concept of human nature*, p. 49f.

13. Mohamed, *Fiṭrah: The Islamic Concept of Human Nature*, p. 51.

14. Mohd Sani bin Badron, 'Ibn alᶜArabī on Fundamental Religious Notions: Natural Disposition (*Fiṭrah*), Divine Law (*Sharc*), True Faith (Imān) and Disbelief (*Kufr*)', *al-Shajarah Journal of the International Institute of Islamic Thought and Civilization*, 4: 1, (1999). p. 97.

15. Badron, ''Ibn alᶜArabī on Fundamental Religious Notions', p. 97.

16. Mahmoud Dhaouadi, *New Explorations into the Making of Ibn Khaldūn's Umran Mind*, (Kuala Lumpur: 1997), pp. 108, 113, 117.

17. Ibid, pp. 109-115.

18. Ibid, p. 110.

19. Ibid, p. 124f.

20. Ibid, pp. 108-117.

21. S. Quṭb, *Fi Zilal al-Qur'ān*, V, (Beirut, 1973), p. 2767.

22. S. Quṭb, *Fi Zilal al-Qur'ān*, VI, p. 3917f; cf. Y. Mohamed, *Fiṭrah: The Islamic Concept of Human Nature*, pp. 55-58; cf. '*Jihad and Fiṭrah* in the Thought of Quṭb and Shariati,' Journal for Islamic Studies, Mellville, 1996.

23. By 'Ignorance' here Quṭb is not referring merely to the kind of ignorance of pre-Islamic Arabia, but he is also referring to contemporary Muslim governments that adopt anti-Islamic systems of rule such as Capitalism and Communism.

24. Hamid Enayat, *Modern Islamic Political Thought* (London, 1982), p. 151; cf. Y. Mohamed, *Fiṭrah: The Islamic Concept of Human Nature*, p. 64f. In my book on *Fiṭrah*, I gave the impression that *Fiṭrah* in the view of Quṭb is dualistic, but I have altered my view, and now try to show in this chapter that it constitutes for him innate purity. The dualistic dimension of human nature for Quṭb is associated with the duality of the human soul. I at first gained the impression that this duality is innate, but I found no passage in Quṭb that explicitly connects it to *Fiṭrah*.

25. Ali Shariᶜati, *The Sociology of Islam*, trans. H. Algar, (Berkely, 1979), pp. 13-37; cf. Shariᶜati, *Man and Islam*, trans. F. Marjani, (Houston, 1981), pp. vi-xiv; cf. Mohamed, Fiṭrah, p. 59f.

26. Ibid, pp. 95-96.

27. Ibid, pp. 80-81.

28. Ibid, p. 89.

The Concept of Man as a "Small World"

YASIEN MOHAMED

his article deals with the concept of man as a "small world", that is, man as a microcosm of the world, or, a small version of the universe. We compare here the views of the Ikhwān al-Safā[1], Miskawayh (d. 1030 A.C. 1421 A.H.), Isfahānī[2] (d. 1050 A.C. 1 p/87 442 A.H.) and Ghazālī (d. 1111 A.C. 1505 A.H.).[3] The first two represent an emanationist view of the creation, and the latter two a creationist view. Whatever the differences in their views, the notion of man as a microcosm of the world is the quintessence of their Islamic cosmology. This notion of the human microcosm is also central to Islamic psychology, which unlike secular psychology, acknowledges that the human microcosm constitutes both a body and soul, and that these correspond to the physical and spiritual dimensions of the universe respectively. The soul or psyche (*nafs*) refers to that aspect of man which represents his personality and is capable of being transformed to higher levels of psycho-spiritual being. The soul that liberates itself from matter ascends to God and becomes a tranquil soul (*al-nafs al muṭma'innah*). The possessor of such a soul has an integrated personality with the body and soul co-existing in harmony; he is also a complete human microcosm, living in harmony with nature and with God.

THE IKHWAN AL–SAFA

Islamic cosmology, as exemplified by the Ikhwān al-Safā is based on a Neoplatonic system of emanation, which is based on four central concepts, those of the One, the Spirit, the Soul and the Material world. In this Neoplatonic system, the human species occupies a position at the top of the terrestrial realm, as it is the culminating point of the cosmos. The more basic aspects of the terrestrial realm precede man: minerals yield to plants, which support animals, until the crowning purpose of this realm, man, is achieved, within whom both spiritual and the physical dimensions of the cosmos are contained as the "small world" (*al-ᶜālam ṣâghīr*), expressing in microcosm the entire cosmos. Man was deemed as such because all the dimensions of the cosmos are within him. Furthermore, and in keeping with Neoplatonic thought, when the human soul is liberated from materiality, it is able to return to God, the Creator of both it and the cosmos. This concept of man as a microcosm is integral to the cosmology of the Ikhwān.

What is meant by the concept that man is a microcosm of the cosmos? It suggests that man is a microcosmic form of the whole universe. That is, both his spiritual and physical dimensions correspond to the physical and spiritual nature of the universe respectively. So, every part of the human body can be compared, and even explained, by the various corresponding parts of the physical universe, and every part of the soul can be compared with every corresponding part of the physical universe which has an affinity to it. Thus, the Ikhwan refer to man as a "small world" (*al-ᶜalam saghīr*), which means that he, both his body and soul together, make up a minute form of the large world.

As has been mentioned, man stands midway between the animal and angel in the Neoplatonic scheme of emanation. His angelic or spiritual aspect is mixed up with his animal or physical aspect. The *latter* element makes man an imperfect creature. But even this imperfect aspect emanates from the One, albeit a lower form of existence. It therefore reflects the One imperfectly. It is by virtue of man's spiritual aspect that he is able to transcend the lower levels of his microcosmic reality and evolve spiritually towards the One. So, when the human soul is liberated from materiality, it is able to return to God. The concept of man as a "small world" became an integral part of the Ikhwān's cosmological doctrine. In describing how various parts of man correspond to various parts of the universe, the Ikhwān demonstrated the connectedness between man and nature. They asserted that the universe is too large for man to study, and that man need only look to himself, and he will find all the elements of the universe within him, that is, in his body and soul.[4] By man coming to realize himself as a small world, he will not only know the world, but also God. The whole universe has been created to serve man's innate urge to return to the Creator, which means that he should develop a positive and respectful attitude to all aspects of the universe. The Ikhwān therefore went to great lengths to describe in precise detail the resemblance between man and various parts of the universe. His body is a prototype of the physical world (including planets, minerals, plants and animals) and his soul is a prototype of the spiritual world (including angels, jinns and demons).[5]

Know, when the ancient sages looked at this physical world with their eyes, and witnessed its phenomena with their senses, and contemplated upon its states with their intellects, and examined the conduct of the (unique) individualities from the general (species) with their insight, and learn from the arts of its particulars by their reflection, they could not find any part of it more complete in frame, or perfect in form, or more analogous to anything else, than man. Since man is altogether a combination of a physical body and a spiritual soul, they found in the constitution of his bodily frame prototypes of all the existents in the physical world... [of its spheres, planets, elements, minerals, plants and animals]. They also found the prototype of spiritual creation of its angels, jinns, man and devils, and the souls of the rest of animals, and the powers of creation act freely in the world; they are analogous to the human soul and its powers act freely upon the body. When these matters of the picture of man became clear to them, they named him a small world (*al-ᶜālam ṣâghīr*).[6]

The Ikhwān draw analogies between man's body and the physical world:

The frame of his body can be compared to the earth: the bones to mountains, the marrow to minerals, the belly to the sea, the intestines to the rivers, the veins to the streams, the flesh to the earth and the hair to plants, the skin where hair grows is like good land, and where no hair grows is like bad land. Man's front corresponds to the east, his back to the west, his right side to the south and his left side to the north. His breathing is like the wind, his speech like thunder, his voice like the bolt of lightning, his laughter like daylight, and his weeping like rain, his despair and grief, like the darkness of night, his sleep is like death; the days of his childhood are like the days of spring, the days of his youth are like the days of summer, his middle-age is like the days of autumn, and his old-age is like the movements of the planets and their turning. Birth and man's appearance are like the rising, his death and disappearance are like the descending.[7]

Thus, the Ikhwān refer to the world as the "big man" (*īnsān kabīr*), since its parts correspond, at a macrocosmic level, with the parts of the small man (*īnsān ṣâghīr*). The authors cite many other analogies to illustrate the similarity between man and the world. The interconnections between the universal bodies (simple and complex) and particular bodies in the world are also compared with the government of a city state.[8] The above quotations give us a sense of the way the Ikhwān saw man as a microcosm of the universe. Such perceptions of man, which are central to their theory of emanation, emphasize man's affinity with and proper relation to the cosmic world. Furthermore, it serves to make man realize his need to liberate himself from matter and become a true microcosm. By so doing, he will realize his true essence, return to God, and complete the chain of being.

Man's true soul will achieve perfection as part of the cosmos, which is gradually unfolding according to a Neoplatonic scheme of creation. Within this scheme, man seeks to return to his ontological point of origin, God. This is man's spiritual ascent towards perfection. His original descent from divine perfection, which involves a certain level of terrestrial imperfection, is the providential fate of all things. This descent to imperfection is irreversible for all creatures, but not for man. Man has been endowed with reason, which enables him to rectify his imperfection, and to aid his soul's ascent to the One. This process does not merely involve a rational apprehension of cosmological realities, but it requires the knowledge and practice of the good. Man's rational faculty enables him to transcend matter, including the body, which is inferior to the soul. Reason enables man to transform his soul to a level of ontological superiority.

Thus, the body and soul are aspects of the human microcosm and refer to the terrestrial and celestial dimensions of the cosmos respectively. The rational aspect of this human anthropology makes it possible to apprehend the meeting point between the Neoplatonic geography of the cosmos and the moral anthropology of the human microcosm. The Ikhwān's theory of cosmic emanation influenced later Arabic writers such as Miskawayh, and their concept of man as a microcosm of the universe became a recurring theme in the writings of Miskawayh, Isfahānī and Ghazālī.

MISKAWAYH

Miskawayh adopted from the Ikhwān their concept of man as a microcosm and their emanationist theory of the universe. Although the two concepts are related, we will deal mainly with their view of man as a microcosm of the universe.

The concept of man as a microcosm is not new in the Ikhwān and Miskawayh; it has its roots in Neoplatonic sources,9 Miskawayh adopted this idea from the Ikhwān, but he was less concerned about giving detailed analogies between the various aspects of man and the various aspects of the cosmos.

Man as a microcosm, with all the various aspects of his body and soul, resembles various parts of the cosmos. He has to transcend the lower forms of his nature to progress in his spiritual evolution towards God. In chapters 2 and 3 of the *Fawz al-asḡhar*, Miskawayh views man as a microcosm of the world, and states that man has parallels with four elements in the world:

Man is a small world (*ᶜalamun ṣâghīrun*) and his faculties are inter-connected. He has parallels to all that is in the big world (*ᶜālamun kabīrun*): to the four elements in the inhabited and uninhabited worlds; on land, sea and mountain; and to inanimate objects, plants and animals, as though he were an abridgement and composition of all that is in it. Some parallels are apparent, and some are hidden and obscure.[11]

Unlike the Ikhwān, Miskawayh does not provide details of how the elements of the human microcosm resemble the cosmic elements. His statement is general, to show that man as "a small world" reflects the whole universe, and that the key to his happiness lies in realizing his small world. This is the key to his ethical theory. Man's cognitive perfection is explained in terms of contact (*ittiṣâl*) with the intelligible world; this is when he becomes a microcosm of the world:

> You become a world apart, and you deserve to be called a small world (microcosm), because the forms of all existing entities would have become realized within you, so that you would have become in a sense identical with them. By your actions you will have arranged them in order in the measure of your capacity, and you will thus become, with respect to them, a deputy of thy Lord, the Creator of all things   you will then constitute a complete world   your perfection will have made you ready to receive the divine emanation forever and always you will have come so close to God that no veil should then separate you from Him   This is the highest rank and extreme happiness. Were it not possible for the individual person to achieve this rank in himself... he would have been in the same condition as the individuals of the other animals or as the individual plant... It would have been impossible for him to achieve eternal existence and everlasting bliss by coming close to God.[12]

As a true microcosm, then, man will attain ultimate happiness, but he must first perfect himself morally, and must therefore rise above sensory pleasures. By so doing, he joins the higher spiritual realm (*al-mala' al-ᶜala*) and receives the illumination of the divine light. He partakes of divine perfection, becoming godlike. Miskawayh concludes that this happiness accords with the love of God, which only the truly virtuous and happy man can attain.[13] Man will then transcend his mortal self and live a divine life.[14] This conception of man as a microcosm of the whole universe is most concisely expressed by Miskawayh, who states:

> When man attains perfection, he performs his distinctive activity upon understanding all existents (*ᶜālim al-mawjudāt kullahā*). Such a man becomes a mirror picture of the world and deserves to be called microcosm (*ᶜālam ṣâghīr*). The forms of all existents will become present in him, and he will become identical to them. He will then become a vicegerent of God.[15]

Man is potentially a microcosm, but by his reason he is able to reach a level where he realizes this potential, becoming a true microcosm. This is not merely a process of rationality and apprehension of reality, but it involves knowledge of the good, and a purification of the soul through the pursuance of good. So, when man fully realizes his potential to be a microcosm, he becomes identical with nature, becomes godlike, and attains supreme happiness.

The concept of man as the microcosm of the world is also identical to that of the Ikhwān, but Miskawayh does not follow the style of Ikhwān, which is to provide detailed descriptions of the affinity between man and nature. Like the Ikhwān, Miskawayh propounds a theory of evolution that has four stages: from the mineral to the plant, to the animal, and finally to man. For man to fully realize the microcosm within him, he has to become identical to the whole of creation, from the minerals to the angels. Without this similarity and connection with nature, man cannot become godlike, nor can he attain supreme happiness. Herein lies the link between man as a microcosm and his spiritual evolution. He has to fully realize his microcosmic state to become harmonious with the rest of creation; his sense of connectedness with nature will enable him to reach the end of his spiritual evolution and attain complete happiness.

Thus, the Ikhwān and Miskawayh have at least four points in common: the concept of the emanation of creation from God, the concept of spiritual evolution towards God, the concept of man as the microcosm of the universe, and the notion that the soul returns to its Creator and attains happiness with its increasing purification from the impurity of matter and worldly pleasures. It is when the rational part of the soul gains supremacy over the lower parts, that man will come to realize his state as a "small world", and then both his body and soul will live in harmony with the physical and spiritual parts of the world.

ISFAHANI

Isfahānī departs from the emanationist view of the world as conceived by the Ikhwān and Miskawayh. God to him is not immanent in the Neoplatonic sense; He is a transcendent God and a personal God to which man can turn directly for guidance. Although God is transcendent, the creation is not detached from Him, but it is a Divine expression, with all its natural, human and supernatural forms. These forms are differentiated in time and space and are not part of the process of emanation.

In this section, we shall limit our discussion to Isfahānī 's concept of man as a microcosm. The following passage shows how Isfahānī adopted the concept of man as a microcosm and placed it within a different context; that is, he believed that man as a microcosm of the larger world is endowed with an affinity to nature and to the cosmos. An understanding of this affinity leads to an understanding of man, of nature, and ultimately of God.

MAN AS A MICROCOSM[16]

Isfahānī adopted the concept of man as a microcosm of the world as he was convinced of man's affinity to nature, the understanding of which is a key to the understanding of the reality of man and God.

> The sages said: God fashioned man as a sensible, intelligible structure according to the pattern of this world, and brought him into being in a way that is similar to everything found in the world, to the extent that it is said that he is a small world, a microcosm of the larger world, in order to guide him to knowledge both of the world and the soul, and thereby to knowledge of the Creator of both. The epitome of man's knowledge of his Creator is to know the world, and know that it is created, and that it has a Creator who is totally other than it—far exalted is God above such a thing.[17]

This is the cosmological way of knowing God. It is a rational way based on the observations of nature. The purpose of creating a microcosm is to know the world: for to know the world is to know God. Knowledge of God can also be achieved through the knowledge of the soul, which leads to both the knowledge of the world and of God. That nature is also the key to the knowledge of the essence of the human microcosm is clearly stated in the Tafʼīl. The human soul as a whole, both its spirit (rūḥ) and its passion, constitutes the microcosm which has an affinity with the elements of the world, and therefore, knowledge of these elements, or existents, is the key to the knowledge of the human soul. Conversely, knowledge of the human soul will lead to knowledge of the universe. Isfahānīʻs reference to the soul here does not preclude the passionate side of soul (and its connection with the body).

Thus, Isfahānī states, "The human soul combines the existents of the world … whoever knows the existents knows his soul". Furthermore (commenting on Chapter 30, verse 8), he states that "if men had to reflect upon their souls they would know the realities of the existents of creation, both transitory and permanent".[18] Therefore, with knowledge of his soul (*rūḥ*), man will have knowledge of the spiritual world and its permanence (*baqāʼuhū*); and with knowledge of his body, man will have knowledge of the physical world and its transience.

Whereas in al-Dharīʽah, Isfahānī introduces the notion of microcosm in the context of the way to knowledge of God, it is in the Tafʼīl that he really expands on this concept in a manner resembling the Rasāʼil. Man as a microcosm is a small model of the big world, sharing similar qualities with the whole world, both respect to his body and soul. His physical characteristics resemble plants and minerals, and his moral qualities resemble the qualities of animals. Unlike the Ikhwān, Isfahānī cites many verses from the Qur'ān to give the concept an Islamic orientation. He states that man is composed of earthly elements: "Who fashioned well everything He created, and originated the creation of man from clay" (32:7). God has combined within man simple and complex elements, making him a microcosm (mukhtasar) of the world. To use another metaphor, he is like an abridged version of a book: the words are fewer, but the meaning is the same. Man is made from the best of the earth; he is like butter in buttermilk, and oil in sesame seed oil. Everything in the world resembles him. His heat, cold, moisture and aridity are like the elements; his body contains minerals, his senses are like the animals, his anger is like the lion, his error is like that of Satan, and his knowledge and worship like that of the angels.

As God has crystallised all wisdom and confirmed His speech in the Preserved Tablet, He has also confirmed it in the hearts of people.[19] Man and the world resemble each other, as it is said, "Man is a small world, and the world is a big man". Man, the small world, resembles the big world, containing minerals, plants, animals, angels, Satan, and the Preserved Tablet of God. Man is also a receptacle for all the good and bad qualities of the world. Distinctive features of all aspects of creation are to be found within man, who can take on these various forms in different degrees and times. He is sometimes as praiseworthy as an angel, and sometimes as blameworthy as an animal or devil. "The potentials united within man make him a vessel for the good qualities of the world: its natural forms, its minerals and its spiritual realities; as a combination of all of these minerals, plants, animals, beasts, devils and angels, he manifests within himself the distinguishable feature of them all".[20]

This kind of detailed description of the material, moral and spiritual qualities of man and their mirror image in the form of plants, animals, devils and angels is absent in Miskawayh's *Tahdhīb* and *Fawz al-asĝhar*. The author's main focus appears to be the theory of emanation and the ascent to the One source. It is however present in the *Epistles* of the Ikhwān, but Isfahānī pays more attention to the similarities between man's moral qualities and the universe.

> Thus, there are some people who are as tyrannical as the lion, as scornful as the wolf, as false as the fox, as wicked as the pig, as submissive as the dog, as collective as the ants, as impudent as the fly, as stupid as the donkey, as meek as the faithful bird, as skillful as the wild ass, as proud as the lion, as jealous as the cock, and who coo as softly as the dove. Some people have a beautiful outward and inward appearance like the citron tree.[21] Then there are the opposite ones who, like gall nuts[22] and acorns, are ugly in appearance but whose inner demeanour is likened to walnuts and almonds. Then there are [also] those who possess beautiful outward appearances but are ugly on the inside, like the colocynth[23] and

the oleander.[24] In relation to animals and insects, the good believer is like the bee that takes the good from the trees but does not pluck the fruit nor break the tree and does not harm another human being. The bee mostly gives benefit to man [in the form of honey] which is sweet in taste and pleasant in smell. In relation to trees, [the good believer] is like the citron tree: its blossom, fruit, wood, and leaves have a pleasant smell and taste. In relation to animals and insects, the hypocrite and the wicked are akin to the louse and the termite, and to plants [surrounded by] weeds without origin, [and are devoid] of fresh air, leaves, shade, or flowers. [Hypocrisy or wickedness] spoils the fruit [that is, the human soul], dries out the trees, and bears fruit that has few leaves, many thorns, and is difficult to reach.[25]

In a manner resembling the style of the Ikhwān, who compared the universal Soul with the government of the soul, Isfahānī compares man with the social and political stratification of a country:

> Philosophers have related many examples of man's essence and its faculties; they illustrate what can only be perceived by the intellect through a sensory picture that approximates human understanding: They said: As a small world,[24] man, as mentioned, is compared to a country-its structure is firm, buildings erect, walls fortified, streets designed, places divided, houses inhabited, paths travelled, rivers flow, and workers employed.[27]

To conclude, Isfahānī adopted the notion of man as microcosm from the Ikhwān using similar analogies. Whereas Miskawayh conceives of the microcosm in the context of theory of emanation, Isfahānī employs it within the framework of a theory of creation. The Microcosm concept is a means to the knowledge of God, and serves to reveal man's ethical qualities with corresponding ethical qualities in the rest of the creation.

The Ikhwān, Miskawayh and Isfahānī share the same view of man as microcosm, but they approach it in different ways. The Ikhwān's theory of the microcosm is viewed within the context of emanationistic cosmology. Detailed and precise aspects of man, his body and soul are compared with the spiritual and material dimensions of the universe. These similes and images of man and the cosmos recur in different forms throughout the *Rasā'il*. Miskawayh adopts the same notion of man as a small world, making it integral to his cosmological world view, but he does not offer any vivid images or similes to illustrate it. Isfahānī microcosm fits into a Qur'ānic scheme of creation: the affinity between man and nature is established through the microcosm, and so is man's dependence on the creation. The notion of microcosm is also employed as a rational way of arriving at knowledge of God and increasing man's faith in Him. Unlike Miskawayh, Isfahānī provides vivid examples to illustrate man as a microcosm of the universe, making the *Rasā'il* the model for his style.

The difference is that Isfahānī's microcosm is not integrated within a Neoplatonic cosmology, but within a Qur'ānic theory of creation. It has practical implications for Islamic epistemology, psychology and ethics, aspects of knowledge which we turn to in subsequent chapters.

COMPARISON WITH GHAZALI

Ghazālī shares with Isfahānī the notion of man as microcosm of the world, and in the *Mīzān* has an identical description of it as in *al-Dharīʿah*. Mention of the microcosm recurs a few times in the *Mīzān,* but Ghazālī does not provide vivid descriptions between man and nature. Ghazālī states:

> Part of God's compassion towards his devotees, is that He has combined within the person of man, despite his relatively small size, the wonders of the world which could be described to be almost parallel to his own wonders, to the extent that he is like a small copy (*nukhah mukhtaarah*) of the form of the world, so that man can reach by contemplating them [the wonders of his individuality], knowledge of God, the most powerful, the illustrious.[28]

Like Isfahānī, Ghazālī also adopts the notion of the human microcosm as a point of departure to get to know the world and God. He compares man's soul with the world, stating that the wonders of man have their parallels in the wonders of the world. Therefore, by reflecting upon the soul one gains knowledge of the world, and hence of its Creator:

> The wonders of the world are composed and created by God. (Since) the parts of the soul correspond with the parts of the world, and these parts of the world are bulging with marvels, the one who examines (these parts) will benefit by having more firm belief and confirmed faith. Thus, God has urged (us) to reflect upon the universe and commanded (us) to contemplate upon the souls, horizons, heavens and the earth.[29]

As mentioned, Ghazālī does not provide vivid descriptions that compare man with nature, but below we find a passage which is not a feature in Isfahānī, where Ghazālī compares parts of human organs to the craftsmen of the world.

> Know, the soul of Adam's children is a microcosm (mukhtasar) of the world. In it, is a trace of every image in the world; his bones are like mountains, his flesh like dust, his hair like plants, his head like the sky, his senses like planets, and the detail of that is long. Furthermore, his interior (*batinihī)* is like the craftsmen of the world. Thus, the strength of

his belly is like the cook, his liver is like the baker, his intestines are like the bleacher (who whitens clothes), and what whitens milk and reddens blood is like the dyer, and the explanation of that is lengthy. Know that all these things are ceaselessly at your service, yet you are heedless, and because you are not aware of them you are ungrateful to He who granted you these bounties.[30]

Since man has both a body and a soul, both animal and angelic qualities, his animal aspect take on the form of certain vices which are identified with the vices of certain animals, including the ox, pig, dog, camel, tiger and fox. And his soul or angelic aspect is akin to his rational faculty by which he apprehends reality. Thus, man's nature is akin to both the animal and the angel, the qualities of his soul could be compared to the animals, angels and the rest of creation. Similar kinds of analogies can be noted in *al-Dharīʿah*. Compare these two passages below:

Ghazālī	Isfahānī
Man has been created on a level between animal and angel. Altogether, he is composed of faculties and attributes. With respect to his nutrition and reproduction, he is like a plant; and with respect to his sensory perception and motions he is like the animal; with regard to his form and stature he is like an engraved picture on the wall. His special faculty for which he was created is his intellect which apprehends realities. One who employs all his faculties to attain knowledge and action is like the angels. It is appropriate to call him a divine angel as God states: *"This is no mortal; he is but a noble angel."* (Q. 2:31). However, if he seeks to satisfy his bodily pleasures and eats like the animal, he will be reduced to a beast and become as temperamental as an ox, greedy as a pig, submissive as a dog, rancorous as a camel, proud as a tiger, sly as a fox, or will possess all of these attributes collectively as a shunned Satan.[31]	But insofar as one only eats and reproduces, man is like a plant. As for the fact that he senses and moves, he is like an animal; and as for his visible form, it is like a picture on a wall. But man's [distinguishing] virtue is [his capacity for] articulation, his superior faculties and their requirements. Thus, it is said, "What is man without a tongue, except a disregarded animal or a form like it?" Thus, man is similar to the angel in respect of his faculties of knowledge, articulation and understanding, and is like the animal in respect to his power of nutrition and reproduction. So, whoever directs his energies towards cultivation of thought, knowledge and action is fit to join the highest ranks of the angels. He is ranked as angelic and Divine-like, as God says: "This is no mortal, he is but a noble angel" (Q. 12:31). But whoever directs all his energy and ambition to the care of his appetitive faculty by pursuing bodily pleasures and by eating like cattle, is thereby only fit to join their ranks. Such a person becomes either as gullible as the ox, as greedy as the pig, as submissive as the dog, as spiteful as the camel, as proud as the tiger, as evasive as the fox, or he combines [all these qualities] and becomes just like the rebellious Satan.[32]

These two passages are similar in content and style. Both compare moral human qualities with animal qualities. In the *Kīmiya* there is a similar comparison. Uncontrolled anger is akin to the dog's behaviour, and uncontrolled desire is akin to the pig's desire. Ghazālī is fond of comparing human vices with certain animals.[33]

To conclude, we have discussed the concept of the microcosm among the Ikhwān, and in Miskawayh (placed within the framework of emanationist cosmology), Isfahānī and Ghazālī (placed within the framework of creationist cosmology).

The Ikhwān's theory is viewed within the context of emanationistic cosmology. Detailed and precise aspects of man, his body and soul, are compared with the spiritual and material dimensions of the universe. These similes and imageries of man and the cosmos recur in different forms throughout the *Rasā'il*. Miskawayh adopts the same notion of man as a small world, making it integral to his cosmological worldview, but he does not offer any vivid imageries and similes of it.

Isfahānī's microcosm does not fit into an emanationistic perspective, but the affinity between man and nature is established through the microcosm, and so is man's dependence on creation. The notion of microcosm is also employed as a rational way of arriving at knowledge of God and increasing man's faith in Him. Unlike Miskawayh, Isfahānī provides vivid examples to illustrate man as a microcosm of the universe, making the *Rasā'il* the model for his style. Ghazālī appropriates from Isfahānī the notion of man as microcosm of the world and provides an identical description of it in one passage. However, Ghazālī is original, though not unique, in comparing human vices with animals, and human organs with the craftsmen of the world. Comparisons between man and nature are more common in the Ikhwān and Isfahānī. Ghazālī and Isfahānī employ the microcosm as a key to the rational knowledge of God.

CONCLUSION

The Ikhwān, Miskawayh, Isfahānī and Ghazālī share the same view of man as microcosm, but they approach it in different ways. The Ikhwān's concept is to be viewed within the context of emanationistic cosmology. Detailed and precise aspects of man, his body and soul, are compared with the spiritual and material dimensions of the universe. These similes and imageries of man and the cosmos recur in different forms throughout the *Rasā'il*. Miskawayh adopts the same notion of man as a "small world", making it integral to his cosmological worldview, but he does not offer any vivid imageries and similes of it. Isfahānī's microcosm does not fit into an emanationistic perspective, but the affinity between man and nature is established through the concept of a "small world", which is also employed as a means of arriving at knowledge of God. Unlike Miskawayh, Isfahānī provides vivid examples to illustrate man as a microcosm of the universe, making the *Rasā'il* the model for his style. Ghazālī appropriates from

Isfahānī the notion of man as microcosm of the world and provides an identical description of it in one passage. However, Ghazālī compares human vices with animals, and human organs with the craftsmen of the world. Comparisons between man and nature are more common in the Ikhwān and Isfahānī. Ghazālī and Isfahānī have both employed the concept as a key to the rational knowledge of God. Isfahānī's analogies compare man with every aspect of the cosmos, including minerals and insects. These analogies are not used merely for stylistic embellishment, but it is an attempt to show the affinity between man and nature and the various elements that make up human nature.

Implicit in this concept of man as a "small world" is a respectful attitude to the universe in early Islamic thought. Since the universe reflects something of the divine, the contemplation of it will lead to a knowledge of God. Because of the intimate connection between man and the cosmos, man can observe in the universe a reflection of himself as a small world, and a reflection of the big world within himself. Moreover, he can apprehend the deeper, spiritual meaning of nature only because he can apprehend the inner, spiritual depths of his own being.

NOTES

1. The Brethren of Purity wrote fifty-one treatises in the 4th/10th centuries known as *Rasā'il* (Epistles) of the Brethren of Purity. The authors are not known, but they were of Sh,c, inspiration and were probably based in Basra. The Epistles had a wide influence on later Muslim intellectual figures, including Miskawayh, Isfahānī and Ghazālī.

2. Isfahānī is an Islamic ethical philosopher who died around the middle of the eleventh century. He wrote an ethical work called *al-Dharī'ah ilā Makārim al-Sharī'ah* (The Means to the Noble Qualities of the Law), which had a great influence on the ethics of Ghazālī. For some detail on his life and works, see Yasien Mohamed, "The Ethical Philosophy of alRāghib alIsfahānī", *Journal of Islamic Studies*, 1996, 6 (1) 51-75. For some information on the impact of his cosmological ideas on Ghazālī, see Yasien Mohamed, "Knowledge and Purification of the Soul. An Annotated Translation with Introduction of Isfahānī's *Kitab alDharī'ah ilā Makārim al-Sharīah.*" (58-76; 89-92) in *Journal of Islamic Studies.* Oxford. 1998; 9 (I): 1-34.

3. This study is a new version of an article dealing with the same concept, but which has been explained within the context of cosmology. See Y. Mohamed, "The Cosmology of Ikhwān al-Safā, Miskawayh and al-Isfahānī" in *Islamic Studies* 39:4 (2000), 657:679. Our present article adds the view of Ghazālī and we limit the discussion and comparison to the concept of man as a "small world". So, for a better understanding of how this concept fits in with cosmological theories of three of these figures, the reader will do well to refer to our previous article.

4. S.H. Nasr, *Islamic Cosmological Doctrines*, p. 98.
5. Ikhwān al-Safā, *Rasā'il Ikhwān al-Safā, II*, (Cairo: 1928), p. 334f. Where man, the small world (al-ᶜālam ṣâghīr) has a dual nature of body and soul, the body is analogous to the city and the soul to the king. Cf. Fakhry, *Ethical Theories in Islam* (Leiden: 1991), pp. 96-98.
6. Ibid, p. 456, 14-15; p. 457, 1-13.
7. Ibid, p. 466,16-21; p. 467,1-4.
8. Ikhwān al-Safā, *Rasā'il Ikhwān al-Safā*, III (Cairo: 1928), p. 215, 22f./ trans. Dieterici, cited in Widengren, "Macrocosmos-Microcosmos: Speculation in the *Rasā'il Ikhwān al-Safā* and some Hurufi Texts", *Archivio di Filosofja Padova*, 48 (1980) 297-312, p. 299. According to Widengren, this passage was "undoubtedly inspired by Stoic popular philosophy" and the social structure is depicted as feudalistic.
9. Jachiwicz, "Islamic Cosmology", in C. Blacker and M. Loewe, eds. *Ancient cosmologies*. London, 1975, p. 146.
10. Windengren argues that the doctrine of correspondence between man as a small world and the world as a big man goes back to an ancient Indo-lranian concept. This correspondence also has an astrological orientation in that every part of the human body is under the protection of one or two zodiac signs; furthermore, the development of the human embryo in every stage is under the protection of a planet. See G. Widengren, "Macrocosmos-Microcosmos Speculation in the *Rasā'il Ikhwān al-Safā* and some Hurūfi Texts", *Archivio di Filosofia Padova*, p. 305. These speculations are apparently integrated into the Neoplatonic structure of the Ikhwān al-Safa.
11. Miskawayh, *al-Fawz al-Asĝhar* (Tunis: 1987), p. 118, 8-12.
12. Miskawayh, *Tahdhīb al-Akhlāq*, ed. C. Zurayk (Beirut, 1966); p. 41, 11-23, p. 42, 1-4, trans. Zurayk, *The Refinement of Character* (Beirut, 1968), p.37f.
13. *Tahdh,b*, pp. 120-122.
14. Miskawayh, *Tahdhīb*, p. 152/trans. Fakhry, *Ethical Theories*, p. 12.
15. *Tahdhīb*, p. 41, 4-20.
16. On Isfahānī 's concept of microcosm and its comparison with Miskawayh and the Ikhwān al-Safā, see Yasien Mohamed, "Knowledge and Purification of the Soul", An Annotated Translation with Introduction of Isfahānī 's *Kitab al-dharīᶜah ilā makārim al-sharīᶜah*", (58-76; 89-92), *Journal of Islamic Studies*, 1998, 9 (1), 1-34.
17. Isfahānī, *Kitab al-Dharīᶜah ilā makārim al-sharīᶜah* (Cairo: 1987) pp. 76, 9-13; 202. Isfahānī states: "God created a small world for every person, both of his body and his soul, and He brought into being in man, an example of every existent in the big world" (p. 202).
18. *Tafl*, p. 62; cf. *al-Dharīᶜah*, p. 202.
19. *Tafl*, p. 76f.
20. *Tafl*, p.84, 10-11; p. 86, 1-2.
21. *Utrujj*, see earliest reference to it in *al-Dharīᶜah*, p. 60, 4, see translation above and footnote for a clear explanation.

22. Also: "oak apples". For a similar passage comparing the moral qualities of man with animals, see *Tafl*, p. 84, 10-11; *Mīzān*, p. 902. See chap. 3, sec. 2.3.
23. *al-Dharī cah*, p. 73, 6, note 4. See translation above.
24. *al-Dharī^cah*, p. 73, 6, note 4.
25. *al-Dharī^cah*, p. 166, 2-15.
26. *al-Dharī^cah*, p. 103, for reference to man as a small world. The body is compared to the city and the intellect to the king. See *al-Dharī^c ah*, p. 67 for a similar idea.
27. *Tafl*, p. 92f.; cf. *al-Dharī^cah*, p. 103, for similar analogies in a slightly different context.
28. *Mīzān*, p. 200, 14-17; cf. Smith, *Kīmiya*, p. 62.
29. *Mīzān*, p. 216; cf. Field, *The Alchemy of Happiness*, p. 31; Ghazālī states that knowledge of the soul leads to a better knowledge of God than knowledge of the body.
30. Ghazālī, *Kīmiyā sa^cā dah*, p. 140, 11-12; p. 141, 1-6. In another passage Ghazālī refers to the idea of microcosm and calls for the study of man's body to have a "more intimate knowledge of God", Cf. Claud Field, *The Alchemy of Happiness*, (Lahore, 1991), p. 31. In the above passage, Ghazālī not only compares man with nature per se, but also with the craftsmen of the world. This is a unique comparison, not found in *al-Dharī^cah*.
31. *Mīzān*, p. 209, 19ff. Cf. *al-Dharī^cah*, p. 86, 6-15, for an almost identical passage. See translation below.
32. *al-Dharī^cah*, p. 86, 6-15.
33. *Kīmiya*, p. 133.

3

Human Nature in Secular Psychology: An Islamic Critique

MALIK BADRI

This chapter will provide an Islamic critique of modern psychology, especially of psychoanalysis, behaviorism and cognitive psychology. It will question their assumptions of human nature, particularly the cognitive aspect, and will conclude with a section dealing with the contributions of the early Muslim scholars to cognitive psychology.

It took modern psychology several decades, since the discovery of Freudian analysis, to come to the realization that human nature is not merely the product of environmental stimulus, or of biological instincts, but of the human mind, which is a powerful force that determines human behavior. This new discovery by cognitive psychologists was revolutionary for modern psychology, but not for Islamic psychologists, who recognized centuries ago the powerful influence of the mind over the body.

The Islamic perspective of human nature and contemplation will be the point of departure for a critique of secular psychology. Contemplation (*tafakkur*) of creation alters human consciousness, which at a profound level, leads to the knowledge of God. It assumes the existence of the human mind (or soul) as distinct from the body, and of the power of the former over the latter. The advances in cognitive psychology, with its research on the effects of mental processes, have long been acknowledged by the classical Islamic scholars. The Islamic perspective to cognitive psychology, however, goes beyond the modern version; it is concerned with both psychological and spiritual wellbeing, leading ultimately to an intuitive knowledge of God.

AN ISLAMIC ASSESSMENT OF MODERN PSYCHOLOGY

In Islamic contemplation, altered states of consciousness are not an end in themselves, as the goal is a deeper insightful knowledge of God as the Creator and Sustainer of the universe. Consequently, an in-depth psychological discussion of Islamic contemplation would fall within the field of cognitive psychology, with special reference to the psychology of thinking.

BEHAVIORISM

The field of cognitive psychology, in its unrefined form, was the focus of the early schools of psychology before behaviorism became dominant. In those days, psychology was used mainly to study people's consciousness, their feelings, the content of their thoughts and the structure of their minds, attending to the question of learning only through these vistas. The behaviorist school introduced a totally new approach, where learning could be studied via stimuli and observable responses. Behaviorism became the basis of psychology; feelings, the components of the mind, and the process of thinking were considered questions that could not be observed directly. The methods used to study them (such as introspection, and the observation and reporting of inner experiencing) were criticized as being vague and unreliable and could not be controlled by experimental procedures. Accordingly, the behaviorists who wanted psychology to become an exact experimental science, like physics and chemistry, restricted their work to phenomena that could be observed in the laboratory, and the responses that could be measured and controlled became the focus of their experimental and scientific concerns. On the other hand, the cognitive and emotional activities which take place inside the human-being were considered something of a closed black box with contents that could not be observed, and for which, consequently, no time should be wasted in studying. Thus, the behaviorist vision of humans was that they were mere machines that, when exposed to specified stimuli, would react with responses which the researcher could control and predict. This approach automatically removed contemplation from being an area of psychological inquiry.

This effort to emulate physical and biological sciences by ignoring a person's spiritual and inner cognitive activities was unequivocally established by J.B. Watson, the founding father of behaviorism. He emphasized that people should be viewed as nothing more than animals; they are different from other animals only in the types of observable behavior that they perform. To be scientific, psychologists should therefore not allow themselves to study humans in any manner different from their work with animals. He writes that,

> [Behaviorism] attempts to do one thing: to apply to the experimental study of man the same kind of procedure and the same language of description that many research men had found useful for so many years in the study of animals lower than man. We believed then, as we believe now, that man is an animal different from other animals only in the types of behavior he displays. The raw fact is that you, as psychologist, if you are to remain scientific, must describe the behavior of man in no other terms than those you would use in describing the behavior of the ox you slaughter.[1]

Influenced by this constricted perspective and encouraged by Ivan Pavlov's contributions to learning by conditioning, behaviorists went on to explain every human mental and psychological activity through the vision of stimulus-response connectionism. Even the process of thinking was explained in terms of network of stimulus-response associations and considered as no more than soliloquy.

> The principal aim of this dehumanization of people was to mold psychology into a scientific cast. Another major objective was the secularization of Western societies and their emancipation from the grip of religion. In this connection, Watson clearly laments the fact that humans do not accept being classified as animals, and naively believe that God created them and that there is life after death. He states:

> Human beings do not want to class themselves with other animals. They are willing to admit that they are animals but "something else in addition". It is the "something else" that causes the trouble. In this "something else" is bound up everything that is classed as religion, the hereafter, morals, love of children, parents, country, and the like.[2]

From what has been said, it is obvious that behaviorism adamantly denies that humans have an innate good or evil nature, and that what they believe in is neither true nor false. Like a dry leaf on a windy day, their nature, values and beliefs are completely determined by environmental stimuli; there is no place in the behavioristic conception for any global ethical truths or moral standards. It also excludes any notion of human freedom of choice and any conscious moral or spiritual decision-making. Talking about contemplation and internal cognitive spiritual notions and feelings within the bounds of such a psychology would be inconceivable. The renowned British neurologist, John Eccles, endorses this criticism of behaviorism, saying:

> During the long dark night of the dominance of behaviorism, words like mind, consciousness, thoughts, purposes and beliefs were considered "dirty" words unallowable in "polite" philosophical discourse. Ironically,

the most prominent philosophical obscenities were a new class of four-letter-words: minds, self, soul, will.[3]

In psychology, however, the complex nature of human behavior and its non-materialistic nature does not allow for such basic units or major underlying concepts. Any attempt to override this fact is inevitably met with failure and soon forgotten. We may take the concept of the conditioned reflex as an example to illustrate the difficulty, because it was regarded as one of the simplest concepts in psychology and was endorsed by many behaviorists.

What is a conditioned reflex? A hungry dog hears the sound of a bell and is immediately given some dried meat. The process is repeated until the dog salivates to the sound of the bell. This salivation to an artificial stimulus, and the bell is known as a conditioned reflex. Conditioning can also be easily applied to humans, such as when they learn to respond reflexively to a flashing light with a knee-jerk, or to the sound of a bell by blinking. Though this phenomenon was described by early Muslim scholars such as Ibn Sīnā and al-Ghazālī, it was first studied experimentally by Ivan Pavlov, the famous Russian physiologist.

Learning by conditioning can explain some aspects of simple learning, but it cannot be taken as a serious unit in psychology because many areas of psychology are not based on such simple stimulus-response connections. For example, social psychology, humanistic psychology, perception, language-learning, and similar fields cannot be reduced to the simple stimulus-response paradigm of conditioning. Similarly, the deep and complex aspects of human behavior cannot be explained by conditioning laws. For example, how could one explain "love" using stimuli and conditioned reflexes? The complex nature of this behavior has no room for such extreme fragmentation.

PSYCHOANALYSIS AND NEUROPSYCHIATRY

Though other dominant perspective and schools of psychology such as psychoanalysis and the biological perspective had, and still have, bitter disagreements with the behaviorists, they are in complete harmony when it comes to secularization and the downgrading of conscious thinking. Classical Freudian psychoanalysis, for instance, sees human behavior as fully determined by one's unconscious sexual and aggressive impulses, which means that people's conscious ideas, their contemplation, their judgments and their reasoning are but by-products of a deeper concealed mind of which they are unaware. Freud considered religion itself as an illusion and a mass obsessional neurosis!

Traditional neuropsychiatry, which is strongly based on an "organicist" biological perspective, also depreciates the significance of conscious ideation, freedom of choice, and the unchanging spiritual moral standards of human being. Biological determinism, in its exaggerated form, claims that anything, normal or abnormal, that people do is fully governed by their inherited genes, their nervous system, and inborn biochemistry. As one researcher describes it, "Behind any twisted idea or action, there is a twisted molecule in the brain". Theoretically, they believe that the way these inborn biological aspects interact with the environment is like a program in a computer's hard disk: if you happen to know all the particulars and variables, you can predict accurately the future behavior of the person concerned. Consequently, they explain much of human ethical behavior; that religion has always considered to be the conscious choices of people and for which they should bear responsibility, in terms of irresistible biological determinism. For instance, several studies have tried to prove that promiscuity, homosexuality and lesbianism are deep-seated biologically programmed urges, and that people should not, therefore, be condemned for following the instincts created by their genes.

If studying Islamic contemplation from the psychological point of view necessarily deals with the conscious inner cognitive thought and feelings of people, then these three dominant perspectives of Western psychology (behaviorism, Freudian psychoanalysis and neuropsychiatry) can offer little or no help. Indeed, two of these perspectives see humans as mechanical creatures dominated by external stimuli or biological and biochemical factors and, according to the third, our conscious thinking and feelings are simply a deception by our unconscious and ego defense mechanisms. It is not surprising, therefore, that these psychological schools and their artificial oversimplification of complex cognitive activities and feelings, despite securing respect for many years by providing scientific explanations of human behavior, have failed to provide satisfactory results. The optimism of fifty years ago has now dissipated, and the social and psychological problems of Western societies are critical, as indeed they are in other countries affected by modernity. The problems are not surprising since the psychology of humankind, with all its complex variables and spiritual aspects, could never be reduced to the chemical and physical data of laboratory experiments.

Precise disciplines such as physics and chemistry have made astonishing advances, not only because of the long period of their historic development – as some psychologists have us believe–but also, and more importantly, because of their purely material nature. These two disciplines build basic units of measurement and comprehensive theories to explain the behavior of matter and energy and their precise interaction. The two factors of matter and energy are fundamental because, without the concept of the atom and its components of protons and electron, the experimental sciences could not have achieved so much. The same thing could be said about the cell as a basic unit in biology, or about the genes in the study of heredity.

The same difficulties we encounter in the reductionism of human emotions in behaviorism prevented psychology from formulating a comprehensive theory like Einstein's theory of relativity in physics or Darwin's theory of evolution. Although recent scientific discoveries have now revealed certain flaws in the latter, it still serves as a general and comprehensive biological theory. Some schools and perspectives in modern psychology, such as psychoanalysis, Gestalt psychology and learning theory, tried to formulate an all-embracing theory, but none succeeded, and their efforts simply became part of the history of Western psychology.[4]

These successive failures were evidently a logical outcome of the unreasonable efforts of modern psychologists to transform their discipline into an experimental science by neglecting people's feelings, consciousness, minds, and mental process, as they had previously removed from them their souls and spiritual essence. This deformed approach was, from the start, strongly opposed by several scholars. The British psychologist, Cyril Burt, for example, is often quoted to have said that psychology lost its soul, then its mind, and finally its consciousness, as if it were preparing itself for its ultimate demise.[5]

COGNITIVE PSYCHOLOGY

One may not be as surprised to see the downfall of this distorted image of humankind in modern psychology as to realize that it took so long for Western psychologists to correct it. Psychology had to undergo a complete revolution to be able to reinstate its "mind" and rediscover its inner conscious cognitive activities. The revolution is the contemporary cognitive revolution. Scholars began to show more interest in thinking and inner cognitive processes from about the middle of the twentieth century, but it took psychology several decades to recognize the superficiality of stimulus-response behaviorism and the unscientific distorted nature of the theories of psychoanalysis. This marked a return to the study of the internal mental activities used by people in analyzing and classifying information taken from their environment.

This new perspective in psychology is particularly important in that it shows the value of contemplation from both the scientific and religious points of view. Though this cognitive approach may be considered a return, to the early stages of psychology, the methods used are much more advanced and depend on technologies especially devised to study human cognitive activities, on recent development in neuroscience and, more importantly, on the computer revolution. Specialized research in these disciplines has clearly exposed the limitations of the concept of mechanical human being as adopted by behaviorism; this concept has been replaced with that of a human being as an "information processor".

When modern scholars compare people's thinking, inner cognitive and emotional processes and memory to a computer, they are describing the fact that they receive various stimuli from their environment, then code, classify and store them in their memory, to retrieve them when they need to solve new problems. In this simple analogy, receiving information from the environment corresponds to typing on the keyboard of a computer or feeding it in some other way. The central processing unit with its loaded software corresponds to the mind with its internal cognitive activity, like thinking and feeling; and the mental or behavioral responses that the person performs correspond to what the computer shows on its monitor. The computer reacts differently to a specific letter struck on its keyboard according to the software program used; similarly, people react differently to specific letter stimuli to which they are subjected in their environment. Following the same logic, as we know exactly what kind of software is loaded in our computers, we should strive to know what "software" is loaded in our minds as it is this "software" which makes us think, feel and behave in the way we do. Thus, the simple behavioristic conception of limiting research in psychology to stimuli that directly bring about responses has been equivocated.

It is interesting to note that although psychology and other social sciences continue to support the secular reductionistic view of human beings according to progressive developments in technology, this computer model of the human being is clearly more realistic than the behaviorist model since it tries to restore to modern psychology its "mind" and "consciousness", yet it obviously falls short of the true spiritual Islamic vision of humankind. Western psychology is still obsessed with an outdated tunnel vision "scientific" model. Furthermore, a paradigm shift of psychology, as in other social sciences, does not bring about a real revolution. Thomas Kuhn, the philosopher who popularized the concept of "paradigm" in his *The Structure of Scientific Revolutions,* said that "the more developed sciences had paradigms, but psychology didn't."[6]

This is obviously true, since in developed sciences a "paradigm shift" results in a real revolution, where the new paradigm overthrows and replaces the old, just as Einstein's theories completely transformed Newtonian physics. In psychology and other social sciences, new paradigms—if we can call them so—generate much enthusiasm and attract many followers, but do not replace the old paradigms that continue to survive and sometimes flourish again a few years later. Thus, though the cognitive revolution is causing major changes in modern psychology, it cannot be considered a real rebellion against earlier concepts.

The real revolution in psychology will come when it regains its "soul" and liberates itself from the constricted scientific and medical models for erecting an image of human nature. Indeed, the interaction of biological, psychological, and socio-cultural factors to produce a "complex" of a thinking and behaving human being—as Western psychology still upholds—can never be as simple as the interaction of hydrogen, oxygen and carbon, which occurs in photosynthesis when plants use solar energy to produce molecules of glucose from water and carbon dioxide.

However, even the revolution of cognitive psychology, which attempted to free the discipline from its constricted approach, still limits itself to this trio of psychological, biological and socio-cultural components of human behavior and mental process. It has also ignored the spiritual components, despite increasing modern scientific evidence regarding its importance. By limiting itself to these three components because they are more easily defined compared with the spiritual aspect, or by simply rejecting the spiritual aspect because it emanates from a religious vision, modern psychology will remain ambiguous, inefficient and at a loss. It is like someone who anticipates the formation of glucose by the process of photosynthesis using the three elements of carbon, hydrogen and oxygen, but excludes solar energy simply because it is more sublime and less concrete. However, it must be stressed that even without the spiritual faith factor and despite the advancement of knowledge, the study of these internal mental processes will always be a highly complex field where stimuli and their responses, causes and their effects interact in a manner which defies any sophisticated method of observation or measurement.

THE MIND-BODY ENIGMA

The study of the internal psychological and mental world of the human being brings us face to face with one of man's most difficult questions: what is the connection between the body and the mind? The answer to this question is a medley of philosophical ideas, religious beliefs, psychological studies, and biological and organic research findings about humankind in general, and the human brain and nervous system in particular.

A PERSPECTIVE ON THE BRAIN (ECCLES)

Though we know very little about the activities of the human brain, the materialists claim that the human being does not possess a "mind", unless this word is used to mean the material "brain" inside the skull. They also claim that what we call a "thinking mind" is nothing but the reflections and "translations" of the minute changes in the chemistry of the brain and its electrochemical nervous pulses—their justification being that people's thinking, and indeed their entire characters, change when the brain is damaged. This stand is obviously supported by behaviorists and other secular psychologists.

The opposing group affirms that there is a "mind" that controls the brain and, ultimately, a person's behavior and thinking. Chief among this group is the neurologist, John Eccles, who won a Nobel Prize for his outstanding research on the nervous system. This scholar and the scientist who uphold his assertion affirm that their research on the activity of the human brain and the nervous system can only be fully explained by the existence of a "mind", a "realizing soul", or what Eccles calls a "self-conscious mind". They contend further that this non-material entity fully controls the nervous and behavioral activity of a human being. If the brain was the only entity governing the human cognitive processes and behavior, as materialists claim, no person would or could contest an action or decision taken by his brain. However, this is clearly not the case. Indeed, if, for example, a male volunteer is electrically stimulated in a certain part of the motor area of the cerebral cortex, he will respond with a jerking movement of his arm. If he is told not to move his arm, and the electrical stimulation of the brain is repeated, he will find his arm moving in spite of him; and if this process is repeated again, he may try to stop the movement of that arm with his other arm. This can be performed experimentally. Eccles would argue: if the brain was the only governing body, then the subject would not have negated what his brain had ordered; however, as this is not the case, then what caused the arm to move and what tried to stop it? Clearly, the brain moved it, and the mind tried to stop it.

Eccles and various other scholars often use the image of the relationship between a broadcasting station and a television set to explain the relationship between the mind and the brain. According to Eccles, the non-material, self-conscious mind continuously scans, probes and controls the brain. If the brain is damaged or if the person is unconscious, the mind will continue to do its job, but the outcome will depend on the quality and efficiency of reception by the brain. Similarly, if a television set develops a fault, the image it conveys will be disturbed or may disappear completely. Therefore, to say that the brain is the only element involved is a very naïve conception, just like the belief of a child that the persons and images that appear on the television screen are inside the television set! This was the exact statement made by my four-year-old niece, Amina, when I told her our guest, ʾHāmid ʿUmar al-Imām, was the distinguished Shaykh who chanted the Qurʾān every morning on Omdurman Radio. She said: "But Uncle, how can such a big man get inside our small radio?"

In the impressive volume, *The Self and Its Brain*, that Eccles wrote with the renowned philosopher Karl Popper, the author comes very close to agreeing with the religious belief about the immortality of the soul. As an open-minded scientist, convinced by his research on the existence of a self-conscious mind[7], he asks himself: what happens to this mind after death?

Finally, we come to the ultimate picture, what happens during death? All cerebral activity ceases permanently. The self-conscious mind that has had an autonomous existence in a sense… now finds that the brain it had scanned and probed and controlled so efficiently and effectively through a long life is no longer giving any message at all. What happens then is the ultimate question.[8]

As Eccles has asserted, what takes place after the death of the brain is the ultimate question that will continue to haunt scholars as well as lay people. It will forever mystify us because God decreed that knowledge about the true nature of the soul or spirit, how it interacts with the body and what happens to it after death, was to be a strictly guarded secret curtailed from us in this world. Indeed, knowing what happens after death would necessarily reveal the secret of our soul and spirit and, if this happened, then the whole religious conviction of this life as a testing place would be invalidated. When asked about the spirit, Prophet Muhammad received the following revelation: "They asked you about the spirit. Say, *"The spirit is of the command of the Lord. It is only a little knowledge about it that is communicated to you"* (17:85). Thus, knowledge of the true nature of the spirit is unattainable. And for this reason, Islam urges the Muslim worshipper to concentrate his contemplative efforts on the attainable. The complete answer to this question will therefore remain unresolved.

Some scholars may believe that trying to tackle this problem from the purely biological aspect may be easier and "scientifically" more straightforward than the more intangible philosophical, religious or psychological aspects. However, the truth of the matter is that the biological perspective is not less complicated; in fact, it could be even more complicated since an in-depth investigation in biology and physics can often end up in philosophy and spirituality. In his valuable book, *The Psychobiology of the Mind,* W. Utall says that all the modern research and discoveries about the workings of the human brain have not brought us any closer to solving the problem of the relation between body and mind.[9] In fact, they have simply added new questions; the basic questions asked in the days of Aristotle, more than 2000 years ago, are still waiting for satisfactory answers.

A PERSPECTIVE ON THE HEART (PEARCE)

Another complication raised by modern biological research about the relation between body and mind is the role of the human heart in influencing the brain and shaping neural behavior. According to Joseph Pearce in his thought-provoking book, *Evolution's End,* the human heart is much more than a pumping station; it is the organ that alerts the brain to carry out appropriate responses. Neurotransmitters, which play an important role in the functioning of the brain, have been found in the heart. He says, "Actions in the heart precede the actions of both body and brain...We know now that the heart...controls and governs the brain action through hormonal, transmitter, and possibly finer quantum-energies of communication."[10]

If what Pearce says is true, then artificial plastic hearts will not be able to do what a real or transplanted heart can do. It would also mean that a person who receives a transplanted heart will somehow behave in ways like that of the donor. Finally, there must be some scientific evidence for the proposed non-localized influence or "remote control" of the heart over the brain and body.

Concerning the first issue, Pearce relies on the authority of Christian Barnard, the heart transplant pioneer, who said: "We must give up the idea of an artificial heart, since we found the organ to be far more than just a pumping station."

As for the second point, Pearce confirms that though the heart is governed by a "higher" order of energy (or a "soul" in Islamic belief), the behavior of the "people getting heart-transplants often dramatically reflect certain behaviors of the late donors." Regarding the possibility of non-localization, he refers the reader to convincing experiments in which two cells taken from the heart are observed through a microscope. In the first experiment in which they are isolated from one another, they simply fibrillate until they die. However, when similar cells are brought near to each other, they synchronize and beat in unison:

> They don't have to touch; they communicate across a spatial barrier...Our heart, made up of many, billions of such cells operating in unison, is under the guidance of a higher, non-localized intelligence...So we have both a physical heart and a higher "universal heart" and our access to the latter is...dramatically contingent on the...former.[11]

According to Pearce, when we are in deep spiritual contemplation, we are drawing from our spiritual universal heart, which influences our physical heart that communicates with our brain and influences our cognitive activities. This, in some respects, is very similar to the views of Abū Hāmid al-Ghazālī in his monumental work *Ihyā' 'ulūm al-dīn* (*The Revival of the Religious Sciences*) in which he clearly states that although the spiritual heart (*qalb*)—which is the controlling center of the soul—is different from the physical human heart, its functioning is related and directed by it. We can thus see how a biological discourse develops into a religious dialogue.

However, as Uttal argues, despite all the recent achievements in science and technology, we are still ignorant of the way the nervous system provides human beings with their consciousness and their sense of being, which are their dearest possessions. This, I believe, is really a matter for contemplation about the creation, with all its psychological, spiritual, and behavioral aspects.

FROM COGNITIVE ACTIVITY TO ESTABLISHED HABITS

We turn to the research of cognitive psychologists and computer scientist in their attempts to understand human internal cognitive activities. Both are concerned with the study of the human capacity to analyze, classify and store information in the memory to retrieve it when needed. They have conducted many detailed studies to examine the process used by a human being in thinking and problem-solving; then, using this data; they have established various programs imitating human cognitive activity. Some have even created a program that tries to imitate the way of thinking of neurotics and psychotics in their adjustments to their environments. These studies have clarified many aspects that the behaviorist had chosen to ignore because they felt it was impossible to identify its contents and have produced many theories and explanations that challenge the naïve concept of stimulus-response psychology. These studies have also opened a window for the Muslim psychologist to learn more about the importance of contemplation and worship, and the concomitant internal mental-cognitive activity associated with them. Psychotherapists and personality psychologists have made use of these cognitive studies that disclose human internal thinking and feelings and examine the formation of observable normal and abnormal human behavior.

As we have mentioned earlier, the behaviorists emphasize the role of the environment as the only influence responsible for the development of the human personality and normal and abnormal human behavior. This is to say, they believe that environmental stimuli directly lead to the behavioral responses. The cognitive psychologists, on the other hand, are more concerned with the meaning produced by these experiences.

They claim that an experience does not automatically provoke a response, except in the case of reflexes – like pulling that hand away when it touches a hot surface. Complex responses that influence people's beliefs, voluntary decisions and observable complex behavior come from previous conceptualizations, emotions and experiences which give meaning to subsequent environmental stimuli. In other words, it is what people think about that affects their beliefs, feelings and consequent behavior. If their thinking is centered on the creation and bounties of the Almighty, their faith will increase, and their deeds and behavior will improve. If it is centered on their pleasures and desires, they will be distracted from their religion and their behavior will degenerate; and if their thinking is about their feats, frustrations, failures, and consequent pessimism, they will be afflicted with reactive depression and other psychological disorders.

Consequently, cognitive psychologists concentrate their therapy on changing patients' conscious thinking, as it is the activity that usually precedes the feelings and emotional responses of normal and neurotic people. In other words, they try to change the "software" used by their minds, as it is the program, they use which gives meaning to what they experience. This internal cognitive activity (automatic thoughts) may be so rapid and spontaneous that the individual does not notice it except after thorough analysis and training.

This research has shown that every intentional action performed by the individual is preceded by an internal cognitive activity. They have also proved that the human mind never stops this cognitive activity at any moment of the day or night, whether the individual is aware of it or not. A classic illustration of this is when someone is unable to find a solution to a problem, so he or she puts it aside and moves onto a different activity; then, suddenly, the solution comes to mind without a conscious effort by that person or any expectation. A famous example of this is Archimedes' sudden discovery of the fluid displacement law. Similarly, someone who fails to remember a name, or a word will suddenly remember it sometime later.

Therefore, it is the internal cognitive activity of a human being, whether conscious or unconscious, that directs observable human behavior. This conclusion was reached by cognitive psychologists after long years of research, overstepping all the psychological schools that tried to confine complex human general behavior into simplistic theories. Furthermore, this cognitive perspective clearly supports what Islam had already established: that contemplation as an internal thought process, is the backbone of faith, which is the source of every good deed.

In addition to this discovery that every action begins with an internal cognitive activity—be it a notion, a memory, an image, a perception, or an emotion – it has also been shown that when this cognitive activity gains strength, it can become a motive or an incentive for action. And if the individual performs this motivated action repeatedly, then these internal ideas can easily and spontaneously make it become a rooted habit. This habit is not necessarily a skill; it can be an emotion, a spiritual feeling, or an attitude. So, if the cognitive therapist wished to treat a patient who suffers from an emotional or other kind of habit, he must strive to change the internal thinking that causes this behavior. If the habit is fear of social situations, for instance, the therapist must identify the negative thinking that causes the patient to respond with this social fear. For example, if the patient imagines that he would look silly if he were to talk or introduce himself to strangers, or if he were to deliver a speech before a group of acquaintances, the therapist can then help the patient change these negative thoughts by showing that their irrational fears have no basis. Furthermore, he can show that the patient's feelings blindly followed his pessimistic thinking, which has wrongly taken complete control over his behavior. When these internal notions are changed, the behavior will change accordingly.

This kind of therapy can also be performed by stimulating responses that are contrary to the negative ideas, fancies, and internal emotions that cause the habit. In the case of fear of social situations, for instance, the therapist can stimulate in the patient a relaxing feeling of security and psychological comfort, while at the same time exposing him to increasing difficult social situations (whether real or imaginary).

On the other hand, if the negative habit causes the patient some pleasure and psychological comfort, such as gambling, drinking alcohol or performing certain deviant sexual behavior, the treatment by countermeasures leads the therapist to stimulate a sense of pain, psychological stress and fear in the patient when he repeats that negative habit. In this type of aversion therapy, an alcoholic or drug addict, for instance, is given injections of a chemical material that will cause him to have nausea and headaches when he drinks alcohol; he may even be exposed to painful but harmless electric shocks. This "reward and punishment" therapy is known as "reciprocal inhibition" and is one of the most successful techniques of modern behavioral therapy.

Though devised by behaviorists, the cognitive therapists have developed it by relating it to the thinking and the conscious feelings of the patient. This marriage of aspects of behavior modification with the recent developments in cognitive therapy is the latest and most successful innovation in psychological therapy.

Cognitive psychology, therefore, affirms that people's conscious thinking and inner dialogues influence their feelings and emotions, and form their attitudes and beliefs – in short, they can even shape their values and vision of life. If the discussion is transferred from the cognitive therapy of the emotionally disrobed to the cognitive activity of normal Muslims, one can clearly see the great influence of the cognitive processes involved in contemplation in remodeling the very psyche of individuals. Furthermore, if the spiritual/faith factor is added—a factor which is a powerful cognitive force totally excluded by modern psychology—one can imagine the momentous change that Islamic contemplation can achieve in purifying the souls and elevating the status of the worshippers. Through contemplation, Muslims can refine their own internal "reward and punishment" psycho-spiritual strategies. They do not require a worldly reward or an electric shock to change their unwanted habits and replace them with more worthy ones. By devoting their internal cognitive and spiritual aspirations to the contemplation of God's majesty and perfection in contrast to their laxity and unworthy behavior, they will certainly develop the sentiment of love of God and the refined feelings of contentment, happiness, and tranquility.

THE CONTRIBUTIONS OF EARLY MUSLIM SCHOLARS

It took Western psychology more than seven decades to return to the "common sense" recognition of the influence of thinking and the cognitive processes in shaping human beliefs, attitudes and external behavior. Indeed, the cognitive principles which have only recently impressed modern psychology, were already known centuries ago, by scholars such as Ibn Qayyim al-Jawziyyah, al-Balkhī, al-Ghazālī, Miskawayh and many others. These scholars mentioned the importance of notions, reflections and ideas that cross the mind and can grow to become drives and incentives that are carried out in real life, and when repeated, become habits. They employed this principle to encourage people to cultivate good habits, to remember God constantly and to contemplate over the heavens and earth. They also said that a person should change harmful, negative notions, before they become fixed desires and drives, because changing a drive or motive is easier than stopping a consequent action, and removing an action is easier than trying to uproot it after it has become a habit. They stated further, akin to the words used by the modern behavior therapists, that treating a habit should be done by training the individual to do its opposite.

In his masterpiece, *Maālih al-Abdān wa al-ᶜAnfus* (*The Sustenance of the Body and the Soul*), Abū Zāhid al-Balkhī showed the influence of contemplation and inner thought on health-a discovery that was only developed more than ten centuries after his death. He even suggested that just as a healthy person keeps some drugs and first-aid medicines at hand for unexpected physical emergencies, he should also contemplate and keep healthy thoughts and feelings in his mind for unexpected emotional outbursts.[12]

In his *al-Fawā'id* (*The Spiritual Benefits*), Ibn Qayyim explicitly says that anything a person does begins as an inner thought, a concealed speech or an internal dialogue, for which he uses the Arabic word, *khawātir* (plural of *khawātir*), meaning, fast, inner, concealed reflections. Modern cognitive psychologists can compare this with the idea of "automatic thoughts". Ibn Qayyim describes how fleeting thoughts, particularly negative ones, develop into human actions and observable behavior. He warns that a lustful, sinful, or emotionally harmful *khawātir*, if accepted and not checked by the person concerned, can develop into a strong emotion or lust (*shahwah*). If this emotion acquires cognitive strength it can develop into a drive or impulse for action. And if not combated by an opposite emotion it will be acted out in reality as external behavior.

Furthermore, if this behavior is not resisted, it will be repeated so often that it becomes a habit. In this respect, Ibn Qayyim believed that emotional, physical and cognitive habits followed the same pattern—a belief which is strikingly similar to the modern approach of cognitive psychologists. Thus, he advises the Muslim to lead a happy and righteous life by fighting the negative *khawātir* of inner fleeting thoughts before they become an emotion or an impulse. However, he warns that these fleeting thoughts cannot be totally removed, for they are as irresistible as breathing. Nevertheless, a wise person who has strong faith in God can accept the good *khawātir* and reject the bad ones.[13] This discourse reads like a summary of modern behavioral cognitive therapy in a modern textbook of psychology, with the addition of the spiritual dimension which is lacking in modern secular psychology. Much of this literature by early Muslim scholars is based on knowledge acquired from the Qur'ān and the *sunnah*, which is molded into useful psychological principles.

In his *Ihyā' 'ulūm al-dīn,* al-Ghazālī says that the Muslim who wants to adhere to good behavior has first to change his ideas about himself and imagine himself in the desired condition. Then he must gradually assume those good manners, even if he feigns what he does, until they become a part of him. When his thinking changes, his behavior will change. He describes the process as follows:

> Good manners can be acquired by practice: by feigning or assuming the actions issuing from those manners at first until they eventually become part of one's nature. This is one of the wonders of the relation between the heart and the organs—I mean the soul and the body. Every quality that appears in the heart will have its influence flowing to the organs so that they act only in accordance with that quality. Similarly, the effect of every action that issues from the organs may reach the heart. And this continues in a circular system.[14]

Al-Ghazālī insists that contemplation is the key to every good deed, because it qualifies all cognitive actions of the believer with the remembrance of the Almighty and the recognition of His favors and grace. Since the origin of every action is a cognitive, emotional, or intellectual mental activity, those who are given to long periods of contemplation will perform their acts of worship and obedience quite easily. While internal cognitive activity is the key to every good and proper action, it is also the source of all disobedience, whether implied or overt.

Thus, to conclude, contemplation in the Islamic perspective makes use of all the cognitive activities employed by a human being in the thinking processes but differs from secular contemplation in that its vision goes beyond this world. Its contemplation of the world leads to the consciousness of the hereafter and the knowledge of God. Islamic contemplation therefore integrates reflection of the mundane with spirituality resulting in a new human experience. Contemplation of the creation is a religious duty that leads to a knowledge of God. It transcends mere sense perception, and the believer can apprehend the Ultimate reality through spiritual insight.

The revolutionary change within modern psychology lies in the recognition that neither the unconscious sexual conflict nor the environmental stimuli per se, cause emotional disorders, but rather it is the perceptions, thoughts and contemplation of a person about these stimuli or experiences which can make him a neurotic. Thus, after many years of wandering in the dessert of soulless theories, psychotherapy is finally returning to the commonsense practice of cognitive healing that has always been used to help the emotionally disturbed, and which was meticulously studied by ancient physicians and healers.

NOTES

1. J.B. Watson, *Behavorism* (London: W. Norton & Co., 1970), p. ix.
2. Ibid.
3. John Eceles, *Evolution of the Brain: Creation of the Self* (London: Routledge Publishers, 1991), p. 225.
4. Malik Badri, *ᶜIlm al-Nafs min Manzur Islami.* (Khartoum: IIIT, 1987).
5. Cyril Burt, in H.J. Eysenck, *Psychology is about People* (London: The Penguin Press, 1979), p. 300.
6. Thomas Kuhn, *The Structure of Scientific Revolution* (Chicago: University of Chicago Press, 1970).
7. Eccles, *Evolution of the Brain.*
8. Karl Popper and John Eccles, *The Self and Its Brain* (London: Routledge Publishers, 1978).
9. W. Uttal, *The Psychology of the Mind* (London: John Wiley Publishers, 1978).
10. J. C. Pearson, *Evolution's End* (San Francisco: Harper Collins Publishers, 1992), pp. 103 and 104.
11. Ibid, pp. 104-105.
12. Abu Zahid al-Balkhi, *Masalih al Abdan wa al-ᶜAnfus*, MS 3741(Istanbul: Ayasofya library). Photocopied by the Institute of Arabic-Islamic Sciences, Frankfurt a. M., 1984.
13. Ibn Qayyim al-Jawziyyah, al-Fawaid, (Beirut: Dar al-Nafaiis, 1981), p. 173.
Abu Hamid al- Ghazali, *Ihya ʾᶜulum al-Din*, (Beirut: Dar al-Qalam, n.d.).

4

Human Nature from a Comparative Psychological Perspective

MUSTAPHA ACHOUI

A plethora of books are available on human nature from a philosophical, moral, or religious perspective, or a mixture of all these. However, studies that have a psychological approach to the subject are rather rare, and those that do exist are usually a little more than an introduction to the study of the psychology of human nature. Some scholars, like Wrightsman (1992), give the following reasons for the lack of interest in the subject among psychologists: Firstly, many psychologists operating within the dominant Western paradigm believe that it is futile to explain behaviour in terms of human nature, and that only laymen tend to explain behaviour as a result of mere human nature. Secondly, Western psychologists, until recently, have not been overly concerned with the so-called "universality of social behaviour". This can be seen in the studies of cross-cultural psychology. Their concern has been with the study of social behaviour in a framework of Western culture, rather than the study of human behaviour in a wider perspective of the human race. Thirdly, Psychological research has centered on the study of experimental social psychology, and on the concepts that can be studied empirically rather than loose concepts. This made laboratory research predominant in Western psychological research, as it forms an important part of empirical studies that are either descriptive or experimental.[1]

Nonetheless, Western scholars, whether philosophers, sociologists, or psychologists, have recently become more and more interested in the subject of "human nature". This has been felt by many scholars such as Stevenson, Chaney, Wrightsman, and Schultz, who have studied the subject of human nature from various viewpoints: philosophical, psychological, anthropological, and developmental.[2]

At the same time, some books and studies have also been published in Arabic, and from an Islamic viewpoint, following various approaches: philosophical, religious, moral, psychological, or anthropological. Among these are works by al-Aqqad, Bint al-Shātī, Barakat Ahmad, Amīr, Sayyid Mursī, Akbar Ahmad, and Al-ᶜAnī.[3]

This essay is intended as a contribution towards an understanding of human nature from a perspective rooted in Islam and the discipline of psychology. It has a two-fold approach: It first seeks to understand human nature through the texts of some Qur'ānic verses and *Hadīth*. Secondly, it adopts a comparative approach between the Islamic and Western perspectives of the human nature, with reference to postulates made by Schultz (1994) and other Western scholars. I have chosen Schultz's work since his examination of a relevant theme contrasted with its counterpart, such as, for example, freedom and predestination; and his enumeration of various opinions by Western psychologists on these dimensions, facilitate a process of review and comparison.

PERSONALITY FROM A WESTERN PERSPECTIVE

In his *Theories of Personality*, Schultz asks several questions about the nature of human personality, concluding that psychologists in the West do not agree upon a single best theory of personality. That is why he uses the word "theories" instead of "theory" in the title. Schultz further stresses that the way human nature is conceptualized by a theorist forms the most important aspect in any theory of personality.[4] He presents 18 theories which he then groups into nine categories or major tendencies, where each has its own approach, postulates, methods of research, concepts and dimensions of personality, and qualities of human nature. These will be the subject of our comparison.

Schultz advances several reasons for the study of personality, the foremost of which is that major problems faced by contemporary humanity, such as famine, pollution, crime, and addiction, are caused by human beings themselves. Understanding human nature then is a prerequisite to solving the root-cause of society's problems, and the study of personality may be a major contribution of psychology to save humanity. Therefore, human nature, seen in a comparative perspective, assumes a great importance on both theoretical and practical levels.

Can psychology in general, and the Islamic approach, have any role to play in saving humanity in this world and the hereafter? I do not claim that I can answer these two questions, but it is not amiss to suggest the important role that can be played by psychology in understanding human nature and personality, and the capability of such understanding to address some problems faced by humanity, such as racism, discrimination, and violence.

Therefore, it may be useful to present an Islamic vision of human nature using the characteristics of human nature articulated by Schultz in his vision of "personality", in addition to other dimensions which I may suggest in this respect. One must, of course, bear in mind that this is merely a relative vision, as it is only a human interpretation. Hence, Schultz rightly points out that the psychological theories formulated around personality have no common ground to answer questions about certain factors and features that might influence human nature and personality—such as freedom or predestination, heredity, or environment, past or present, individuality and uniqueness or universality, balance or growth and optimism or pessimism.

I have chosen to present an Islamic vision of these dimensions, based on my understanding of some Qur'ānic verses and *Ḥadīth* texts, adding some dimensions not mentioned by Schultz and other non-Muslim researchers. The objective is to formulate these dimensions in a comparative perspective.

CHARACTERISTICS OF HUMAN NATURE FROM AN ISLAMIC PERSPECTIVE[5]

In discussing the characteristics of human nature from an Islamic perspective, we must note that:

> To formulate an Islamic vision about the characteristics of human nature and personality as a modern (Western) psychological concept, we have to clarify the Islamic attitude about three major dimensions with their ramifications: The Creation of Man, The Life of Man, and The Destiny of Man (in the hereafter).

> The study of man from an Islamic perspective should recognize three more dimensions, closely related to the previous ones, with a possible mutual effect. The relationship among these dimensions may not be causal but could be relative in a statistical sense. These dimensions are spiritual, physical-biological, and behavioural.

THE SPIRITUAL DIMENSION

What is meant by "spiritual" here is the aspect of "faith". That is, the belief in Allah, His angels, messengers, scriptures, the day of judgement, and destiny (good or bad). These are the articles of faith which bear no discussion or compromise. But "faith" is higher in degree than "Islam", as it is what is settled in the heart and endorsed by deed. There is no room in Islam for talking about faith that is separate from deeds and behaviour. The Qur'ān reproached the believers for expressing their "belief" and stopping short of action.

O, ye who believe! Why say ye that which ye do not? Grievously odious is it in the sight of Allah that ye say that which ye do not. (61:2-3).

It is clear that the Qur'ānic verses that deal with faith are all coupled with actions and deeds. "Faith" is what is settled in the heart, confessed in words and endorsed by "deeds", as is attested by a *Hadīth* of the Prophet (SAS):

Faith is some and seventy, (or some and sixty) branches: the highest is to say there is no God but Allah, the last is to remove obstacles of the road." (Accepted Hādīth by consensus).

This is what we mean by the spiritual aspect. The metaphysical aspect of faith is a basic dimension, but it cannot be measured, as it is within the knowledge of Allah. However, the actions can be observed and measured.'

THE FORMATIVE DIMENSION (PHYSICAL-BIOLOGICAL)

The Holy Qur'ān specifies that the first man (Adam) was created from clay.

He who has made everything He has created most Good: He began the creation of man with clay. (32:7).

Man We did create from a quintessence of clay. (23:12).

Indeed, the Holy Qur'ān repeats seven times the fact of creating man out of clay. The origin of propagation in man is the drop of sperm, as it is clearly stated in *sūrah* al-Insān and al-Qiyāmah. Several verses describe the physical-biological dimension in the creation of man, in the embryonic and other stages of life.

We have enjoined on man kindness to his parents: In pain did his mother bear him, and in pain did she give him birth. The carrying (of the child) to his wearing is (a period of) thirty months. At length, when he reached the age of full strength and attains forty years, he says "O my Lord! Grant me that I may be grateful for thy favour which Thou hast bestowed upon both my parents, and that I may work righteousness such as Thou mayest approve; and be gracious to me in my issue. Truly have I turned to Thee and truly do I bow (to Thee) in Islam. (46:15).

The Holy Qur'ān has also described the creation of hearing and sight and other physical characteristics and functions.

Have We not made for him a pair of eyes and a tongue and a pair of lips and shown him the two highways? (99:8-10.)

THE BEHAVIOURAL DIMENSION

Modern psychology is broadly concerned with the study of behaviour. Thinking is a form of behaviour, so is remembering or writing or any other form of activity performed by man, be it simple or complex, concerned with worship or common transactions.

The behaviour of man, his education, development and change is the objective of heavenly messages to ascertain the worship of the Creator. The study of this behaviour by observation, experimentation, analysis, and induction is the concern of various branches of psychology.

The Qur'ān is concerned from the very beginning to end with the behaviour of man in this world and with his destiny in the hereafter, which depends on his behaviour.

It is noticeable that all branches of faith except the principles of faith are concerned with behaviour and treatment. Even the bases of worship in Islam, like sâlāt, fasting, *zakāt* (almsgiving) and hajj are all an expression of behaviour which has two sides: internal and external, or spiritual and material. This expression is an interactive and complementary process that aims at moderation and balance in the behaviour of the Muslim and the believer. Good deeds represent a higher level of behaviour exercised by a man of faith, as the benefactor worships the Lord as if he can see Him and is certain that Allah can see the man in the act of worship.

While the unseen is only known to Allah, the visible behaviour is the field of psychology. Anyhow, from the Islamic point of view, it is enough to judge by what is visible, leaving what is unseen to the will of Allah. In this connection a *Hadīth* by the Prophet (SAS) says,

When you see a man frequenting the mosques then say he is a man of faith.

What is unseen is not a substitute for what is a visible behaviour. So, when one openly commits a vile act, he cannot justify it by saying that the intention is good. Actions are directed by intentions, but only when those intentions are good and do not lead intentionally to harm.

THE THIRD ELEMENT OF THE BEHAVIOURAL DIMENSION

I believe there is a difference between the spiritual and metaphysical dimensions of behaviour. The definition of behaviour in modern psychology is rather inadequate, as it does not take into consideration the dimension of faith which depends on intention. Yet, modern psychology has recently become more interested in the cognitive (rational) aspects of behaviour, even the spiritual aspect, though to a very small extent. Therefore, we may add to these two dimensions (behavioural and cognitive) another dimension: we may call this the faith dimension in behaviour. Here the emphasis is on the realization of the importance of the role of intention, and the reward a man may get when he behaves in a certain way, starting from an attitude of faith.

In this connection, al-Shatibb says,

> Actions are governed by intentions, and these in behaviour are considered forms of worship and habits. There are numerous proofs to this. Suffice it to say that intents differentiate between habits and worship; and in worship between what is obligatory or otherwise, and in habits between what is mandatory or elective; what is permitted or considerable and prohibited; what is sound or unsound, etc. One action may have a certain intent and is considered a form of worship; then it may have another intent and it becomes blasphemy, like falling prostrate to Allah or to an idol. Moreover, when a deed is joined to an intent, the prescribed judgements are joined likewise. When actions are devoid of intent then judgements are equally unattached, like the acts of a man in his sleep or those of the unconscious or the deranged.[6]

Though intent is basic in worship, the psychological study of behaviour is not carried out through the study of the intention but through the study of the observable behaviour, its results and consequences. When the intent is in itself an intrinsic behaviour, then it could be studied through interview and questioning or other techniques of psychological research. In fact, behaviour is often a reflection of intentions.

THE METAPHYSICAL DIMENSION

This dimension deals with aspects that the Muslims should not be overly occupied with, as it is enough to believe in them in the manner they were described in the Qur'ān and in the *Hādīth*. These aspects include the belief in resurrection, heaven and hell, angels and jinn, and imparting the spirit into man. These two sources give enough information to make further research unnecessary.[7]

COMPARING THE ISLAMIC AND CONTEMPORARY WESTERN PERSPECTIVES

The following are some of the basic issues I want to use in comparing the modern psychological attitudes about the characteristics of human nature and personality, with the Islamic attitude, based on the Holy Qur'ān and the *Hadīth* texts. I hope to enlarge this study, so it becomes a basic reference to understand human nature and its characteristics, the human personality and its dimension from a comparative psychological perspective. This is done by constant reference to the Qur'ān and the *Hadīth* texts, and the basic references in Western thought which gave rise to psychological concepts about the characteristics of human nature and personality:

Does man have free will in belief, opinion, and behaviour, or is he governed by predestination?

Is man eternal or nihilist?

Does man have two dimensions (material-spiritual) or one dimension only (material)?

Does man have an absolutely good or absolutely evil nature? Or does he have a nature open to good and evil attractions at the same time?

Is man's behaviour based on intentions alone, on deeds alone or on both?

Is man's past more influential in his behaviour, or is it his present, or future, or all of these?

Is optimism the basis of human nature, or is it pessimism?

Does man try to achieve balance, or is he in a state of constant growth?

Is the environment (learning) more influential in the behaviour of man or is it heredity?

Is every man unique in qualities and character or are there universal and comprehensive qualities in human nature and character dimensions?

The above are the basic questions in visualizing a model of human nature from an Islamic perspective. Therefore, I shall try to answer these questions one by one about this vision, comparing it to other visions within a modern psychological frame, with special reference to the basic personality theories discussed by Schultz (1994). I shall use this book in its treatment of the various visions of the major theories about the psychology of personality, such as: the analytical, the behavioural, the traits, the humanistic, and the cognitive. These theories are found in most texts about general psychology or modern books on the psychology of personality. In this respect, I do not find it necessary to go beyond Schultz's book on the subject.

FREE WILL OR DETERMINATION

Allah the Almighty created Adam in the best of models. He endowed him with mind and set him above all other creations, giving him knowledge of what he did not have (the names) and gave him complete freedom in paradise on one condition that he should not taste the fruit of a certain tree. Adam failed the test. Perhaps the aim of that test was to show Adam that his knowledge was limited, and that he was open to forgetfulness and temptation.

If man has limited knowledge, he must also have limited freedom. The fact that Adam was limited by one condition in paradise denotes his freedom had limitations. His forgetting and tasting the fruit of that tree is a sign that his knowledge was limited too.

The question of free will and determinism was discussed in *Kalam* (Islamic philosophy), and the various Islamic schools of thought are not in agreement about it. There are numerous details about the argument in major books on the subject. But we have to be satisfied with the clarification in the Qur'ān that freedom carries its own consequences and responsibilities; and that if man has a choice between faith and disbelief, then he has to bear the responsibilities of that choice. If he is free in his behaviour, then he should also bear the consequences of his chosen behaviour. Thus, we read in the Qur'ān:

> *Say, "The Truth is from your Lord"; Let him who will, believe, and let him who will, reject. For the wrongdoers We have prepared a Fire whose (smoke and flames) like the walls and roof of a text will hem them in: if they implore relief, they will be granted water like melted brass that will scald their faces. How dreadful the drink! How uncomfortable a couch to recline one! (18:29).*

Belief and disbelief are two types of behaviour connected with freedom of the mind and the will. We cannot talk about the freedom of will without having the ability to choose between belief and disbelief in the general sense of the words and in the religious sense as well, nor can we talk about responsibility devoid of the freedom of will and mind, or the freedom of behaviour. Therefore, the *Hadīth* testifies that no responsibility is imposed on a boy until he becomes of age, or the sleeper until he wakes, or the mad man until he regains his normal senses.

This freedom of behaviour between belief and disbelief, with all that goes between positive and negative behaviour (irrespective of absolute value judgement) may explain to us why man is variously described in the Qur'ān; some of these descriptions are positive, some are negative.

Therefore, man's liberty entails responsibility. Despite this complete freedom in belief and behaviour, the Qur'ān tells man very clearly that his abilities are limited, and consequently his freedom is also limited in certain fields. Man cannot choose when to be born.

In pain did his mother bear him, and in pain did she give him birth (46:15).

Nor can man choose when or where to die.

When their term is reached, not an hour they can cause delay, nor (an hour) can they advance. (7:3).

Nor does anyone know in what land he is to die. (31:34).

While we find the Qur'ān calling to adopt the causes and laws of Allah in the society and the world in general, the Muslim maintains the conviction that there is a cause of all causes Who is not caused by any cause, and that is Allah the Almighty, Who has power over everything, and on Whom all depend, to Whom all matters refer, and Whose Will comes above every will. Therefore, the behaviour of the Muslim should not be separated from this vision, even though he has to adopt the causes.

Nor, say of anything: I shall be sure to do so and so tomorrow, without adding: so please Allah. And call thy Lord to mind when thou forget and say: I hope that my Lord will guide me ever closer than this to the right road. (18:23-24).

So, how do theories of psychology stand on this subject? If we were to investigate theories of personality in modern psychology, we would find a lack of agreement on the subject. The Freudian theory, for instance, believes that man has no free will. That is to say that man is controlled by the unconscious, as he or she is in constant struggle with the unconscious forces like the instincts (such as sex and aggression) which he can never conquer. The role of the ego, according to Freud, is to coordinate between the pressures of the Id (instincts and desires) and those of the super ego (conscience and morals). This Freudian attitude about the freedom of man is not accepted by a neo-Freudian, Erich Fromm (1900-1980).[8] Though he was a follower of the psychoanalytic approach, Fromm has a positive attitude towards the free will of man, as he believes that personality is not formed by social, political and economic factors alone since man has certain psychological characteristics which can help to form his own nature (personality) and his society as well.

The Behavioural school shares the analytical school in their belief in determinism. Though not in agreement with Freud about the existence of internal forces that control personality, Skinner[9] (1904-1990)—as a forerunner of modern behaviourism—believed
that man's behaviour is like a pre-programmed instrument whose activity and function are decided beforehand. Therefore, man has no freedom in behaviour or spontaneity, as his behaviour is controlled by stimuli received from his environment.

Despite their different theoretical starting points, both the Analytical and the Behavioural schools do not believe in man's freedom. In contrast, the trait theory, represented by the American psychologist Gordon Allport[10] (1897-1967), held a moderate attitude. Allport believed that man is capable of controlling his future with a degree of freedom. But he also believed that the behaviour of man is defined by traits and personal inclinations that are difficult to change once they were formed.

If we turn to the Humanistic theory, we find that its advocates, like Abraham Maslow[11] (1908-1970), stress the free will of man, who has the potential of choosing the way to satisfy his needs and realize his capabilities. Therefore, man, according to this theory, is responsible about the degree or level of the growth he achieves.

The Cognitive theory, represented by modern psychologists led by George Kelley[12] (1905-1967), believes that man is free in choosing, controlling, and modifying his behaviour when there is a need for it. He is also free to revise his old concepts and replace them by new ones. According to this theory, man is always looking towards the future.

Finally, the theory of social learning, represented by Albert Bandura[13](1925) holds a moderate attitude about the freedom of man. Bandura believes that people are not powerless entities monitored by the forces of society, nor are they absolutely free that they can do anything they choose to do. Man and his environment mutually affect each other.

To sum up, we find wide disagreement among modern theories of psychology about the freedom of man. Most of these theories hold a moderate attitude, and say that the behaviour of man, though stemming from a will, is subject to hereditary forces (biological) and social forces (environmental) that influence that behaviour and direct it despite man's will. In fact, most psychologists agree that the major determinants of personality are biological as well as environmental factors.

An overall observation of the above indicates that existing theories ignore the will of Allah in directing and determining the destiny of man. They also ignore the spiritual determinants (belief in Allah) and their effect on personality and behaviour. To correct this shortcoming, one may refer to the Qur'ānic vision explained above. For more details, one may also refer to the various Islamic schools of thought, such as the Muʿtazilb and the Ashʿarb.

ETERNITY AND NIHILITY

Schultz does not approach this dimension, nor do psychologists in general, as they consider it a metaphysical subject, within the realm of philosophy. Though basically a metaphysical subject, eternity forms a variable influential on the behaviour of man.

The person who has a firm belief that he is answerable about his behaviour before Allah, and that he will be held accountable for his deeds on the Day of Judgement, which will destine him to eternity in paradise or in hell, will certainly have a different behaviour from a man who has no belief in paradise or hell, nor in eternity either. When no difference is detected in reality between the behaviour of the believer and the non-believer in eternity, then that difference may be ascribed to various factors, among which is a weak belief in the Day of Judgement.

DOES MAN HAVE ONE MATERIAL DIMENSION OR TWO DIMENSIONS (MATERIAL-SPIRITUAL)?

Schultz does not mention this point when dealing with aspects of human nature treated by various psychologists. Yet, a survey of opinions by psychologists on this point shows lack of agreement. Some are concerned with physical and biological aspects only. Others add the behavioural aspect to these two. The spiritual aspect connected with faith hardly finds many followers in modern psychology. Yet, the American Psychological Association recognizes religious psychology as one field in modern psychology.

To look at man as a being of various dimensions—physical, biological, spiritual and behavioural—that interact and are integrated, may fill a gap in modern psychological theories which look at man from a narrow viewpoint, limited by biological factors (hereditary and biochemical), and social and environmental determinants.

DOES MAN HAVE AN ABSOLUTE GOOD OR ABSOLUTE EVIL NATURE?

Again, Schultz does not approach this point in his above-mentioned book. This is probably because this is a philosophical and moral question, and not a psychological one. To deal with it would entitle a value judgement and a moral attitude, which many psychologists try to avoid. It is also due to a strong desire to separate psychology in subject and method from philosophy and ethics. Yet, it is not possible to completely separate psychology from philosophy and ethics. Therefore, I believe that the Islamic vision of man is an objective one, since it looks at man from various perspectives. Man is not all good or all evil, but is claimed by forces of good and evil, and he is always fighting against the evil tendencies. The Islamic view of man is concerned with individual differences in this field, and with the aspect of faith in the nature of man. No matter how good the man may be, he cannot be immune to evil; and no matter how evil the man may be, he cannot be completely deprived from any good. However, the type of education, the environment, the biological effects and values held by man are the factors that direct man towards good or evil, where one tendency dominates. Some Muslim scholars add to this the Satanic inducement and its negative effect on man's behaviour, which may lead him to commit evil deeds. To avoid such inducement, one has to pray for divine protection against the accursed Satan. This behaviour, again, does not fall within the frame of Western psychological theories. In brief, man is not all good or all evil. He is a mixture of angelic and satanic qualities. Therefore, he is a different being, neither an angel nor a devil: He is a Man.

To explore the attitude of modern psychologists about the relation of good and evil to man, we find Maslow in his Humanistic theory affirming that the innate human nature is basically good, but Maslow does not rule out the existence of evil among the human beings. Freud was extremely pessimistic. He maintained that he found "little 'good' about human beings on the whole."[14] Freud had a positive belief that aggression and sex are two instincts of a biological origin, and that they form a basic component of the human nature (Schultz, 1994).

IS THE BEHAVIOUR OF MAN BASED ON INTENTIONS AND DEEDS; ON INTENTIONS ALONE; OR ON DEEDS ALONE?

The question of intention is not a concern of psychology, as it is a religious concept connected with the practice of worship. We are told in the Qur'ān that the purpose of creating man and jinn is to worship the Creator, and the concept of worship in Islam comprises all forms of behaviour where the intention thereof is to come closer to Allah and worship Him. This relation was qualified by the quotation from al-Shatibī. Though modern psychology is not concerned with intentions, it does not ignore drives and incentives and their influence on behaviour. But Schultz does not mention this dimension in the vision of human nature by various psychologists, nor its influence on behaviour and personality.

We are told by the *Ḥadīth*: "Deeds are by intentions, and every man is requited in accordance with what he intended." But in Islam, especially in jurisprudence, consideration is of deeds and their consequences, not of intentions. The intention is basic in "worship" only, and the reward is in the hands of Allah. This distinction is basic to avoid misbehaviour on the pretext of good intention. These intentions cannot be judged by persons or organisations, irrespective of their status.

Briefly, then, all deeds in worship are seen through the lenses of intentions, which are known only to Allah and the doer of those deeds. The rewards or punishments of the human being are seen through consequences of deeds, not through intentions. The more the deeds match the intentions, the better the reward.

WHICH IS MORE INFLUENTIAL IN MAN'S BEHAVIOUR: HIS PAST, PRESENT, FUTURE ASPIRATIONS, OR ALL THREE?

Modern psychological theories about personality vary a great deal about the influence of the past or the present on the formation of the individual's personality. Some theories lay more emphasis on childhood (from birth to 12-13 years). Other theories feel that personality is free from influence of the past, as it may be influenced by events and experiences of the present, and by hopes and aspiration of the future.

The Analytical theory, especially the Freudian tendency, feels that the past of the individual is basic in forming the personality, and that the Id, which is the major part in forming the personality, is an inherited physiological factor, and that the stages of psycho-sexual development is also inherited. It is well known that the Freudian theory lays more emphasis on the Id, the unconscious, in the formation of personality. It believes that the psycho-sexual stages of development which the child experiences from birth to puberty are basic in the formation of personality, for the present and the future. Freud rather thinks that the first five years are the primary factor in forming the personality of the adolescent person.

In addition to this emphasis on heredity, the Analytical theory does not deny that part of the personality is acquired by learning at the early stages of life, and through interaction with the parents in particular. It is also well known that Freud's pupils and early followers like Alfred Adler and Carl Jung strongly opposed Freud's extremist vision of personality and his overemphasis on the sex and aggressive instincts as decisive in the shaping of personality types. This is not the place to review all criticisms of Freud, but we may point out that Adler, for instance, has a more balanced view, as he holds that the formation of personality is a result of the past and the present of the individual. Similar to this attitude is that of Jung, Eric Fromm and Eric Ericson, as they all see the importance of the various stages of life, not the early stages alone, which is the Freudian position.

The Traits theory, led by Gordon Allport, puts more emphasis on the present in the formation of personality. Therefore, Allport thinks that personality is more influenced by present events and by the look to the future more than what happened in the past.

The Humanistic theory, as expressed by Maslow, has a balanced attitude on this subject. He recognizes the importance of early childhood experiences in enhancing or obstructing the development of personality. But he does not think that we are victims of those experiences. Maslow is one of few psychologists who lays more emphasis on various stages of life, especially the middle period.

The Behavioural theory has a similar balanced attitude like that of the Humanistic theory on this subject. The forerunner of modern behaviourism, B.F. Skinner, believes that past experiences have an equal influence on our behaviour and personality as do present experiences. This makes the behavioural attitude another balanced attitude on this subject.

THE ATTITUDE OF ISLAM

Islam pays great attention to the childhood period as it has a vital role in the formation of personality and behaviour. Yet, the relevant texts do not seem to indicate that the individual is destined to remain a prisoner of his past. The historical Islamic experience clearly shows that Islam was able to change the behaviour and personality of the Prophet's companions who embraced Islam out of belief and conviction, leading them in a new direction. Islam could also radically change entire nations and civilisations in the field of creed and belief in particular. While man is answerable about his past, there is room for repentance to change the consequences of that past if it was marred with sins and bad deeds. This change could be achieved by performing good deeds, quitting sins and evil deeds and proclaiming repentance. Islam views the period of childhood as the time for learning and training. It is the period when the person is not held answerable until he reaches puberty.

The future is an important dimension in the formation of the personality of the Muslim. This is because the future in Islam is not limited to this world alone, but it extends to the Day of Judgment. Therefore, the future is a significant dimension in the formation of the Muslim personality and directing it to good deeds in the present and the future.

The best summary of the Islamic attitude on this subject may be found in the following verse from the Qur'ān:

But seek, with the (wealth) which Allah has bestowed on thee, the Home of the Hereafter, nor forget thy portion in this world: but do thou good, as Allah has been good to thee. (28:77).

It is also expressed in the wisdom of the saying, "Do for your present world as if you were to live forever, and for your life in the hereafter as if you were to die tomorrow."

DOES THE ENVIRONMENT (LEARNING) OR HEREDITARY FACTORS HAVE MORE INFLUENCE ON MAN'S BEHAVIOUR?

Islam recognizes the influence of heredity (the biological factor) in the nature and personality of man. Modern science has shown that sperm and egg carry within them the hereditary qualities that shape the individual in various stages of his or her life. This is alluded to in the following verse of the Qur'ān:

It is He Who has created man from water; then has He established relationship of lineage and marriage: for thy Lord has power (over all things); (25:54).

The Jalalain exegesis reads "water" to denote "sperm and egg", and the "relationship of lineage" points to the father's side, while "marriage" denotes the mother's side. That is to say, the biological is caused by heredity and the social is caused by marriage. Thus, there is reference to the biological (hereditary) and the social (caused by marriage).

In addition to heredity, Islam puts great emphasis on the role of parents and society in the formation of the personality of man. The *Hadith* tells us that "No one is born except on innate character: His parents turn him into a Jew, a Christian or a Magian." The *Hadith* affirms the influence of both heredity and environment in the formation of personality. The Qur'ān reproached the unbelievers for following their forefathers' behaviour in general, and their deviant beliefs in particular.

When they do aught that is shameful, they say "We found our fathers doing so"; and "Allah commanded us thus." Say: "Nay, Allah never commands what is shameful; Do ye say of Allah what ye know not?" (7:28).

Judging by several experiences in the history of individuals, groups and nations, it is clear that man's personality is capable of learning, changing and excelling in various stages of life. The foremost example proving this is the change effected by Islam in the souls of people of various ages, and in the changed conditions of tribes and nations upon embracing Islam. Therefore, Islam does not endorse a belief in the decisive influence of the past, but it keeps the doors open for soul-searching to accommodate and align oneself with the teachings of Islam. So, Islam discards what came before, and opens new horizons, through repentance and asking forgiveness, that restore hope to man. Islam does not encourage a belief in the decisive influence of environment and learning: it holds that both heredity and learning have their own significant effect.[15]

Yet, a general overview of the texts would show that the thrust of the Islamic concern is with learning and environment rather than with heredity. Islamic teachings assert the capability to change at both the individual and social level.

THE STAND OF MODERN PSYCHOLOGICAL THEORIES

There is a large discrepancy among psychologists on this issue, to a degree of contradiction at times. Some would give more importance to heredity, denying significant influence on the environment. Others give the environment great all the power to influence the formation of personality and relevant psychological qualities like intelligence, and emotion. After twenty years of disagreement, an integrative approach that recognizes the influence of traits and individual needs in addition to the influence of environment in the formation of personality and behaviour has emerged.[16]

IS OPTIMISM OR PESSIMISM BASIC IN HUMAN NATURE?

When Allah created Adam and informed the angels about this new creation who was to become vicegerent the earth, the angels asked the Almighty how He could put someone on Earth who would cause evil and bloodshed.

> *Behold, thy Lord said to the angels: "I will create a vicegerent on earth." They said: "Wilt Thou place therein one who will make mischief therein and shed blood? Whilst we do celebrate Thy praises and glorify Thy holy (name)." He said: "I know what ye know not." Qur'ān* (2:30).

Though the angels wondered about the wisdom in creating Adam, the Almighty ordered the angels to fall prostrate before Adam as Allah the Almighty knows what the angels do not know about the creation of Adam.

Although Adam forgot the order of the Almighty while he was in Paradise with his wife, Allah pardoned Adam after he repented. Even after the fall of Adam and Eve from Paradise, and after the death of Abel at the hands of his brother Cain, and after the bloodshed and disobedience committed by man against his fellow man throughout the ages, humanity is not all evil. Nor is it all good. A man's deeds will largely be good or bad based first and foremost according to his nature (biological or hereditary determinants), then according to his

education and learning; and lastly according to his deeds and faith. The Holy Qur'ān wholly encourages good deeds and the realization of the vicegerency of Allah on earth despite the pressures and difficulties of life. We find in the text of a *Hadith* that the Prophet (SAS) encourages optimism and discourages pessimism. "No omen but the good one. They said: "and what is a good omen?" He said: "The good word you may hear."[17]

Briefly, then, Islam is all a call for optimism and rejection of submission of dejection, even for those who have sinned greatly.

Say: "O my servants who have transgressed against their souls: Despair not of the Mercy of Allah: for Allah forgiveness all sins for He is oft-Forgiving, Most Merciful." (39:53)

THE ATTITUDE OF PSYCHOLOGICAL THEORIES ON PESSIMISM AND OPTIMISM

The Analytical School

Freud is extremely pessimistic about human nature. He describes man in negative terms, saying that he is destined to struggle with his inner forces (instincts) all the time, and is doomed to become a victim of struggle, restraint, and anxiety. Contrary to this, Carl Jung is optimistic about human nature since he sees man capable of growth, improvement, and development. The same attitude is adopted by Adler, Erich Fromm, Murrey, and Horney.

The Traits School

Allport describes man in optimistic terms. He believes in man's capability of improvement, and in social reform. Raymond Catell has a slightly different attitude from Allport.[18] In his youth, Catell was more optimistic about man's ability to solve the problems facing society, through gaining the knowledge necessary to control the environment. But reality was not up to Catell's aspirations, so he concluded that both human nature and society have deteriorated.

The Humanistic School

Followers of the Humanistic school have a positive attitude towards this issue, as they are all optimistic about the human nature. Therefore, they emphasise the psychological health rather than the psychological disturbances, the growth and development rather than stagnation and fossilisation, the positive aspects of man rather than his weaknesses and shortcomings.

The Behavioural School

Though Skinner and other behaviourists believe that the environment controls the behaviour of man, they affirm that man is responsible for designing this environment and the formation of its various aspects, like buildings, tools, clothes, food, government institutions, social system, language, habits, etc. Therefore, man can introduce modification into that environment to realize his own interests. Therefore, man becomes the controller and controlled at the same time. Or, according to Skinner, man designs a controlling culture, but he ultimately becomes a product of that culture.

The Cognitive School

Represented by its forerunner George Kelley (1905-1967) this school believes that man is a rational being who can form concepts through which he can see the world and formulate a unique approach to reality. Kelley believes that man himself plans his own destiny, and that he is not a victim of that destiny.

DOES HUMANS ENDEAVOUR TOWARDS BALANCE OR ARE THEY IN CONSTANT DEVELOPMENT?

We gather from the Holy verses that man is in constant growth physically and psychologically (emotionally and mentally) until he becomes forty years old. Then he gradually deteriorates, also physically and psychologically, until he dies.

> *If We grant long life to any, We cause him to be reversed in nature: Will they not then understand?* (36:68).

Despite this general law of growth, the Holy Verses and the *Hadith* texts all encourage the search for knowledge and the education of the soul in the various stages of life, though responsibility begins with puberty and ends with death. The various schools of psychology have the following stands:

The Analytical School: Freud believes that man is forced to restore balance and keep a state of physiological equilibrium in order to protect the organism against stress and strain. This is an instinctive force which constantly leads the organism to feel stress, and it therefore tries to lessen that stress and achieve pleasure. Contrary to that, Carl Jung believes that man is in a state of constant growth, and that major changes in personality begin to appear in his midlife, between

35-40 years of age.

Adler believes that man constantly endeavours to achieve supremacy, and that such endeavour increases rather than decreases stress. Contrary to Freud, Adler believes that to relieve stress in not the only drive that man has, because the endeavour towards excellence demands greater effort, which is opposite to the state of balance characterized by relief of tension and stress. Moreover, Adler believes that the endeavour for excellence is an individual and societal process. Briefly, all followers of psychoanalysis, except Freud, emphasize growth rather than balance as a quality of human nature and personality.

<u>The Traits School</u>: Allport thinks that the main object of life is not to release tension, as Freud maintained, but to raise that tension which sets man looking for new aims and new challenges. When man achieves one objective, he has a new drive to face another challenge for another objective. The reward in the process, according to Allport, is not the achievement itself, but the process of meeting the challenge. The same holds true in the endeavour to reach an objective. What matters is the effort, not reaching the objective. Therefore, man is constantly in need of new objectives to move and drive him, and to keep a necessary level of tension in the personality.

<u>The Humanistic School</u>: The followers of this school believe that man is in a state of constant growth and development. Maslow thinks that man is driven by innate needs which graduate, in a pyramid fashion, from basic physiological needs like food, drink, propagation, sleep and breathing up to the need for safety, for a sense of belonging, love, appreciation and up to the need for self-realization, which lies at the top of all needs. Maslow further thinks that this final need is not realized except in the middle of a lifetime, and only by a small percentage of successful people.

<u>The Behavioural School</u>: The Behaviourists are not concerned with inner drives and tensions which move man to realize objectives or make some achievement, because they believe that behaviour is formed by learning, which, in turn, is formed by external factors. This leads to the denial that innate (hereditary) or internal (subjective) factors drive man to achieve some objectives. An objective, according to Skinner, is not individual, but social. Though Behaviourists affirm that basic behaviour is formed in childhood, they do not deny the possibility of modification or change of that behaviour during adolescence which lead to acquiring new forms of behaviour. Briefly, then, the Behaviourists have a moderate attitude towards the issue of "balance-growth.

DOES THE INDIVIDUAL HAVE A DISTINCTIVE QUALITY AND PERSONALITY, OR IS THERE UNIVERSALITY IN HUMAN NATURE AND PERSONALITY?

Most psychologists who write about personality agree that it is characterised by individuality and consistency throughout the time. But they disagree about individuality/universality, as a quality of human nature:

The Analytical School: Freud recognizes the quality of universality in the human nature, as he believes that everyone goes through the same stages of psycho-sexual development, as he is moved by the same forces and instincts (the Id). Yet, Freud affirms that a part of the personality is distinctive. Therefore, the ego and the super ego, though performing the same role for every individual, differ from one person to another because they were formed through personal experiences. Jung has a similar attitude to that of Freud, but he differs in explaining this dimension of personality. Jung believes that there is a difference in personality until the middle period of the lifetime. After that, there is a universality in the formation of personality, as no distinctive types of personality appear after the middle period of life. Differing from Freud and Jung, Adler clearly affirms the distinction and individuality of the personality. Fromm stands in between. Fromm believes that there is a universal and comprehensive quality in the personality, which is seen in a common social quality within a certain culture. At the same time, Fromm believes that everyone is different from the other.

The Traits School: Allport believes that everyone differs from the other, because each has his own traits and capabilities which clearly denote his character and set him apart from the others. Yet, Allport does not deny the existence of common traits among people.

The Humanistic School: Maslow believes that needs and drives are common among people (universal). But the ways these needs are satisfied differ from one person to another, because this is a behaviour that can be learned. Therefore, Maslow and Rogers stand on the middle ground of this subject.

The Behavioural School: Because the formation of behaviour is one by learning, individuals differ from one another, as experience forms behaviour, and people have different experiences, especially in childhood. Therefore, we cannot find two persons behaving in exactly the same manner. That leads the Behaviourists to say that distinctiveness is the basic quality of human nature and personality.

THE ATTITUDE OF ISLAM TOWARDS UNIVERSALITY IN HUMAN NATURE AND PERSONALITY

We clearly see from the Qur'ān that people were created out of one soul. This is repeated four times in *surah* al-Nisā ': 1, al-An^{c}ām: 98, al-A^{c}rāf: 189, and al-Zumar. Yet, Islam recognizes differences among people, whether in physical aspects, psychological aspects, or both. Responsibility for deeds and behaviour in Islam is individual:

> *O mankind! We created you from a single (pair) of a male and a female, and made you into nations and tribes, that you may know each other. Verily the most honoured of you in the sight of Allah is the most righteous of you. And Allah has full knowledge and is well acquainted (with all things)* (49:13).

We may see by this verse that differentiation is on two levels: individual and societal (nations and tribes). The Almighty made the difference in colour and language a sign to those who are capable of thinking.

> *And among His signs is the creation of the heavens and the earth and the variations in your languages and your colours; verily in that are Signs for those who know. (3:22).*

About the differences between people, which is now called "the individual differences", we read,

> *Their Prophet said to them: "Allah hath appointed Talūt as king over you." They said, "How can he exercise authority over us when we are better fitted than he to exercise authority. And he is not even gifted with wealth in abundancy?" He said, "Allah hath chosen him above you and hath gifted him abundantly with knowledge and bodily prowess. Allah granteth His authority to whom He pleaseth. Allah is all embracing, and He knoweth all things." (2:247).*

We may conclude from the above verses that human nature and personality are based on differentiation, though the origin is one (one soul), and that this differentiation is based on physical, psychological, and spiritual levels of the individual, and on social and racial groupings, i.e., tribes, nations, colours, and languages.

Finally, we can visualise the model of human nature from an Islamic perspective, and in accordance with the above-mentioned qualities and dimensions. The major aspects of this model are the following:

> Emphasis on the spiritual aspect and its influence, as a belief concept, on behaviour. The direct relation between faith and behaviour cannot be

severed.

The integration and interaction among spiritual, biological and physical aspects determine the personality and behaviour of the individual.

Man has a free will in some issues and is predestined in others at the same time. Apparently, the environment is more influential than hereditary in the formulation of behaviour and personality, thus recognizing the influence of both heredity and biological factors.

The Islamic view emphasizes the importance of growth, change, and learning in the formation of personality and behaviour rather than the realization of balance, which basically aims at relieving tension and achieving pleasure.
Despite the negative aspects in the personality and behaviour of man, the Islamic perspective of personality is more optimistic than that of some psychologists. It calls for optimism, the desertion of pessimism and dread, and resisting despair, dejection, and bad dreams.

Despite the emphasis of the Islamic perspective on the origin of creation from one soul, the difference on spiritual, psychological, biological and physical levels is considered more important than similarity or typicality of personality and behaviour. The Islamic position calls for competition among people in the field of good deeds.

Islam considers the present and future of personality and behaviour more important than the past. The period from childhood until puberty is not accountable before the Islamic law (*Sharb^cah*), but the education, parents' responsibility and social institutions are of basic importance in this period according to Islam.

CONCLUSION

It is difficult to put a conclusion to the issue of human nature from a comparative perspective. So, this is a conclusion to the essay and not to the issue. Muslim scholars have, for a long time, ignored the study of human nature and human sciences, despite the importance of these disciplines in the development of civilization, and even though man is the center of the Qur'ānic message, as it is his responsibility is to establish the vicegerency of Allah on earth.

This essay may help those interested in the subject to make postulates about human nature from a psychological perspective in general, and the relative theories on human personality and social behaviour in particular. These postulates must be liable to testing and empirical or logical study or both, and liable to comparison among cultures and religions. This may form a theoretical basis for further studies on the subject, and for theoretical psychological and empirical studies relating to personality and social behaviour from an Islamic perspective.

In fact, the "Islamisation" of psychology must begin with laying the theoretical bases of a psychological vision of human nature on the one hand and defining the subject matter and methodology of psychology on the other. It is obvious that a vision of human nature from a psychological point of view cannot be separated from religious, philosophical and moral issues, but we have kept the treatment of the psychological aspect of human nature separately for the purpose of convenience.

Finally, there is a need for further studies to clarify the attitudes of various Islamic schools of thought on the issues related to a vision of the human nature. Muslim psychologists and others are required to lay the theoretical bases to the understanding of human nature in a manner helpful to induce theories and applications.

NOTES

1. See S. L. Wrightsman, *Assumptions About Human Nature*, 2nd Ed. (Newbury Park: Sage Publications, 1992).

2. Cf. L. Stevenson, *Seven Theories of Human Nature*, 2nd ed (Oxford: Oxford University Press, 1987); N. Chaney, *Six Images of Human Nature* (Englewood, New Jersey: Prentice-Hall, 1990).

3. Abbas al-Akkad, al-*insān fi al-Qur'ān al-karīm* (Cairo: Dārul Nahdha, n.d); Bint alShātī Aisha, *al-Qur'ān wa Quathaya al-insān* (Beirut Dar alcIlm Lilmalyeen, 19*82); ;* Barakat Ahmad Lutf,, *al-Tabia 'aal-Bashariaya fi al-Qur'ān al-karīm* (Al Ryadh: Dar Al-Marrikh, 1981); Amīr cAbdul Azziz, *al-Insān fi al-Islām* (Oman: Dar al-Furquan, 1984); Ismacil al-Faruqī "Nadhariayat al-insān fi al-Qur'ān al-karīm", *Al-Tawhīd* 94 (1984, Rajab-Sha 'ban); Sayyid Mursī, *al-Tarbiya wa al-tabia 'a al al-Insāniya fi al-Fikr al-Islāmi wa Bardhi al-Falsafat al Gharbiya* (Cairo: Dar-al Ma 'arif, 1988); Akbar Ahmed, *Nahwa cIlm al-insān al-Islāmi*, trans. Abdul Ghani Khalaf Allah (Herndon, Virginia: IIIT, 1990); Al-cAnī Nizar, al-Shakhsiay *al-Insān fi al-Islām* (Oman: IIIT, 1998).

4. D. Schultz and S.E. Schultz, *Theories of Personality*, 5h ed. (Pacific Grove: Brooks/Cole Publishing, 1994).

5. I have intentionally chosen to say "an Islamic" not "the Islamic" perspective to show that this is only a relative position, related to my own understanding of the texts, and I leave the door open for other research endeavours in this vital field where co-operation is a basic need. I would further point out that this comparison, between the Islamic vision and the western visions of the human nature, is a comparison of my relative understanding of the Islamic perspective with another relative understanding of the Western psychologist, concerning the human nature and personality, based on their philosophic and religious background: Christian or Jewish. It is not a comparison of the absolute with the relative or divine knowledge with human interpretation. I would also like to point out that the Islamic vision of the human nature and its characteristics, and of the personality of man, is too vital and comprehensive to be summarised. All operations of amplification simply aim at making such a comprehensive vision more understandable, in order to use it as a theoretical frame of reference for theorising and conducting research in various human and social fields. A few comments on conducting this study: It is necessary to mention at this point that this comparison is of a relative (attitude of Western psychologists) to a relative (Islamic understanding of my own). Secondly, non-Muslim psychologists have a starting point based on a religious or philosophic background, which they often hide, though they are affected by those bearings, consciously or unconsciously. For this vision, this theoretical vision of mine, which stems from an understanding of Islamic texts, to be more comprehensive, it must be supported by empirical research using (Muslim and non-Muslim) samples, taking into consideration such background variables as age, education level, and gender. Another basic point to study is the relationship between theoretical vision and actual behaviour, which originally stems from such theoretical vision, in one way or another.

6. Al-Shatibī Abū Ishaq, *al-Muwāfaqā fi Usul alSharÍah, II«* (publisher unknown.

N.d.), 323-4.

7. Throughout my contemplation of the Holy Qur'ān, I have not found a single verse that encourages the Muslim to ponder over the metaphysical aspects. In fact, the entire Qur'ān is a call to ponder over the creation of the Almighty (earth, mountains, clouds, stars, animals, and man himself) so this observation could serve as a proof of the existence of the Creator, first, and to use those creations in the service of man, second. Therefore, the "spirit" in the metaphysical sense of the word is not open for pondering and scientific research. "They ask thee concerning the spirit. Say the Spirit is a concern of my Lord: Of knowledge it is only a little that is communicated to you." (17:85). The third point is that this concept of the various dimensions of the human nature has three further dimensions, namely: past, present and future.

8. Schultz and Schultz, *Theories of Personality*, pp. 152-193.

9. Ibid., pp. 351-377.

10. Ibid., pp. 197-218.

11. Ibid., pp. 275-299.

12. Ibid., pp. 325-347.

13. Ibid., pp. 381-406.

14. Ibid., p. 58

15. *Sūrah al-Maʿārij*, p. 19-34.

16. E.J. Phares, *Introduction to Personality* (New York: Harper Collings College, Publication, 1991).

17. Related by al-Bukhār, in *The Book of Medicine*

18. Schultz and Schultz, *Theories of Personality*, pp. 219-245.

5

The Place of Human Nature in Ibn Khaldūn's Thinking

MOHAMAD DHAOUDHI

IBN KHALDŪN'S FORGOTTEN NOTION

Ibn Khaldūn's well-established positivist approach to the study of societies, cultures and civilisations seems to have given the following impression to many researchers and scholars of his heritage: in his explanation of societies' and civilisations' dynamics, the author of the *Muqaddimah* dealt only with objective[1] external laws, rules and factors, such as *al-ᶜasâbiyyah*, royal authority, religion, or Bedouin and sedentary milieus. Consequently, he has been often described, and rightly so, as the greatest sociologist and historian[2] not only of the Arab Muslim civilisation of the Middle Ages, but of all civilisations preceding his own time. In establishing his New Science of the "out there": the social objective reality (as it is often called by modern social scientists), principally through his positivist outlook of social phenomena, Ibn Khaldūn appears to have remained strongly attached and influenced as well by his view of the internal, "in there" human nature.

Ibn Khaldūn's notion of human nature and its deterministic impact on his assumptions, conceptualizations and theories of societies and civilisations have been largely if not completely neglected by those who have studied Ibn Khaldūn's work. We have hardly encountered a study that preoccupies itself seriously with the subject of human nature in Ibn Khaldūn's thinking.[3]

This is due, of course, to the prevailing positivist spirit of the author's works, especially in his *Muqaddimah*. In all of them he stands out primarily as historian, sociologist, political scientist, and economist. In brief, he is a careful observer of the "out there" social reality: societies and civilisations' dynamic forces. His comprehensive (global, multidisciplinary) approach as well as his avant-garde, positivist-rational (and, rationalizing) terminology, methodology, and conceptualization of social phenomena like *alᶜasâbiyyah* (group feeling), are outward evidence of his striking

90

empirico-positivist scholarship.[4]

Referring to the author of the *Muqaddimah* only by those titles, though understandable, certainly leaves out some rather important dimensions of the thinking of this encyclopedic scholar of the Middle Ages. His concept of human nature and its implications on the individual's behavior and civilisation's destiny must not be discarded or neglected in any rigorous analysis of Ibn Khaldūn's works. Yet indifference[5] toward the Maghrebi sociologist's intimate vision of human nature is widespread, and one can speculate that positivist, modern social scientists would perceive this aspect of his thinking as obscure, subjective, irrational, and unpersuasive. Nonetheless, this vision is an important element in explaining, for example, his empathy with the Bedouins, on the one hand, and his manifest hostility to the sedentaries, on the other.[6] Thus, Ibn Khaldūn's psychology of man becomes basic for a better understanding of his wide-ranging thought.

IBN KHALDŪN'S CONTRIBUTION TO THE UNDERSTANDING OF HUMAN NATURE

Psychology's Place in Ibn Khaldūn's Work

The author's famous scholarly treatise (*The Muqaddimah*) on man as a social being, societies' dynamics, and the moving forces of human cultures and civilisations, among others, has neither a separate chapter nor even a section on "the Psychology of Man". Chapter III of the *Muqaddimah* deals with Politics, and section I of Chapter V adequately covers the subject of Economics. This is a further specific reason why Ibn Khaldūn's vision of man's basic human nature has not drawn attention from those who have studied his social thought. Nonetheless, Ibn Khaldūn's psychological knowledge of man can surely be found scattered[7] throughout the *Muqaddimah*. In it, one encounters not only the author's typeset of human nature but also its actual varying effects on the dynamics of human societies and civilisation as well. Thus, the interactions of the social and the psychological forces are not only the shaping factors of human personality as modern psychology asserts, but also of societies' and civilisations' unfolding. In this sense, Ibn Khaldūn's view of social psychology has a larger frame and scope of analysis that goes beyond the realm of the individual to cover human societies and civilisations. This perception of the author of the *Muqaddimah* makes one realize that he is more than just a rigid socio-historian.

Ibn Khaldūn's Typology of Human Nature

No doubt there are a number of references to human nature in the *Muqaddimah*. But the difficult task lies in identifying with precision specific categories referred to by the author. Nonetheless, in reading Ibn

Khaldūn's statements on man's nature, one can identify three categories or types of human nature.

Human nature as reflected in *al-fiṭrah*

In Islamic thought, *al-fiṭrah* is either that human state devoid of bad traits and customs at birth (creation) or, at worst; it is that human state that predisposes human nature more toward virtues than vices. Ibn Khaldūn's use of the concept of *al-fiṭrah* is inspired by the Qur'ān as well as by the *Ḥadīth*.[8] In these two basic Islamic sources, the notion of *al-fiṭrah* still appears to mean, also, a balanced human inclination that lives according to the laws of the natural divine order.

The Qur'ān sees Islam as the best match for *al-fiṭrah* as defined above. Thus, Islam is referred to in the Muslim Holy Book as "*dīn al-fiṭrah*", that is, the religion whose teachings, laws, rules, ethics et al. are inspired by the very balanced (primitive/Bedouin)[9] state of human nature. In other words, Islam as an ethico-religio-cultural and social system meets and satisfies the basic innate ("fiṭrah")/primitive human needs on which depend not only the harmony of the individual and his or her human collectivity, but also that of the entire divine order.

The *al-fiṭrah* type of human nature seems to correspond to Rousseau's "*L'homme est ne' bon*". It is Ibn Khaldūn's yardstick by which he measures the quality of human individuals, groups, societies, and civilisations. The closer they remain to the primitive/ innate state of human nature, the better they are. It may be argued here then that the explanation for Ibn Khaldūn's hostile attitude toward the sedentaries is that they are seen as having corrupted their good, primitive, innate human nature, while his admiration of the Bedouins stems out of their apparent closeness to the primitive goodness of human nature,[10] the *al-fiṭrah* state of human existence.

The Dualistic Human Nature

Ibn Khaldūn's second type[11] of human nature resembles in its dynamics *al-ᶜasâbiyyah*. The latter is a conflicting set of historical moving forces that often clash with each other, thus creating a chain of conflicts and antagonisms. Viewed that way, the dynamics of *al- ᶜasâbiyyah* offer a compelling explanation of human history as an endless chain of exhaustion, rotation, and evolution. Likewise, the author's second view of human nature shows the conflicting nature of human beings' make up. The roots of the conflicts are the result of the dualistic components that constitute human nature itself.

As in the first type, the Qur'ānic vision inspires Ibn Khaldūn's understanding of the second type of the nature of man. He writes: "It should be known that God put good and evil into the nature of man. Thus, He says in the Qur'ān, 'We led him along two paths'" (90:10). So human nature has an equal inclination toward doing good and evil. With this even emphasis of good and evil elements, the Qur'ānic perspective appears to give human nature a fundamental dialectical characteristic. The latter would imply that man's own nature makes out of him a being always in a state of change, conflict, ascent, and decline. Man cannot be other than a dynamic creature: incapable of escaping the human condition whose characteristics are endless tension, agitation, and confrontation. Ibn Khaldūn translates the human duality into animalistic as well as human dimensions. On the one hand, the former refers to such things which humans share with species of animals like food, dwelling, movement, senses, and many other things.[12] On the other, man's capacity to think and reason is his most distinct human quality.[13] Conflicts and tensions arising out of these two poles are uniquely human. With this type of a dichotomist human nature, man has a strong chance of being involved in wrongdoing. In Ibn Khaldūn's terms, man has the capacity to move away from his initial good (primitive) human nature. However, he can presumably avoid this either by dedicating his personal good inclinations to improve himself, or by relying on religion as a guiding model for good behavior. "Evil is the quality that is closest to man when he fails to improve his customs and when religion is not used to improve him".[14]

In this way, Ibn Khaldūn seems to consider religion (particularly Islam) as a system which can preserve human nature closest to its primitive good state, while allowing for the evolution of the individual as well as the collectivity. With such an interpretation of his thinking, the religion of Islam would allow humankind "to have its cake" (the preservation of the innate good human nature) and "eat it at the same time" (develop it without corrupting it through the compelling processes of civilisations). Thus, neither Ibn Khaldūn's esteem for Bedouins nor his strong Islamic belief should be seen as just a mere coincidence. They are, we believe, intimately related to the strong link between *al-fiṭrah* and Bedouin states as outlined here. Nonetheless, Ibn Khaldūn's committed belief in the good effect of religion on human nature does not invalidate his notion of the duality of human nature (by transforming it to pure goodness— "one dimensional nature"), but rather that religion will encourage the preservation of much of that innate human goodness[15] as witnessed among the Bedouins.

The Aggressive Human Nature

Ibn Khaldūn bluntly stated that the roots of human aggression as well as injustice are to be found in the animalistic side of human nature; "Because aggression and injustice are in the animalistic nature of man." Like some contemporary ethnologists and psychologists[16] studying man's and animal's behavior, the author of the *Muqaddimah* considers aggression as a fundamental inborn feature whose infrastructure is widely observed among all living beings, including man: "Aggression is in the nature of living beings. God has given each of them a defensive organ".[17]

Yet man not only manifests what may be labeled "reflexive aggressive response for survival" towards other humans. Ibn Khaldūn's observations and experiences enabled him to unveil other complex forms which human aggression could take. He had noticed injustice committed by humans, not because their physical survival was at stake, but rather, it appeared to be the result of a sort of—what we could call "Hobbesian"— human readiness to do injustice to others. He writes, "He who casts his eye upon the property of his brother will lay his hand upon it to take it, unless there is a restraining influence to hold him back."[18] Viewed this way, human nature's animalistic components are far from being conducive to harmonious cooperation, social solidarity, and evolution. On the contrary, he considers them to be fundamentally destructive and disruptive to man's collective and individual advancement.[19] In looking at these three forms of human nature, one can assert that there is an unambiguous Qur'ānic/Islamic influence on the author's thinking concerning man's nature. The first type (*al-fiṭrah* state) and the second one (the dual nature) are drawn from the Islamic outlook on the range of human nature as expressed especially in the Qur'ān. These two categories depict man's nature at its very primitive and natural state either as good—more or less— or neutral (dualist) towards good or bad actions. In both cases, human nature is overwhelmingly dialectical.

However, the third type of the Human Nature is a strikingly ugly one. Man falls into this state when he becomes dominated by his animalistic (materialistic) desires. Every extravagant materialism bears within it the seeds of its own destruction. The corruption of the primitive goodness of human nature is one of the most important casualties[20] of the sedentarization process. In the luxurious sedentary milieu, man is transformed from a human being to an animal.[21] When this takes place, the undermining of Islamic as well as Bedouin/natural values becomes a *fait accompli*.

Thus, nothing is left (neither *al-ᶜasâbiyyah* nor religious guidance) in the luxurious sedentary culture to preserve the essential goodness and dualism of the primitive human nature. The ultimate fatal decline of human civilisation becomes inevitable. According to this frame of analysis, Ibn Khaldūn's *Muqaddimah* can be assessed and evaluated on two fronts: Firstly, there are in the *Muqaddimah* the visible stated socio-historical forces which explain, among others, societies and civilisations' growth and decline. Secondly, there are also in the *Muqaddimah* tacit and latent statements of a psychological nature which make human nature (in its three forms) an essential contributing factor (through the actions of the social actors) in societies' and civilisations' growth and decline.

Human Nature's Dynamics
Al-fiṭrah is the type of human nature Ibn Khaldūn favoured.[22] This is seen

to represent the primitive, Bedouin cum natural, and good human nature. From this outlook of human nature, one could infer that man's potential inborn good nature would remain closer to *al-fiṭrah* state if the outside milieu's structure and living conditions are fundamentally Bedouin (primitive) or Islamic in character.

The second type of human nature is a dialectical one. Good and bad human tendencies are continuously in confrontation. As such, human nature is very precarious and offers little resistance to the influence of its milieu. The direction it takes is externally determined.[23] It swings one way or the other depending on the nature of its surrounding environment.

Finally, man's good human nature is transformed to type III if his external social milieu is deprived of both the Bedouin/simple living conditions as well as Islamic teachings, values and practices.

IBN KHALDŪN'S THREE TYPES OF HUMAN NATURE AS TOOLS OF RESEARCH

Can these sub-categories of human nature be put to use in understanding the theory of civilisation's rise and fall? This is what we attempt to do in the following pages of this chapter that will deal with the main forces behind the Arab-Muslim civilisation's rise and fall.

When the three sub-notions of human nature are correlated with civilisations' rise and fall, one finds on the one hand that Ibn Khaldūn linked Arab-Muslim civilisation's rise not only to the presence of a strong "*ʿasâbiyyah*" and Islamic belief among the early Arab Muslim Bedouins, as commonly claimed by Khaldūnists, but also to their good/innate/primitive human nature (types I +II).

On the other hand, Ibn Khaldūn was also convinced that the Arab Muslim civilisation's (and all civilisations for that matter) breakdown is due to excessive materialism which disintegrates *alᶜasâbiyyah* and weakens religion and animalizes human nature (type III).

Looking closely at these factors of civilisations' rise and fall,[24] one can identify two patterns as shown in Table I below: (1) in the case of the Arab Muslim civilisation's rise, the variable of good human nature (Types I+II) appears to be there first since the human personality is, by Ibn Khaldūn's Qur'ānic definition, born with them. The development of *al-ᶜasâbiyyah* and then religion follow suit later. (2) As for as the causes of Arab-Muslim civilisations fall, the corruption of human nature., (type III) seems to follow the disintegration of *al-ᶜasâbiyyah* and religion's abatement, thereby causing the decline of the sedentary civilisation.

Bedouinity and its Dynamics

For Ibn Khaldūn, the very rise of Arab-Muslim civilisation appears to have been contingent on the three conditions (see Table 1) which existed among the earlier founders (Bedouins) of the new empire. He describes the Bedouins as people whose worldly affairs do not go beyond basic necessities. Their nature is preserved free from distorted habits (and thus are closest to the state of *al-fiṭrah*). They are people who quickly accept religious truths and right guidance. Co-operation is strong among them because of the prevailing spirit of *al-ᶜasâbiyyah*.

Bedouinity appears to mean to Ibn Khaldūn what primitiveness has or had meant for many social scientists and philosophers. By inference the Bedouin/ primitive human nature is the closest to man's original good nature (types I + II), and *al-fiṭrah* is largely equivalent to Rousseau's concept of "*L 'homme est ne bon*". This state of good human nature does not seem, however, in the long run to be equipped to preserve its own entity against external influences. Bedouins aspired towards a sedentary lifestyle and not vice versa. This is confirmed in the contemporary world where there is a large rural migration to urban centres in spite of public awareness of the dangers of the urban habitat. This strong, perhaps, innate inclination tempts the *al-fiṭrah* state. Human nature's "Bedouin" state was not made easily preservable. In other words, it is at the mercy of outside conditions.

Islam and Human Nature's Goodness

The socio-cultural system based on Islamic teaching that developed appears to have been compatible with many of the Bedouin community's main characteristics. Firstly, the Qur'ān has emphasized that Islam is the religion of *al-fiṭrah* (*din al-fiṭrah*),[25] the natural good human nature. As such, it is compatible with Bedouiness as described earlier. Secondly, throughout the Qur'ān and the *Ḥadīth* it is made clear that a Muslim must never be dominated, or worse, obsessed by insatiable materialism. However, he should not feel guilty when enjoying it moderately. In this sense, the Islamic ethic appears to allow for a greater share of materialistic goods and possessions than the Bedouin lifestyle could then offer. With this additional nuance, Islam still remains, however, firmly opposed to an excessively materialistic lifestyle. Thirdly, Islam strongly encouraged the development of strong Islamic ties among all Muslims: the spirit of *al-ᶜasâbiyyah*. But the basis of the Islamic solidarity is no longer the blood ties of *alᶜasâbiyyah*. Its new foundation is the new Islamic value system. With this new concept of solidarity, the grounds are laid for a broader sense of solidarity among all Muslims, be they of Arab or non-Arab origin.

Islam's socio-cultural teachings encouraged maintaining some important features of the Bedouin community's values. Despite some modifications, the similarities between the two cultural orders made tensions and conflicts on these points unlikely, and so we find Ibn Khaldūn observing that "the Bedouins are quick to accept religion's truths and right guidance".

Seen this way, Islam may be considered as a global system by which the original Bedouin Arab-Muslims were able to move away from their confined, restrictive Bedouin milieu, yet preserve the goodness of human nature.

Thus, I believe that for Ibn Khaldūn, Islam's most significant social impact and role among the Arabs is that it enabled them to take up the role of world leadership. Without the spirit of religion, he concedes, the Bedouin Arabs could not even acquire royal authority, let alone world dominance. As such, Islam constituted a revolutionary event (combining the three forces of civilisation's rise) that completely transformed Arabia's qualitatively and made it a world power in less than one century. More than fourteen centuries later, the Arab Islamic fact is there to be reckoned with not only in the Middle East but on the world scene at large.

Ibn Khaldūn's vision of the good, Bedouin human nature and of Islam as its adaptable protector should explain the undisguised hostility that he consistently manifested toward the sedentary population. By definition, sedentary culture represents a distant evolution from the natural, simple Bedouin state (types I + II) of human existence. The sedentary urban complex is in stark contrast with the Bedouin social order. Sedentary culture has more than the basic necessary goods which the Bedouin community needs for its physical existence. Indeed, luxury is a typical characteristic of sedentary civilisation, and obsession with materialism a dominant feature. This obsessive materialism (*al-Taraf*) is the most corrupting element to the very primitive goodness of human nature. Therefore, Ibn Khaldūn offers a materialistic explanation of *the quality* of human nature as civilisation develops.

CIVILISATION'S DECLINE AND ITS RELATION TO AL-ᶜASABIYYAH, RELIGION'S WEAKNESS AND HUMAN NATURE

Sedentary Civilisation's Economic Problems

In a sedentary culture, individuals, groups and collectivities are strongly affected by economics, and obviously modern materialistic civilisation is no exception. Because of this, sedentary citizens, as Ibn Khaldūn (p.286) argues, tend to look and strive for more and more luxury. This tendency is more than confirmed in present, urban-based societies. This collective orientation puts financial pressure both on the rulers and the ruled of the sedentary culture. The compelling drive towards luxury becomes irresistible throughout the entire fabric of the affluent civilisation Ibn Khaldūn offers an adequate description of the mechanics of the economics of this type of civilisation. He writes:

We have stated before that the city with its large population is characterized by high prices in business and high prices for its needs.

These are then raised still higher through the customs duties; for sedentary culture reaches perfection at the time when the dynasty has reached its greatest flourishing, and that is the time when the dynasty levies customs duties because then it has large expenditures. The customs duties raise the sale prices, because small businessmen and merchants include all their expenses, even their personal requirements, in the price of their stock and merchandise. Thus, customs duties enter in the sale price. The expenditure of sedentary people, therefore, grows and is no longer reasonable but extravagant. The people cannot escape this because they are dominated by and subservient to their customs.[26]

Sedentary Civilisation's Social and Moral Problems

The sedentary population's obsession with luxury deals a devastating socio-cultural blow. The collective normative order regulating the socio-cultural system is bound to loosen up in favor of a new assertive/aggressive individualism. With it, the chance of a state of anomie (weakening of *al^casâbiyyah*) is greatly enhanced.[27] On the one hand, the sedentary individual desires more and more luxury but he often fails to satisfy his expanding needs. Put in modern sociological terms, the sedentary person is under the pressure of ever rising expectations.

This anomic situation has a direct impact on sedentary society's statistical rate of deviance and crime, as Emile Durkheim has shown in the 20th century. As in modern civilisation, the wide spread of criminality and deviance was seen as a symptom of the breakdown of a socio-cultural system. This is often linked by modern social scientists to the phenomenon of social disorganization whose psychological and social results are outlined by Ibn Khaldūn:

> Corruption of inhabitants is the result of painful and trying efforts to satisfy the needs caused by their (luxurious) customs; (the result) is the bad qualities they have acquired in the process of satisfying (those needs) and of the damage the soul suffers after it has obtained them. Immorality, wrongdoing, insincerity, and trickery, for the purpose of making a living in a proper or an improper manner increase among them. The soul comes to think about making a living, to study it, and uses all possible trickery for the purpose. People are now devoted to lying, gambling, cheating, fraud, theft perjury and usury. Because of the many desires and pleasures resulting from luxury, they are bound to know everything about the ways and the means of immorality; they talk openly about it and its causes and give up all restraint in discussing it.[28]

The problems of sedentary civilisation mentioned above are not by any means the only ones that threaten society's social fabric. Sedentary civilisation's increasingly permissive sexuality is one of the gravest threats to society's solidarity (*al-^casâbiyyah*). The relations between luxury, pleasures and sexual activities are expressed by Ibn Khaldūn in this manner:

> Among the things that corrupt sedentary culture, there is the disposition towards pleasures and indulgence in them, because of the luxury (that prevails). It leads to diversification of the desires of the belly for pleasurable food and drink. This, followed by diversification of the pleasures of sex through various ways of sexual intercourse such as adultery and homosexuality, leads to the destruction of the species.[29]

The Steps Leading to the Corruption of Human Nature

Within the context of sedentary culture just outlined, Ibn Khaldūn's spells out how human nature leads to deterioration and corruption. He enumerates four modifications that push human nature to the ultimate loss of its humanity, when it is animalized (as in type III).

<u>Man's Strength:</u> This concept is considered essential to the very identity of man as a human being. Ibn Khaldūn writes

> Man is a man only in as much as he is able to procure for himself useful things and to repel harmful things and in as much as his character is suited to making efforts to this effect.[30]

<u>Sedentary Man's Character:</u> Through his observations of sedentary people, Ibn Khaldūn finds negative transformations in the sedentary personality/character. Those special changes juxtapose the sedentary individual personality profile with the natural, good, Bedouin human character. The opposition between these two types of personality characteristics (types I +II with type III) is spelled out in detail throughout the *Muqaddimah*. Here is one of the descriptions of the character of the sedentary human:

> The sedentary person cannot take care of his needs personally. He may be too weak because of the tranquility he enjoys or may be too proud, because he was brought up in prosperity and luxury. Both are blameworthy.[31]

Ibn Khaldūn continues to illustrate the opposition between sedentary (unnatural, "unfitric") and Bedouin (natural, "fitric") characteristics by citing the government soldiers as a case in point:

> It is in this sense that those government soldiers who are close to Bedouin life and toughness are more useful than those who have grown up in a sedentary culture and have adopted its character traits. This can be found

in every dynasty. It has thus become clear that the stage of sedentary culture is the stopping point in the life of civilisation and dynasties.[32]

The Corruption of Religion: As pointed out earlier, immersion in sedentary life weakens, to say the least, society's restraining collective control system. In Ibn Khaldūn's time, the normative socio-cultural tissue was profoundly regulated by the principles of Islamic culture. But with the spread of sedentarisation, many of the Islamic religious values and norms were bound to be either entirely or partially abandoned by a great majority of the sedentary population.

Thus, the process of weakening religion sets in. Ibn Khaldūn comments on the relation between religious decline and the spread of luxury in societies this way:

> He [the sedentary person] then usually becomes corrupt with regard to his religion, also the (luxurious) customs and his subservience to them corrupt him, and his soul becomes stamped by habits of luxury, as we have stated.[33]

Man becomes Animal: Ibn Khaldūn maintains that the sedentary, bad accumulative effect reaches its extreme negative impact when man's noble and distinct humanity is transformed into an animal. He describes this ugly human transformation (type III) in this manner:

> …when the strength of a man and then his character and religion are corrupted, his humanity is corrupted and he becomes, in effect, transformed into an animal.[34]

Man's animal state appears to mean the lowest level human nature (type III) can fall into. With it, not only the state *al-fiṭrah* is lost but also its duality. Once the animal has taken over, the whole direction of man's behavior changes, and this is a clear sign that the social solidarity (*alᶜasâbiyyah*) and the system of religious values have weakened and disintegrated to a point of no return. This, as he often points out, has always been the universal pattern of the process of all ailing materialistic human societies and civilisations. Importantly, it is in line with the Islamic perspective of how civilisations rise and fall. Islam has distinguished man from all other living beings by according to him his spiritual, thinking and reasoning dimensions.[35] Consequently, man's excessive materialistic involvement is strongly condemned by Islam since it overshadows these distinct human traits and triggers an imbalance in the human condition. Religion's role becomes critical here. When behavior is not guided by religious ethics, the deformation, animalisation and dehumanization of man's entity is the inevitable result. As such, the disfiguring effect of the materialistic, sedentarising cultural process is not only confined to the macroscopic (societal) structural levels of societies and civilisations, but it undermines as well the microscopic (personality of the individual) level by setting out a denaturalizing (anti-*fiṭrah*) process on a large social scale. Once that macro-microscopic (social psychological) process has pushed the personality structure of the collectivity from its good, natural state towards the corrupt side (ending in type III of Human Nature), there is no hope left for the civilization of luxurious sedentary cultures to avoid weakness, disintegration and a final collapse.

Human Nature between Western Thought and Ibn Khaldūn's Thought: The question of what is human nature is as old as humanity itself. A number of thinkers from all civilisations have dealt with the question but without decisive success. To take just Western civilisation as an example, one may single out such names as Plato, Aristotle (from Antiquity), Saint Augustine and Saint Thomas (from the Middle Ages) and Machiavelli, Hobbes, Locke, Rousseau, Freud, Hegel, Marx, Weber, Durkheim, Parsons, Sartre and Levi-Strauss (from modern times). On the one hand, some of those have defined man's nature through his innate capacities[36] alone (mainly in the Enlightenment period). On the other, some contemporary social scientists emphasised external behavior as a reflection of man's human nature.[37]

Importantly, Ibn Khaldūn, as we have seen, combined the two perspectives. He believed that man inherits a human nature (of types I + II) of good standing at birth. But this is by no means a fixed one. It changes its character or temperament under external influences. Human nature of type III is a result of this process. Thus, the temperament of human nature is plastic and flexible. Ibn Khaldūn's type III of human nature is clearly dualistic in nature: He noted that aggression and injustice are in the animal nature of man,[38] and "To man, instead, He [God] gave the ability to think and the hand".[39] This duality is the root of all difficulties and controversies hindering the reaching of a consensual view of human nature by all interested thinkers. The confusion is not confined to the philosophical thought of ancient times, but it continues to prevail in contemporary times as well. In general, modern Western scientific studies of animals and men are far from agreement and thus settling the issue of human nature once and for all.

On the one hand, some have shed more light on certain specific similarities that unite man and the animals. On the other hand, some have outlined the subtle but very critical differences that separate man's world from that of the animals. There are those, however, who have spoken out loudly of man's combined animal and human nature: "Consider our lives. All other activities we share with the other inhabitants of the planet.

Animals, birds, reptiles, fish, and insects also struggle for power, as we do. They organize themselves in social groups. Many build. Some control their environment by ingenious inventions... They play games. Some have power we shall never possess and can scarcely comprehend. Cunning and skillful, that they are. Yet collectively they learn little that is new and individually almost nothing. Their skills are intricate but limited. Their art, though charming is purely decorative. Their languages consist of a dozen signs and sounds. Their memory is vivid but restricted. Their curiosity is shallow and temporary, merely the rudiment of that wonder which fills the mind of a human scientist or poet or historian or philosopher. They can't conceive of learning and knowledge as limitless activity administered by the power of will...we are Homo sapiens: Man the Thinker.[40]

Modern Western thought's resistance to accept man's dualistic (animal/human) nature should be understood against the background of the relationship between humans and the animals in much of Western thought. Although there are important exceptions, particularly among Christian theologians, one can also find an equating of humans and animals that stretches back as early as Aristotle: "It is impossible to determine the exact demarcation between them".[41] In modern times, Darwin asserted that man's nature is conducted by instinct rather than by God-implanted consciousness.[42] Still closer to us is Lorenz who asks us to accept with humility our place in nature with other animals.[43] These one dimensional assumptions about man's animal nature help explain why, for instance, Marx did not extend his notion of conflicts and contradictions (as central forces for societies' dynamics) to include the non-materialistic (particularly the spiritual) side of man as a factor in the making of history. For the author of *The Capital,* man's antagonisms and conflicts cannot stem from man's internal configuration, i.e., his dualistic nature. But in disregarding this vision of human nature, man ends up like a feather that the wind pushes or pulls as it wishes. But has man's (the individual) role and place in history making been like that? Marx, the historian, should know better.

As should be clear by now, Ibn Khaldūn's type II of human nature is in opposition to the above Western view of man's nature. First, man is dualist (the animal and the human side coexist in man's entity) by nature. Second, man remains human in good standing when his distinct human traits (particularly his thought and religious inclination) are not overpowered by excessive materialism, which Ibn Khaldūn equates with animalism. As such, human nature *per se* is a phenomenon riddled[44] by tensions and conflicts. It is the human actor's initial source of his dynamism. When that dualist yet balanced human nature becomes imbalanced, human societies and civilisation, Ibn Khaldūn asserts, can neither rise, nor can their decline, disintegration and fall be delayed.

Viewing man's nature as dualist has the following implications. Firstly, the phenomenon of dialectics can no longer be restricted only to societies' entity through class struggle as Marx claimed. Instead, it would cover the very nature of man. If opposition between and within nature's elements is the striking common feature of this universe, it would be unjustifiable to exempt man's nature from the analysis. Secondly, in his dialectical interaction with the outside world (the macroscopic level), humanity has proven throughout its long history that it is capable not only of resisting the challenges of external forces but that it is able to change them as well. Humanity's will and determination to meet that challenge appears to derive from the dynamism of its dualist nature: the microscopic level. Thirdly, when man is pulled and pushed not only by external forces but by his internal ones as well, his behavior deserves to be described meaningfully as a complex one. Finally, when man's behavior is understood to have two layers of dialectical influences (the microscopic and the macroscopic levels), then it is easier to understand, paradoxically perhaps, why his behavior is often so very difficult to comprehend, let alone to predict.

NOTES

1. It will be shown throughout this chapter that Ibn Khaldūn's perception and reactions to social phenomena were both objective and subjective.
2. See particularly A. Toynbee in *Study of History*. Vol III. (Oxford University Press: 1948); see also Y. Lacoste in *Ibn Khaldūn* (Paris: Francis Maspero, 1956).
3. There is a very limited reference to human nature as discussed here in Abdullah Shrait's book: *Al-Fikr al-Akhlakī cinda (Ibn Khaldūn's Moralist Thought)*, SNED: Algers, 1975: 178. Shrait admits that the *Muqaddimah* does not have a specific chapter or section on morals. The latter has to be inferred, as we have done here, regarding human nature.
4. A.S. El Messidi points out that solid and exhaustive scholarship was a general phenomenon in the Arab-Islamic cultural heritage of Ibn Khaldūn's time. Messidi mentions al-Ghazalī, Ibn Sibawaih, al-Rāzī, and al-Jurjāni as examples of scholars who had written sophisticated works in their disciplines well before Khaldūn's. In this sense, Ibn Khaldūn had only followed suit but in new fields: history, sociology, economics, politics, and psychology, to which he devoted his *Muqaddimah*. See *al Fikr al-ʿArabī*, II, July/August (1980), pp. 8-38.
5. The modern Western positivist spirit must have played a role in the lack of interest in the less obvious side of Ibn Khaldūn's thought.
6. Y. Laoste's great admiration for Khaldūn's talent and depth of vision has not kept him from criticizing Khaldūn's unabated religious commitment. Lacoste, the admirer of Ibn Khaldūn's empirical and positivist approach

to the study of social phenomena, found Ibn Khaldūn's evident mysticism embarrassing.

7. One can say Ibn Khaldūn's *Muqaddimah* has, as do other great works, both obvious and more subtle sides. The latter's importance can be fundamental to the understanding of any great work. Both E.L. Hussari in *Dirasat fi Muqaddimah* Ibn Khaldūn's and A.A.Wahid Wafi in *Abdulrahman Ibn Khaldūn* mention Ibn Khaldūn's chapter on psychology and education, but neither of the two authors deals directly with Ibn Khaldūn's notion of human nature, the subject of this study.

8. On the one hand, the Qur'ānic verse (30) of *sūrah al-Rum* spells out in this way the relation between the *al-fiṭrah* state and the religion of Islam: "So set thou thy face steadily and truly to the Faith, establish God's handiwork according to the pattern on which He has made mankind: no change (let there be) in the work (wrought)." On the other, the *Ḥadīth*, "Every infant is born in the natural state. It is his parents who make him a Jew or a Christian or Heathen", equates the Muslim state of the human being with his natural state (*al-fiṭrah*). Accordingly, the human being is a Muslim at birth. It appears from the second meaning of *al-fiṭrah* given here that his nature has certain dialectical dimensions (good/bad).

9. It is assumed here that Ibn Khaldūn saw a significant correlation between *al-fiṭrah* and the primitive or Bedouin state of the human individual, and this in turn with the state of the collectivity. Ibn Khaldūn's admiration of the Bedouins is thus partially explained explained.

10. Positivist modern social scientists may cite this typecast as an example of Khaldūn's subjectivity and value judgment in his study of social human phenomena.

11. In spite of its dualistic nature, Ibn Khaldūn still considers human nature (of type II) as belonging along with the *al-fiṭrah* state (type I) in the range of the good human nature. This is because types I and II are not overly dominated by animalistic/ materialistic inclinations and greed which are the criteria set by Ibn Khaldūn for the ugly, devilish human nature (type III) that will be discussed later. Furthermore, from an Islamic point of view (which Ibn Khaldūn is certainly influenced by), it is through a good, balanced human duality (staying in the middle of extremes i.e., *al wassatia*) that man can be at his best. It will be shown at particularly the end of this study how important the concept of a dualist human nature is in understanding human behavior and the dynamics of history.

12. Ibn Khaldūn, *Muqaddimah*, p.47.

13. ibid. p. 4214.

14. ibid. p. 92.

15. This human state (where the good overpowers the bad somewhat) is a positive conflict resolution of man's dualistic nature which enables man eventually to be a builder rather than a destructive being. This is basic for civilisation's rise and continuous advancement. But contradictions within man's nature remain an intrinsic factor to consider when discussing the dynamics of the individual and human history.

16. K. Lorenz and S. Freud are among the well-known ones.

17. Ibn Khaldūn, *Muqaddimah*, p. 46. Unlike Lorenz who saw aggression as a general feature of human nature, Ibn Khaldūn linked it specifically to the animal side of man's nature. For him, human nature has two dimensions (the animalistic and the human sides) while for Lorenz it is one dimensional (animalistic).

18. Ibid., p. 47.

19. Ibn Khaldūn's position on the forces of human progress does not appear to go along with the modern materialistic vision that strongly correlates progress mainly with materialistic achievements. This vision of Ibn Khaldūn is in line with the "new outlook" on development in some circles of today's world. The increasing emphasis on human development (instead of only economic development) is a trend that seems to be close to Ibn Khaldūn's implicit perception of human progress and evolution. In other words, his severe criticism of materialistic progress (when it is not balanced by humanistic spiritual values) underlines Ibn Khaldūun's great concern for the quality (maintaining the good human nature) of human advancement.

20. Read especially "Bedouins are closer to being good than sedentary people" in *Muqaddimah*, p. 94.

21. Ibn Khaldūn, *Muqaddimah*, p.289. By today's scientific criteria this is a moral judgment on Ibn Khaldūn's part. But morality's erosion among Western modern social scientists can be traced to two principal factors: Firstly, the modern ethic of science that separates science from human morality; Secondly, the spread of the notion of relativity particularly among contemporary anthropologists and sociologists who have made immoral acts the whole issue of morality that distinguishes between bad and good. See the implications of Maurice Cusson. "La theorie de la immorale", in *Le controle social du crime*. (Paris: Presse Universitaries de France, 1983: 97.

22. In *al-fiṭrah* state, though dialectical in nature (good and bad), the element of goodness in man appears to have a greater likelihood of dominating. This is a good reason for Ibn Khaldūn to favor it.

23. "Man is a child of the customs and the things he has become used to", in Ibn Khaldūn, *Muqaddimah*, p. 95. He also sees human nature as a changing phenomenon (type I to type III) in response to external conditions.

24. While Ibn Khaldūn astutely articulates the forces leading to civilisation's rise and fall (as seen in table I), materialistic civilisation's dead end is supported by Islam's view that no one/nothing is eternal in this universe: "Everything on this earth is bound to perish." The Qur'ān: *Sūrah* 55, verse 26.

25. This is in contrast with the view that claims Ibn Ibn Khaldūn restricted the negative effect of luxury and materialism on civilisation to the ruling classes—such as the kings and their entourage—and not to the general population. See Shrait's: "Ibn Khaldūn's Moralist Thought" cit. p. 285-

86.

26. Ibn Khaldūn, *Muqaddimah*, p.288. Ibn Khaldūn's description of those correlates of sedentary civilisation is remarkably true of today's advanced sedentary societies. Thus, civilisations' and societies' falls are not caused only by internal and external revolutions and attacks, but also by internal psychological determinants.

27. Ibid., p. 288

28. Ibid., p. 286. This quotation offers much for constructing a Khaldūnian theory of crime and deviance. Despite this, it is still a neglected domain of Ibn Khaldūn's thought.

29. Ibn Khaldūn, *Muqaddimah,* p. 288

30. Ibid.

31. Ibid.

32. Ibid., p. 289.

33. Ibid., p. 280. Religion's (Islam's) role is two-fold according to Ibn Khaldūn: Firstly, it helps strengthen *alcaâabiyyah*; and secondly, it allows human nature to be in a good state.

34. Ibid., pp. 288-89

35. Ibn Khaldūn appears to believe that these dimensions can be fruitfully cultivated for man's betterment when he is not dominated by materialism. See Chapter 6 of the *Muqaddimah* cit., beginning p. 333.

36. Pennock & Chapman, p.297.

37. Ibid.

38. Ibn Khaldūn, *Muqaddimah*, p. 47.

39. Ibid., p. 46

40. Highet, pp. 7-8

41. Bock, p. 9

42. Ibid., p. 7

43. Highet mentions Montaigne's explanation of this Western attitude of considering man as a beast: "It is safer to leave the reins of our conduct in the hand of Nature than to keep them in our own", p. 34, *Man's Unconquered Mind.*

44. E. Morin: *Le paradigms perdu: La Nature humaine.* Paris: Editions du Seuil, Paris, 1973: p. 22. See chapter 2: "L 'hypercomplexite".

Part II

The Islamic Concept
of Soul, Spirit
and Heart

6

Nature of the Soul:
The Philosophy of Mulla
Ṣadrā

FAZLUR RAHMAN

In his work, "On the Soul," Aristotle defines the soul as "the first entelechy (or perfection) of a natural organized body possessing the capacity of life."[1] This definition clearly means that the soul is a form or function of an organized body and is incapable of independent, separate existence. But in the same work Aristotle poses the question as to whether the soul may not be the entelechy of the body in the sense in which a pilot is the entelechy of a ship.[2] This question reflects Aristotle's hesitation as to whether the human intellect may not be separable after physical death, while the rest of the soul perishes, and it is probable that he believed in the survival of the human intellect after it is developed by purely intellectual operations. His great commentator and systematizer, Alexander of Aphrodisias, explicitly holds this view, i.e., that the human mind achieves immortality by contemplating eternal objects.[3] Plotinus, who believes in the existence of the World Soul (of which individual souls are modifications), rejects the Aristotelian definition of the soul as entelechy of the body.[4] In the amalgamation of Aristotelianism and neo-Platonism created by later Hellenic philosophy, particularly as expressed in the neo-Platonizing commentators of Aristotle, the human soul was credited with indestructibility, although the Aristotelian definition of soul as entelechy was also subscribed to.[5]

Among the Muslim philosophers who were heirs to this philosophic tradition of later Hellenism, al-Fārābī explicitly identifies the human soul at the beginning of its career as a faculty or power inherent in the body and not as a spiritual substance capable of existing independently of the body. When, however, the human soul-the material intellect-develops into an actualized intellect and can think immaterial forms, al-

108

Fārābī designates it as "acquired" intellect. The "acquired" intellect emerges as a part of the intelligible universe and survives physical death. According to al-Fārābī, therefore, human souls which have not developed into actualized intellect cannot survive bodily death, since they are mere "powers" in the body. This doctrine of the transformation of the human soul into an immaterial, immortal entity appears to be similar to the doctrine of Alexander of Aphrodisias. In other words, for al-Fārābī, whereas the human soul in its initial stage is the entelechy of the body in the first of the two Aristotelian senses, it becomes entelechy of the body in the second Aristotelian sense (i.e., in the sense in which a pilot is the entelechy of a ship) at the end of its developmental career.[6] The souls of the heavenly bodies are, however, eternally entelechies of their bodies in the second sense, since they never were mere powers or potentialities immersed in their bodies.[7]

For Ibn Sīnā, the human soul, although it is only a potential intellect at the beginning of its career, is nevertheless an immaterial spiritual substance capable of existing independently of the body.[8] The body is there to serve the purpose of its realization as actual intellect, but after that it becomes a positive hindrance. Ibn Sīnā, therefore, holds that it is better to define the soul as entelechy of the body than to define it as form of the body; this is because "entelechy" comprises both types of soul, that which is the form of the body and hence inseparable from it—as in the case of the vegetative and animal souls—and that which is separate (or separable) from it, as the human soul. But this means that the term "entelechy" is ambiguous; therefore, when we say that something is an entelechy, we do not know thereby what kind of soul it is—whether it is capable of existence by itself or not.

Again, according to Ibn Sīnā, the definition of the soul as "entelechy" (although he thinks that this is the best possible and most comprehensive definition of the souls "in this world of ours") besides being ambiguous, does not include all the souls, e.g., the souls of the heavenly spheres, which neither work through a physical organ—since they are eternally immaterial substances—nor do they possess sense-perception, while their intellect is also eternally actual and not potential and passive as the human intellect.[9] It is obvious that, basically, these objections arise against Aristotle who was the author of the soul's definition as entelechy of the body, who at the same time regarded the souls of the heavens as eternally and movers of the heavenly bodies.[10] When we have defined the soul as entelechy of the body, Ibn Sīnā goes on, we have only defined the soul as a relation, for entelechy, actuality or perfection is entelechy, actuality or perfection of something viz., of the body, possessing organs. This definition, therefore, does not yield the nature of the soul-in-itself, i.e., whether it is a separate substance or not. In order to prove that the human soul is an immaterial spiritual substance, Ibn Sīnā has, therefore, recourse to his famous argument whereby a person, under certain suppositions, can affirm his own ego without affirming the existence of his body.[11]

Ibn Sīnā's conception of the human soul as an immaterial substance ab initio (most probably motivated by religious considerations) raised fresh objections against him to which an Aristotle or an al-Fārābī was not subject. One of his contemporaries asked him: if the human soul is a separate substance from the start, why is it not an actual intellect and only a potential one, since the only condition of something being an intellect and intelligible in actuality is that it be separate from matter? To this, Ibn Sīnā replied that for something to be an actual intellect, it is not sufficient to be separate from matter but to be absolutely separate from it, i.e., that matter should neither be the occasion of its coming-into-existence nor the vehicle of its subsistence.[12] The unsatisfactoriness of this reply continued to be a target of criticism and Mulla Ṣadrā rejects Ibn Sīnā's view in various contexts.

Mulla Ṣadrā, who is highly neo-Platonic in his theory of knowledge, as will become clear in the following chapters, nevertheless accepts Aristotle's definition of the soul as entelechy of the body. According to him, since the soul is not eternal but originated (a proposition in whose acceptance he is at one with the entire Aristotelian tradition), it cannot be separate and independent of matter, for to say that the soul is separate and independent of matter is only compatible with belief in the pre-existence of the soul, as Platonists and neo-Platonists believe. Ibn Sīnā is, therefore, self-contradictory when he accepts the one but rejects the other. At the same time, Ṣadrā also rejects Ibn Sīnā's view that the soul is a relational concept and not a substantive one. Since the soul, at its birth, is in matter, its soul-ness cannot be construed as a relation as though it had an independent existence of its own and then came into a relationship with matter. Again, if the human soul were an independent substance, it would be impossible to integrate the soul and body, so as to form a natural physical species as the concept of "perfection" requires, and therefore the analogy of the pilot and the ship falls to the ground.[13]

However, the relationship of the soul to the body is not like that of any ordinary physical form to its matter. All physical forms inhere in their matters in such a way that the two do not constitute a composite (*murakkab*) of two existentially distinguishable elements but are totally fused together to form a complete unity (ittihād) in existence, and as a result, the form works simply and directly in matter. As opposed to purely material forms, however, the soul works on its matter through the intermediacy of other lower forms or powers. This phenomenon, viz, where one power or form works on matter not directly but through other forms, is called "soul." Ṣadrā, therefore, says that the soul is the entelechy of a material body insofar as it operates through faculties, and he insists that the word "organs" as it appears in the Stagirite's definition of the soul cannot mean physical organs" like hands, liver or stomach, for example, but faculties or powers through which the soul works, as, for example, appetition, nutrition, and digestion.[14]

It is obvious that this novel interpretation constitutes a grave violence against Aristotle, since his language clearly attributes the quality of "being organized" or "possessing organs" to "the natural body," which makes the soul, strictly speaking, a function of such a body, while Ṣadrā attributes the quality of having "organs" or "faculties" to the soul. This position is, indeed, a radical departure from Aristotle and should be regarded as a first step toward the final idealization of Ṣadrā's account of the soul. Ṣadrā claims that this interpretation of the word "organs" removes the difficulties experienced by the definition of the soul as entelechy in covering all the cases -from plants to heavenly spheres-since all souls work on their bodies not directly but through faculties. Further, it raises the soul from the status of a purely physical form to a form which, although in matter, is capable of transcending it, for the extent of its immanence in matter is less than that of a simple physical form. These considerations should not lead us to think, however, that Ṣadrā has produced this definition for extraneous reasons for, as will become apparent soon, this way of looking upon the soul is intimately related to his doctrine of "emergence" or "substantive change" which lies at the root of his system.

Indeed, the ability of Ṣadrā's definition to comprehend the souls of the heavens is a by-product and is relevant only from the point of view of the Peripatetic philosophy. Otherwise, whereas according to the Peripatetics, the souls of the heavens are eternally actual and, therefore, are not in need of a bodily organ to actualize them and hence are not entelechies of their bodies except insofar, as their bodies occupy different positions in their revolutions, according to Ṣadrā, these souls are only potential like earthly souls even though the degree of their potentiality is less than that of earthly souls.[15] Indeed, as we have shown in Chapter V of Part I, the heavenly souls, together with their bodies, are Ḥadīth or originated according to Ṣadrā, and subject to continuous movement and change. Concerning Ibn Sīnā's doctrine on the heavens, Ṣadrā says:

> Among (the failures of Ibn Sīnā) is his assertion that the heavenly souls have no perfection waiting to be realized except in certain extraneous matters and non-essentials, viz (different) relations of positions for their bodies. For a man of insight who has grasped the truth, this is a base-less opinion and a false belief. This is because the soul, so long as its psychic being remains deficient and not perfectly realized in point of its proper individual (level of) existence, is in need of the body to serve as its instrument for the attainment of its existential perfection, and it must cling to it.   How can a man of perception and insight believe that a

(pure) intellective substance can allow itself to be imprisoned in a bodily relationship, deserting its abode of light for (this) tenebral world merely for the sake of acquiring extraneous relationships with physical positions-and this despite their (the philosophers) doctrine that the higher does not occupy itself with the lower?[16]

Thus, for Ṣadrā, celestial souls are, in principle, as much entelechies of their bodies as earthly souls. Ṣadrā's own account of the soul rests on his fundamental principle of "emergence" or "substantive change" (*istihālah jauhariyah*). He, therefore, holds that the soul is bodily in its origin but spiritual in its survival (*jismiiniyat al-hudūth, yuhaniyat al-baqā'*).[17] The same principle demands that, since the soul emerges on the basis of matter, it cannot be absolutely material, for "emergence" requires that the "emergent" be of a higher level than that which it emerges out of or on the basis of. Consequently, even the lowest forms of life—like plants, although they are attached to and dependent upon matter, cannot be themselves entirely material. On the contrary, they use their matter or body as their instrument and constitute the first step away from the material to the spiritual realm (*malakūt*).[18]

Being entelechy of the body means that the soul renders the genus "body" into a species, i.e., a living body. This means that "body" must enter into the definition of plant, animal, and man, as Aristotle and Ibn Sīnā say. However, since, for Ibn Sīnā, the term "soul" applies only to a relation and not to a substance, he thought that the body was extrinsic to the soul when considered as a substance. He, therefore, denied physical resurrection.[19] But certain later Muslim philosophers, like al-Suhrawardī, went farther off the track. They did not see that the "body" in this context had to be taken in the sense of a genus and not in the sense of a material substratum—as Ibn Sīnā had insisted—and when they saw the material substratum to be perishable, they declared the body to be dead-in-itself and devoid of life which, they thought, was merely accidental to it—i.e., they did not consider "body" as part of the definition of a living being.[20]

Again, being entelechy of a special type of body means that the soul falls into the category of substance, since such a body cannot be constituted without the soul. This argument comes from Ibn Sīnā. Ibn Sīnā, however, had given another proof, referred to above, based on direct consciousness of the self, to establish that the human soul is a spiritual substance, independent of the body. Yet, in strange contradiction to this proof, when Ibn Sīnā was asked if substantiality is a constitutive factor of the soul, why are we not able to affirm its substantiality as self-evident, without inference, he replied, "About the soul we know nothing except that it governs the body: in its essence, it remains unknown. Now substantiality is constitutive of that essence...but what is constituted by substantiality is unknown to us and what is known to us is not constituted by substantiality."[21] It is obvious that Ibn Sīnā is thinking here of the general definition of the soul as entelechy of the body and does not refer to his special proof which is based on direct experience of the self.

After Ibn Sīnā, the question was raised and discussed whether the substantiality of the soul is given in direct self-consciousness. Al-Suhrawardī, since he believed Aristotelian categories to be purely subjective, asserted that in the direct experience of the self all that was given was a self-aware or self-luminous being to which all other concepts like substance, differentia, etc. were extrinsic.[22] He, therefore, describes the self only as a self-luminous being, of the nature of light. Ṣadrā approaches this question from his principle of the primordiality of existence (asālat al-wujūd) discussed in Chapter I of Part I, according to which the only reality is existence and essences are constructed by the mind.[23] According to him, whenever soul is conceived as a concept and is defined, it will be found to be an essence. In direct self-experience, however, soul is only given as pure existence, and since existence has no genus, it is not given in experience either as a substance or non-substance. Direct, intuitive experience is the only way, for Ṣadrā, to know reality, for discursive inferential reasoning can only know essences in an adequate manner (bi al-iqtinā'), and not existences, which are unique.

According to Ṣadrā, both human and animal souls are free from matter and hence capable of existence independently of the body. We shall discuss the question of the human soul later, but the doctrine that the animal soul is capable of independent existence is not found even in al-Suhrawardī and appears to have come from Ibn ᶜArabī, to whom, as our previous discussions have shown, Ṣadrā's debt is immense. The reason for this doctrine, in part, is to prove that simple human souls which possess hardly any intellective activity, but simply work with imagination also survive, as we will elaborate in Chapter V of the present Part on eschatology.[24] But Ṣadrā absolutely holds that a being endowed with imagination is independent of natural matter even though it is not independent of a certain kind of extension and quantity (miqdar) which, however, is not material. This view, in turn, rests on his doctrine of the ᶜĀlam al-Mithāl (World of Images), according to which, an image, although not spiritual, is not material either, is not directly subject to substantive mutation as the world of physical forms and, therefore, exists by itself independent of matter. Ibn Sīnā himself, although he gave an elaborate argument in his al-Najāt and al-Shifā' to show that an image requires a material organ to be imprinted in and that therefore imagination could not survive physical death, said in al-Mubahathat that "If the percipient (faculty or organ) of perceived forms and images were a body or a bodily power, then either that body will suffer separation (tafarruq, i.e., discontinuity) of parts when nutrition enters upon it or it will not. The second alternative is false because our bodies are subject to ceaseless corrosion (by fatigue) and augmentation through nutrition."[24] His conclusion was that such a faculty must be non-material.

But after Ibn Sīnā a whole new development takes place, whose terms go back to al Ghazālī, but which explicitly starts with al-Suhrawardī, according to which images had an independent existence and life of their own in the World of Images (ʿĀlam al-Mithāl) situated ontologically between the spiritual (intelligible) world of pure ideas and the world of coarse matter and material bodies.[25] This development made it easier for Ṣadrā to believe that imagination—the World of extended figures—was not part of the material realm. Ṣadrā, therefore, holds that self-consciousness is not restricted to the rational soul, i.e., man—as philosophers had held—but was a concomitant of imagination as well. Ibn Sīnā was puzzled when asked whether animals have self-consciousness and whether an animal being has a principle in it which preserves that being's identity throughout life even though its body was in constant change. He replied that perhaps animals are not conscious of themselves but only of the objects they perceived and reacted to, or maybe they have a vague awareness of themselves through perception of external objects. On the second question, he was extremely hesitant and pointed to several alternatives among which he did suggest that animals (and perhaps plants) may have an irreducible original factor.[26]

Be that as it may, Ṣadrā categorically affirms that animal souls are capable of survival, because they are separate from matter—thanks to the fact that they have imagination—and that their separateness is not inconsistent with attachment to the quality of extension (or "pure body") which is necessary for an image. Ṣadrā uses the age-old argument for the identity and persistence of the human soul, according to which human bodies are in perpetual change while the inner psyche remains the same, to prove the identity and persistence of the animal soul, since animal bodies are also in perpetual flux while their inner psyche remains the same. It is obvious, says Ṣadrā, that this argument applies to animals as it applies to man.[27]

Similarly, the philosophers' argument from self-knowledge to prove that the human soul is separate from the body, is applied by Ṣadrā to the animals—those higher forms of animal life where sense-perception, some kind of memory-image, and voluntary movement are found. Since animals flee from things causing pain and pursue things giving pleasure, they must have an adequate idea of these things in terms of their images. In doing so, animals must necessarily perceive themselves.[28] Following the neo-Platonic model, Ṣadrā asserts that in sense-perception itself, it is not the external object which is directly perceived; the external object is rather the occasion for the creation by the soul of a perceptible form from within itself. This is much more so in the case of unperceived forms or images which the soul creates by itself. Hence the animal soul is independent of the material body. Again, the animal's self-knowledge is direct, continuous, and independent of its knowledge of the external objects, exactly as is the case with man.[29] Ṣadrā even goes so far as to apply Ibn Sīnā's argument about the immateriality of the human self on the basis of direct self-consciousness to the animal soul. The only difference between man and animal is that the former is capable of intellection which the latter is incapable of; but then even many men are equally devoid of intellectual capacity and work by sheer imagination.[30]

Ṣadrā's view that animal souls are capable of detachment from their bodies— indeed, he insists, they are in some sense detached from their bodies because they are of the order of "actual imagination (khayal bi al-fiᶜl)," as distinguished from developed human souls, which are "actual intellect (ᶜaql bi al-fiᶜl)"—is based on the important doctrine of the "World of Images (ᶜĀlam al-Mithāl)," developed after al-Ghazālī by al-Suhrawardī, Ibn ᶜArabī, and others. According to this doctrine, the ontological structure of reality comprises three worlds—that of pure ideas or intellectual entities on top, of pure images or figures in the middle, and of material bodies at the lowest rung. Developed animals and undeveloped humans are of the order of the middle world of pure figures: although they cannot rise to the status of pure intellects, they nevertheless belong to the "other world (al-ākhira)" compared to this material world which is subject to that perpetual flux to which even the human and heavenly souls are subject so long as they have any intercourse with the physical and are not developed and transformed into pure imagination. But at the same time, it is difficult to see how imaginative souls can be completely freed from matter and cease to be subject to perpetual material flux if they have not become pure intellects—a condition stated recurrently by Ṣadrā—and have found final repose in the eternal realm and being of God.

The development of the soul, according to Ṣadrā, is marked by successive stages of increasing unity and simplicity—an application of his principle of substantive motion. Whereas the faculties of plants are diffused throughout their body, the sensitive soul of animals achieves a higher grade of unity, since the sensitive soul, at the level of sensus communis, is able to combine all sense perceptions. However, the sensitive soul operates through bodily organs which are diverse and spatially localized even though the subject of perception are not these organs but is the soul itself. Imagination is the first "separate" faculty and does not work through any bodily organ. Imagination, however, entails the extension of the image (although the image does not occupy real space and is not material); and hence not being totally free from some notion of spatiality, it does not possess unity and simplicity proper.[31]

This doctrine of the progressive simplicity and unity of the soul clearly belongs to the neo-Platonic type of thought, although it is not foreign to Aristotelianism. At the level of the human conceptual thought, the soul achieves an adequate measure of unity, for a concept is neither localized anywhere in the body, nor is its object material or in matter; it is pure form without matter and in its intention it denotes an infinity of objects to which it is applicable. A concept is, therefore, truly spiritual. However, concepts as such are mutually exclusive and are therefore plural. Although concepts emerge from the soul (as we shall see in the following chapter), nevertheless a knowledge of external, physical objects—which are the paradigm of the absence of unity—is necessary for their emergence. Concepts are therefore connected in some sense with physical objects. It is only when the soul truly becomes "mind" or "acquired intellect," i.e., when it becomes creative of concepts independently of knowledge through the instrumentality of the body, that it becomes genuine unity and achieves a "simple" level of being which belongs originally to separate intellects.[32]

At this point Ṣadrā attacks Ibn Sīnā's doctrine of the "simple intellect" and its relationship to the psychic or conceptual intellect and says that, according to Ibn Sīnā, the only difference between these two levels of intellect is that what the simple intellect has as a unity—without a temporal succession of concepts but with a logical and causal order –the conceptual intellect possesses in inferential and temporal order and, further, that the simple intellect creates these concepts whereas the conceptual or psychic intellect only receives them. Ṣadrā accuses Ibn Sīnā of not having properly understood the nature of the simple. For Ibn Sīnā, the simple principle creates concepts, but these latter do not actually exist in it but outside it; whereas, for Ṣadrā, the simpler a principle is, the more it is able to contain in a simple form, all the things below it.[33]

The consequences of this difference appear both on the question of God's knowledge (which, according to Ibn Sīnā, is accidental and external to the Divine Essence, while, according to Ṣadrā, divine knowledge is inherent in God's essence in a simple manner, as we have seen in Chapter II of Part II), and on the question of the relationship of the soul to its faculties. That the soul operates through different faculties is undeniable. The "latter-day" philosophers like Abu al-Barakat, Fakhr al-Dīn al Rāzī, al-Ijī, and others, however, misunderstood the basis on which earlier philosophers affirmed the different faculties of the soul and thought that their basis was that every faculty, being simple, produces only one type of act.[34] This is not true; the real principle for the differentiation of faculties is either the fact that one type of action can exist—e.g., nutrition—without the other—e.g., growth, or the fact that two types of action are positive but contradictory as, e.g., assimilation of food and its expulsion.[35] Otherwise, different acts can be performed by the same faculty as, for example, nature, although simple, creates motion in a body when it is out of its natural place but produces rest in it when it is in its natural place. Starting from this misunderstanding, these philosophers and theologians came to deny multiplicity of faculties and powers in natural objects.[36]

Faculties, however, are not independent or quasi-independent entities possessing essential differentiae, as vegetative or animal species do. Their differentiation is merely through accidents of the human soul in the sense that some of them function in time prior to others, and through localization of different functions through different organs. Faculties, as such, do not exist; yet Ṣadrā does not say that they are distinguishable only conceptually, and thinks that they are, in a sense, real.[37] How, then, are we to conceive of their relationship to the soul?

Ṣadrā says, "The soul is all of the faculties."[38] This is not to be understood to mean that the soul is the collection or aggregate of the faculties, since an aggregate for Ṣadrā has no existence apart from the particulars which make it up. It is rather to be understood based on Ṣadrā's general principle, discussed several times earlier in this work, that "a simple nature is everything."[39] That is to say, what the multiplicity is *at one level of existence,* unity is precisely that at a simpler, higher level of existence. Faculties are the "modes (shu'ūn)" or "manifestations (mazāhir)" of the soul: at their own level, the faculties are real, at the higher, simpler level, they are swallowed up by the soul, whose creations they are at the lower level but wherein they exist as a unity at the higher level. They are related to the soul as servants are related to the king or as angelic beings and cosmic intelligences are related to God.[40]

That the soul, as the true spiritual self, is a unity in all experience is affirmed by philosophers and the attacks of Fakhr al-Dīn al Rāzī upon them that they regard faculties as subjects of experience as though "in a single human person there exists a host of cognizers" are simply puerile.[41] What is true is that philosophers, including Ibn Sīnā himself, have sometimes talked as though these faculties were independent existents and hence misunderstandings arose about the proper relationship between the soul and its faculties. The fact is that the soul does not emerge as a genuine and complete unity until it reaches the status of the acquired intellect. Two difficulties prevented Ibn Sīnā from the achievement of this insight. First, as has been pointed out earlier, he did not quite understand the nature of a simple principle. Secondly, Ibn Sīnā did not accept the principle of substantive change (haraka fi al-jauhar), which could have led him to hold that at the level of acquired intellect, the soul achieves a new order of existence and emerges as a pure intellect.[42] Al-Suhrawardī, although he enunciated the principle of "more perfect" and "less perfect," did not come to the idea of substantive change and hence he experienced the same difficulty in defending the unity of the soul. In fact, he believed that vegetative functions, since they are physical (and everything physical is, for him, dead-in-itself), are not due to inherent powers or faculties of the soul, but emanate directly from the "Giver of Forms," i.e., the Intellect or Pure Light, and that faculties only prepared the subject for the reception of these forms. Now, there is an obvious difference between that which prepares and that which causes or necessitates (i.e., between the receptive and the productive principles), the heating power of fire, for example, is not just preparatory for the heating operation but necessitates or causes it.[43]

The truth is that, in accordance with the principle of substantive change or transformation, which is also expressed by the doctrine of the systematic ambiguity (*tashkīk*)[44] of existence, the soul first emerges as vegetative, then as perceptive and locomotive at the animal level, then as potential intellect, and finally as pure intellect when the term soul is no longer applicable to it. The soul has its being at all these levels and at each of these levels it is the same in a sense and yet different in a sense because the same being can pass through different levels of development.[45]

Ibn Sīnā had given an excellent example of the relationship between the soul and its faculties from the physical realm when he said that a body may be so related to fire that the former may be only heated by the latter, or it may be so related to the fire that the latter both heats and illuminates that body—in which case, the higher state, the illumination, becomes the cause of the former state, the heating—or, finally, it may be so related to the fire that the sun not only heats and illuminates that body but sets it aflame – in which case, the flame becomes the cause (together with the original fire) of both heat and illumination. Nevertheless, Ibn Sīnā himself, while describing the relationship of the soul to the body, had used contradictory language: on the one hand, he describes the faculties as emanating from (*fuād*) the soul, which is regarded as their source (*manba'*), while on the other he described the soul as a mere link (*ribāt*) integrating the faculties and their activity and called it the meeting point (*majma'*) of the latter. Now this latter conception is against the idea of the soul as a genuine, transcendent simple entity.[46]

Indeed, when the soul achieves its highest form as true unity, it contains all the lower faculties and forms within its simple nature. The commonly held view that when the soul becomes fully developed and separate, it negates and excludes the lower forms, is a cardinal error; many philosophers misconstrue the meaning of "abstraction" as "removal" or "negation" of something.[47] True unity and simplicity does not negate but comprehends everything. That is why the soul, at the highest stage of its development, resembles God, for God, in His absolute simplicity, comprehends everything.[48] Such a soul begins to function like God and creates forms from within itself: indeed, at this stage, the Perfect Man becomes the ruler of all the worlds—physical, psychic, and intelligible— as Ibn ʿArabī, has it. The Perfect Man, according to Ibn ʿArabī, must function directly through the simplicity and unity of his mind, and not through instruments, in order for his will to be obeyed by the entire creation. Such a Perfect Man is the Perfect Saint. But should this Perfect Man choose to work through external instruments—i.e., as a prophet—and enunciate external laws and commands, he may be obeyed by a segment of the creation and disobeyed by another segment. This is nothing surprising and does not detract from the perfection of the Perfect Man, since this is the very nature of functioning through external instruments as distinguished from functioning through the unity of the inner mind. For God Himself, when He decided to work externally through commands and instruments, was disobeyed by a part of His creation, viz., Satan. But at the level of His Divine Unity, where instruments are non-existent, God's obedience is assured by definition, as it were, for there, since his Unity includes all, Satan himself is part of it.[49]

According to Ṣadrā, just as the soul comes into existence as an individual as a power in matter -although not as a power of matter—so it retains its individual character even when it is severed from the body and becomes a member of the Divine Realm. As we shall see later in his doctrine of eschatology, he rejects the transmigration of souls as well as the view that after death, the individual souls dissolve themselves in the ocean of Eternal Being.

NOTES

1. Aristotle. *De Anima*, 11, 1 ,412 a 27; 412 b, line 5.
2. Ibid., 413 a, lines 8-9.
3. Aristotle. *De Anima*, ed. Bruns (Berlin, 1887), p. 108, lines 19 ff.
4. *Enneads,* IV, 7, 85, IV, 3, 21 (cf. 1,1,8; I, 6, 5; IV, 6, 3, etc.).
5. See particularly the commentaries of Themistius, Simplicius and Philoponus on Aristotle's De Anima (cf. my *Avicenna's Psychology*) Oxford, 1952, Introduction).
6. See my *Prophecy in Islam* (London, 1958), Ch. I, Section 1.
7. *Al-Fārābī, al-Madīna al-Fadila* (Beirut, 1959), p. 53, line 1 ff.
8. See my *Prophecy in Islam* (London, 1958), Chapter I, Section 2.
9. See Avicenna's *De Anima*, F. Rahman, ed.,(Oxford, 1959), p. 12, lines 9 ff.
10. Aristotle, for example, Physics, 259 b 20 ff. on the continuous motion of the heavens.
11. *Avicenna's De Anima*, p. 16, lines 2 ff.
12. Asfar, I, 3, p. 458, lines 7 ff.
13. Asfar, IV, 1, p. 12, lines 4-13.
14. Ibid., p. 16, line 4-P. 18, line 7.
15. For example, Asfar III, 1, p. 17, lines 8-13; ibid., I, 3, p. 120.
16. Asfar, IV, 1, p. 348, line 16; ibid., IV, 2, p. 116, lines 2-10.
17. Ibid., IV, 1, p. 4, lines 3 ff.; p. 35, last line ff.; p. 121, lines 4 ff.; p. 123, lines 16-22; ibid.) p. 326, line 6-p. 327, line 3.
18. Ibid., p. 16, line 14-P. 17, line 1.
19. *Avicenna's De Anima,* p. 16, lines 2 ff.; p. 255, lines 1 if.; for his denial of physical resurrection, see his R. Adawiya (Cairo, 1949).

20. Ibid., p. 26, lines 3 ff.
21. Ibid., p. 46, lines 12-15.
22. Ibid., p. 46, line 16-p. 47, line 4; al-Suhrawardī, *Opera Metaphysica*, p. 115, lines 6 if.; ibid., II, p. 112, line 13; p. 114, lines 5 if. The difference between the statements of Opera I and II is obvious, for in the one, self-consciousness is not constitutive of, but lies outside of, the self, but in the latter this duality is denied. See my *Selected Letters Of Shaikh Ahmad Sirhindī*, (Karachi, 1968), Introduction, p. 14, lines 9 ff. 26.
23. References in the preceding note to al-Suhrawardī.
24. Asfar, IV, I, p. 228, lines 6-9.
25. See my *Sirhindī*, Introduction, op. cit., p. 62, lines 10 ff.; see also my article, "Dream, Imagination, and ᶜĀlam al-Mithāl, Islamic Studies (Karachi-Islamabad), Vol. IV, No. 2, pp. 167-80.
26. Asfar, IV, 1, p. Ill, lines 2 ff.; p. 113, lines 5 ff.
27. Ibid., p. 42, line g-p. 44, line 15. This, however, contradicts his own and more basic view that both body and soul are in constant flux.
28. Ibid., p. 44, lines 1 ff.
29. Asfar, IV, I, p.43, lines 8 ff.
30. Ibid., p. 44, lines 8 if.; see ibid., p. 48, lines 4-7, where animals are credited with "actualimagination (*khayal bi al-fiᶜl*)."
31. See references in the three preceding notes, and Chapter III below on Imagination.
32. On the development of the Intellect, see Chapter IV below.
33. Asfar, Ill, 2, p. 117, lines 3 ff.; ibid., I, 1, p. 369, last line if.; see also Chapter IV of this Part below, and Chapter II of Part II above on God's knowledge.
34. Asfar, IV, I, p. 60, lines 3 ff.
35. Ibid., p. 60, lines 12 ff.; ibid., p. 64, lines 11-15.
36. Ibid., p. 63, lines 1 ff.
37. Ibid., p. 65, lines 13 ff.; p. 68, lines 1 ff.
38. Ibid., p. 51, line 6; p. 121, lines 4 ff.; p. 123, lines 16 ff.; p. 221, lines 5 if.; p. 135, line Ip 136, line 5.
39. Ibid., p. 121, lines 8-9; see also Chapter I, Section C, Part I.
40. Ibid., p. 137, lines 16 ff.; ibid., p. 139, lines 13 ff., and reference to the "Epistles of the Brethren of Purity."
41. Ibid., p. 65, lines 19 ff.
42. Asfar, IV, 2, p. 116, lines II ff.
43. Asfar, IV, 1, p. 108, lines 16-18.
44. Asfar, IV, 2, p. 21, lines 12 ff.; ibid. p. 61, lines 7 ff.-p. 63, line 6, etc.
45. References in the preceding note.
46. Asfar. IV, 1, p. 48, line 2 ff. (cf. p. 35, line 4 ff.); see Avicenna's De Anima. p. 261, lines 7 ff.
47. On the meaning of "abstraction" see the following three chapters.
48. Asfar. IV, 1, p. 121, lines 8-11; ibid., I, 3, p. 277, lines 16 ff, particularly p. 379, lines 11- 16.
49. Ibid. IV, 1, p. 140, line I-p. 142, line 6.

7

The Nature of Man and the Psychology of the Human Soul

A brief outline and framework for
Islamic Psychology and Epistemology

SYED MUHAMMAD NAQUIB AL-ATTAS

Man has a dual nature, he is both body and soul, he is at once physical being and spirit (15:26-29; 23:12-14). God taught him the names (*al-asmā'*) of everything (2:31). By the 'names' we infer that it means the knowledge (*al-ᶜilm*) of everything (*al-ashyā'*). This knowledge does not encompass knowledge of the specific nature of the essence (*al-dhāt*) or the inmost ground (*al-sirr*) of a thing (*shay'*) such as, for example, the spirit (*al-rūḥ*); it refers to knowledge of accidents (sing. *ᶜaradī*) and attributes (sing. *sīifah*) pertaining to the essences of things sensible and intelligible (*mahīsūsat* and *maᶜqūlāt*) so as to make known the relations and distinctions existing between them, and to clarify their natures within these domains in order to discern and to understand their meanings, that is, their causes, uses, and specific individual purpose. Man is, however, also given limited knowledge of the spirit (17:85), of his true and real self or soul, (41:53) and by means of this knowledge he is able to arrive at knowledge about God (*al-maᶜrifah*) and His absolute oneness; that God is his true Lord (*al-rabb*) and object of worship (*al-ilāh*) (3:81; 7:172). The seat of knowledge in man is a spiritual substance which is variously referred to in the Holy Qur'ān sometimes as his heart (*al-qalb*), or his soul or self (*al-nafs*), or his spirit (*al-rūḥ*), or his intellect (*al-ᶜaql*). In virtue of the truth that man knows God in His absolute unity as his Lord, (7:172) such knowledge, and the reality of the situation that necessarily follows from it, has bound man in a covenant (*al-mithāq; al-ᶜahd*) determining his purpose and attitude and action with respect to his self in his relation to God (7:172). This binding and determining of man to a covenant with God and to a precise nature in regard to his purpose, attitude, and action, is the binding and determining in religion (*al-dīn*) which entails true submission (*al-islām*).[1] Thus knowledge and religion are natural correlates in the nature of man, that is, the original nature in which God has created him (al-fiṭrah). Man's purpose is therefore to know and to serve God (*ᶜibādah*, 51:66) and his duty is obedience (*ṭāᶜah*) to God, which conforms with his essential nature created for him by God (30:30).

But man is also 'composed of forgetfulness (*nisyān*)'—as a Prophetic tradition says,[2] and he is called *insān* precisely because having testified to himself the truth of the covenant he sealed with God, which entails obedience of His commands and prohibitions, he forgot (*nasiya*) to fulfill his duty and his purpose. Hence according to Ibn ᶜAbbās with reference to a passage in the Holy Qur'ān (20:115) the term *insān* is derived from *nasiya* when he said that man is called insān because, having covenanted with God, he forgot (*nasiya*).[3] Forgetfulness is the cause of man's disobedience, and this blameworthy nature inclines him towards injustice (*zulm*) and ignorance (*jahl*) (33:72). But God has equipped him with the powers and faculties of right vision and apprehension, of real savouring of truth, of right speech and communication; and He has indicated to him the right and the wrong with respect to the course of action he should take so that he might strive to attain his bright destiny (90:8-10; 46:26; 16:78; 32:9; 67:23; 23:78). The choice for the better (*ikhtiyār*)[4] is left to him. Moreover, God has equipped him with intelligence to know and distinguish reality from non-reality, truth from falsehood, and rectitude from error; and even though his intelligence—or rather his imaginative and estimative faculties—might confuse him,[5] and provided he is sincere and true to his noble nature, God, out of His bounty, mercy, and grace, will aid and guide him to attain to truth and right conduct. The supreme example of this is the case of the Prophet Ibrahim, upon whom be peace (6:74-82). Man, thus equipped and fortified is meant to be the vicegerent (*khalīfah*) of God on earth (2:30) and as such the weighty burden of trust (*amānah*) is placed upon him -the trust and responsibility to rule according to God's will and purpose and His pleasure (33:72). The trust implies responsibility to rule with justice, and to 'rule' means not simply ruling in the socio-political sense, nor in the controlling of nature in the scientific sense, but more fundamentally in its encompassing of the meaning of nature (*al-ṭab ᶜah*): it means the ruling, governing, controlling and maintaining of man by his self or his rational soul.

The terms heart (*qalb*), soul or self (*nafs*), spirit (*rūḥ*), and intellect (*ᶜaql*) used in relation to the soul each conveys two meanings; the one referring to the material or physical aspect of man, or to the body; and the other to the non-material, imaginal and intelligential or spiritual aspect, or to the soul of man.[6] In general, and from the ethical point of view, the first meaning denotes that aspect from which originates the blameworthy qualities in man, and they are the animal powers which in spite of their being beneficial to man in some respects, are in conflict with the intellectual powers. The attachment of blameworthiness to the animal powers inherent in the physical aspect of man should not be confused with the idea of denigration of the human body, which is indeed against the teachings of Islam. The human being is created 'in the best of moulds', but without true faith and good works he is worse than the lowly beasts (95:4-5). It is against these non-beneficial aspects of the animal powers that the Holy Prophet urged us when he alluded to the greater struggle (jihad) of man, for they are the enemy within.[7] The second meaning refers to the reality of man and, to his essence. To this meaning refers the well-known Prophetic tradition: 'whosoever knows his self knows his Lord.'

The real essence of man originated from the worlds of dominion (*al-malakūt*) and of command (*al-amr*) (36:83; 23:88.). When it inclines itself towards the right direction, the divine peace (*al-sakīnah*) will descend upon it (2:248; 9:26, 40; 48:4) and the effusion of divine liberality will successively be diffused in it until it achieves tranquility in the remembrance of God and abides in the knowledge of His divinity, and soars towards the highest levels of the angelic horizons. The Holy Qur'ān calls this state of the soul and tranquil soul (*al-nafs-al-muṭma'innah*) (89:27). The faculties or powers of the soul are like armies engaged in constant battles of alternate success. Sometimes the soul is drawn towards its intellectual powers and encounters the intelligibles whereby their eternal truths cause it to affirm its loyalty to God; and sometimes its animal powers drag it down to the lowest foothills of the bestial nature. This vacillation in the state of the soul is the state of the soul that censures itself (*al-nafs al-lawwāmmah*) (75:2); it is in earnest struggle with its animal powers. By means of knowledge, moral excellence, and good works it is possible for man to attain to the angelic nature, and when he does, he no longer has in common with his fellow man the animal nature in him except in outward form and fashion. But if he falls into the degrading depths of the bestial nature and remains captive in that condition, then he is severed from the nature common to humanity and appears as man only in shape and construction. This is the state of the soul that incites to evil (*al-nafs al-ammārah bi al-sū'*) (12:53).

In its specific sense, and when referring to the heart, the first meaning indicates the pine-shaped lump of muscular flesh situated to the left side in the breast. It is the circulator of blood to every part of the body and the fountainhead of the subtle vapour that is the vehicle of the physical animal spirit. Through this vehicle the animal spirit rises from its fountainhead in the heart to the brain through the veins to all parts of the body. This spirit is the conveyor of animal life and is common to all animals. When it passes away it causes the death of the external senses involving that of the body as a whole. As for the intellect, it performs abstractions of objects of the external world and contemplates the realities of things, and its functions are localised in various regions of the brain. The soul or self sometimes denotes the individual, concrete existence of a thing or person.[8]

With reference to the meanings of the four terms used in relation to the soul when they pertain to the soul of man, they all indicate an indivisible, identical entity, a spiritual substance which is the reality or very essence of man. In this sense they point to a unifying principle referred to as the *kamāl* or perfection of a being, to the mode of existence of that which transforms something potential to something actual.[9] This entity, which is a spiritual subtlety (*al-latḅfah al rūḥ̄āniyyah*), is a thing created, but it is immortal; it is not measured in terms of extent in space and time, or of quantity; it is conscious of itself and is the locus of intelligibles; and the way to know it is only through intellect and by means of observing the activities that originate in it. It has many names because of its accidental modes or states (*aḥ̄wāl*). Thus, when it is involved in intellection and apprehension it is called 'intellect'; when it governs the body it is called 'soul'; when it is engaged in receiving intuitive illumination it is called 'heart'; and when it reverts to its own world of abstract entities it is called 'spirit'. Indeed, it is in reality, always engaged in manifesting itself in all its states.

The soul possesses faculties or powers (*quwā*) which become manifest in its relation to bodies. In plants they are the powers of nutrition (*al-ghādhiyyah*), growth (*alnāmiyyah*), and generation or reproduction (*al-muwallidah*). These powers, in their general and not their specific senses, exist also in animals; and in man, whose body belongs to the animal species, there are powers of volition or action at will (*al-muḥbarrikah*), and perception (*al-mudrikah*) in addition to those of nutrition, growth, and reproduction. All these powers belong to the soul, and in view of their common inherence generally in the different bodies as well as their separate inherence specifically in accordance with the natures of the different species, the soul is somewhat like a genus divided into three different souls respectively: the vegetative (*al-nabātiyyah*), the animal (*al-hayawaniyyah*), and the human (*al-insāniyyah*) or the rational (*al-nātiqah*).

The powers peculiar to the animal soul are motive and perceptive, each of which is of two kinds. The motive power operates as the arouser of action (*al-bāᶜithah ᶜalā alfiᶜl*) on the one hand, and as itself active (*fāᶜilah*) or actuator on the other. As the arouser of action, it directs movement attracted by what it considers beneficial or harmful. When attracted by what it imagines to be something beneficial to it, its desire for it arouses its active power to attain it. When attracted by what it considers to be harmful to it, its aversion for it arouses its active power to avoid or overcome it. It is appetitive (*nuzuᶜiyyah*), and its activity is directed by two sub-faculties: the faculty of desire (*al-shahwāniyyah*), and the faculty of anger (*al-ghadabiyyah*). As actuator, it initiates and communicates movement starting the operation of the nerves, muscles, tendons, and ligaments towards fulfilling its purpose in accordance with what it desires or opposes.[10]

As for the perceptive power, this comprises the five external senses (*al-ḥawāss*) in the developmental order of touch, smell, taste, sight, and hearing respectively. These perform the function of perception of particulars in the external world. In addition to these, there are five internal senses which perceive internally the sensual images and their meanings, combine or separate them, conceive notions of them, preserve the conceptions thus conceived, and perform intellection of them.[11]

The perceptive powers of the internal senses may be classified into three kinds: some perceive but do not retain their objects; some retain objects but do not act upon them; some perceive their objects and act upon them. Perception is either of the form or the meaning (i.e., the intention or denotation) of the sensible objects; and the senses that retain their objects either retain their forms or their meanings; and those that act upon their objects act upon their forms or their meanings. The perceiver sometimes perceives directly and sometimes indirectly through another perceptive power. The difference between the form and the meaning is that the form is what is first perceived by the external sense, and then by the internal sense; the meaning is what the internal sense perceives of the sensed object without its having been previously perceived by the external sense. In the act of perception, the perceiver perceives the form of the external object, that is, an image or representation of the external reality, and not the reality itself. What is perceived by the senses is then not the external reality, but it's like as represented in the senses. The external reality is that from which the senses abstract its form. Similarly, with regard to the meaning, the intelligible forms are representations of realities that are imprinted upon the soul, because the intellect has already abstracted them from the accidental attachments that are foreign to their natures, such as quantity, quality, space, and position.[12]

The existence of the internal senses is established by way of intuition (*al-wijdān*).[13] The first of these internal senses receives the information brought in by the external senses and combines and separates internal images or representations of the external sensible objects. It is the common sense (*al-ḥiss al-mushtarak*),[14] also called the phantasy (fantasia). The common sense directly receives the data of the five external senses. It is necessary that the external sensible objects be first present to the external senses before they can be perceived by the common sense. It perceives only their individual sensible particulars, and not their intelligible universals, and it is able to sense pleasure and pain, both as perceived in the imagination as well as in the external sensible objects. It gathers together the sensed forms, combining and separating similar and dissimilar forms so as to make perception possible. This perception of forms, which are internal images or representations of the sensed objects, is called phantasy, and its recorder is the sensitive imagination (*al-khayāl*) or the representative faculty (*al-khayāliyyah*). The common sense, it may be further noted, only receives the data provided by the external senses, gathering together similar as well as dissimilar ones, but does not retain what it receives.

The function of recording and retaining the images or forms of the external objects received by the common sense belongs to the second internal sense called the representative faculty which we just mentioned. This faculty retains the images representing the external objects when the objects are no longer present to the external senses, and thus records the information received by the common sense from the external senses and preserves their images, their individual and collective meanings, and representations already existing therein for presentation to the third internal sense, which is the estimative faculty (*al-wahmiyyah*).

This faculty perceives of the individual, sensible particulars, their particular, nonsensible meanings, like enmity and love, and performs the function of judgement concerning right and wrong and good and bad pertaining to its objects as if they were sensible objects of the external world. The estimation is where judgements and opinions are formed, and unless governed by the intellect, it and the imaginative powers related to it are the sources of errors of judgement.[15] By means of this faculty, for example, the soul denies the intellectual substances that are not bounded nor located; by it the soul affirms the existence of a void encompassing the universe; and by it also the soul is made to accept the validity of syllogisms based on sophistical premises and to differ in the arrival at the conclusion. The estimative faculty presides over judgements not in the analytical way that characterises intellectual judgements, but in the imaginative way determined by memory images through a process of association from past experience, or not by memory images, but by an instinctive interpretation of the image perceived by the soul without going through any process of association from past experience.[16]

Just as the representative faculty conserves forms which it receives from the common sense, the fourth internal sense, called the retentive and recollective faculty (*al-hāfizah* and *al-dhākirah*), retains meanings and conserves them for the estimative faculty which perceives these meanings. The retentive faculty retains particular meanings and memorises them for close inspection and appraisal by the perceiver for so long as they remain in it. When they become absent from retention and the perceiver wishes to recall them, then it is called the recollective faculty. The relation of the retentive faculty to meanings is like the relation of the representative faculty to sensible things whose images are formed in the common sense.

The fifth internal sense is the imaginative faculty (*al-mutakhayyilah*). It perceives forms, then combines and separates them in an act of classification; adds to them and takes away from them so that the soul may perceive their meanings and connect them with the forms or images. It is the natural disposition of this faculty to perform the function of appraisal in orderly or non-orderly fashion, so that in that way the soul may use it to formulate any order it pleases. The soul uses this faculty for the purpose of classification by means of combining and separating its objects, sometimes through the practical reason and sometimes through the theoretical reason. Its essential nature is to perform the function of combining and separating, and not of perception. When the soul uses it as an intellectual instrument it is cogitative; and when it is used according to its natural disposition it is imaginative. The soul perceives what this faculty combines and separates of the forms through the mediacy of the common sense as well as through the mediacy of the estimative faculty. In its developed form this faculty apprehends ideas beyond the spheres of sense and sensual images. It is a specifically human faculty not found in the lower animals. By means of this faculty are established principles of necessary and universal application.

The fifth internal sense, then, has a dual function which is related to the animal and the human souls respectively. In this sense, this faculty has two aspects: an aspect to the senses, and an aspect to the intellect. In the former case it receives sensual forms as the sense perceives it, that is either as a reality or as something metaphorical. As a reality it presents the form as it is in itself; as a metaphor it presents the form not as it is in itself, but as the form is seen by it to be as it is in itself, for example, a mirage. In the latter case it receives the intelligible forms as the cogitative faculty apprehends it, that is, as true or false. As something true it is the form as it really is; as something false it is the form not as it really is but as the form is perceived by it to be as it really is, for example, magic or heresy, or any other erroneous judgement of facts.[17] In relation to the animal soul it is the faculty of sensitive imagination (*al-mutakhayyal*) which is productive of technical and artistic skills; in relation to the human soul it is the faculty of rational imagination (*al-mufakkirah*). In relation to the human, rational soul this faculty is cogitative. It functions as the manager of the data of theoretical reason, combining and arranging them as premises from which it deduces informing knowledge. Then from this knowledge it derives conclusions, and from two such conclusions it derives another and combines them yet again acquiring new conclusions and so on.[18]

These then are the five internal senses explained in a brief and general way. With reference to their classification into three kinds we may now identify them: the perceiver of forms is the common sense, and its conserver is the imagination or representative faculty. The perceiver of meanings is the estimation, and its conserver is the retentive and recollective faculty. That which perceives and acts upon its objects is the imaginative faculty, while that which only perceives and does not act upon its objects is the estimation and the common sense. These internal senses do not have specific sense organs as intermediary instruments performing specific functions like those of the external senses, but they are of an imaginal and intellectual nature and have connections with physical intermediaries, and their various functions are localised in the anterior, posterior, and middle regions of the brain.[19]

The faculties of the soul are not separate entities, each acting differently apart from the soul itself. They appear to be so and perform different functions—some of them prior in time to others—not because they are essentially different from each other, but because of the localisation of functions through different organs, and whose functions become actualised at different times, as well as due to the different states in which the soul is involved. In this respect, the faculties of the soul are in reality the soul itself as it manifests itself in accordance with its various modes.

The human, rational soul also possesses two powers which are both aspects of the same intellect. One of these is active (*ᶜamilah*), and the other cognitive (*ᶜalimah*). In so far as it functions as the active intellect it is the principle of movement of the human body. It is the practical reason and directs individual actions in agreement with the theoretical faculty of the cognitive intellect. In relation to the motive power of the animal soul, which is responsible for the exertion of willing that desire or aversion shall issue in action, it produces human emotions. In relation to the perceptive power and its representative, estimative, and imaginative faculties, it manages physical objects and produces human skills and arts; and in relation to its faculty of rational imagination it gives rise to premises and conclusions. In so far as it governs and manages the human body, it induces ethical behaviour in man involving the recognition of vices and virtues.[20]

The soul may be considered as having two aspects in relation to receiving and giving effects: an aspect towards what is lower in degree than itself, such as the body; and an aspect towards what is higher in degree than itself, such as the world of spirit whence it originated. In connection with what it receives from what is above it for its benefit and its action, it is a recipient of effects; and in connection with what is below it, the soul cannot be a recipient, but a giver of effects.[21] From this aspect of the soul that inclines towards what is lower issues ethical principles and the notion of vices and virtues for the guidance of the body; and from the aspect that looks to what is higher it receives knowledge. As a recipient of the creative power of knowledge through intellection and intuition it is the cognitive intellect. The power of the cognitive intellect is speculative (*naẓariyyah*). It is predisposed to the management of universal forms absolutely separated from matter; its purpose is the abstraction of intelligibles from matter, space, and position; it acts upon concepts of concepts such as the secondary intelligibles (*alma͑qūlat al-thāniyah*).[22] If the universal forms are not completely separated from matter, but are separated only in various degrees of separation which still have material connections, such as concepts of objects of the external world of the primary intelligibles (*al-ma͑qūlāt al-ūlā*),[23] then it will affect their absolute separation by means of abstraction. If the universal forms are in themselves abstract, then it takes them as they are.

The process of abstraction of sensibles to intelligibles, which is an epistemological process towards the arrival at meaning, undergoes various grades of completion leading to perfection. It begins already in the initial act of perception by sense; then it attains to a slightly higher degree of completion by means of the imagination, and a more refined one by the estimation even before attaining to complete and perfect abstraction by the intellect.[24]

The sensible, particular forms that have already been imprinted in the estimation, imagination, and sensation before the arrival of intelligible, universal forms in the intellect, reside in physical entities representing perceptive powers and faculties whose functions are localised in the body. When these forms are present in these faculties and are retained by their conservers, they serve as intellectual forms, or forms whose complete abstraction requires the exercise of the intellect. As to the relation of the intellect to the rational imagination, the contents of the imagination serve the intellect as potential intelligibles, becoming actual intelligibles when the intellect appraises them; not in the sense of being transformed into another form from their state of potentiality in the imagination, or of being transferred therefrom, for they remain as they are in the imagination and maintain their character as images. Only that when the intellect appraises the images, they produce an effect like the effect that comes about when light falls upon sensible things enveloped in darkness making them visible. Thus, the actual intelligibles are something else other than the forms of the imagination, which only serve to generate other forms in the intellect when the intellect appraises them, that is, considers, compares and analyses them, and then abstracts them from their material attachments and arrives at their universal meanings. The intellect first distinguishes their essential natures from their accidental attachments, their similar and dissimilar characteristics, then from the many meanings in the similars it is able to arrive at their single universal meaning; and from the similar meaning in each of the dissimilars it is able to arrive at their multiple meanings. The intellect then has the power of deriving many meanings from the single, and a single meaning from the many. This intellective activity becomes manifest in our formulation of the logical divisions of genus, species, and differentia; the formulation of our syllogisms that enable us to arrive at conclusions; the formulation of definitions.[25]

In respect of its being a recipient of effects from what is above it, the speculative power of the cognitive intellect has many relations and operations. It is not a merely passive recipient, for that which is a recipient of something else is a recipient in terms of power and act.[26]

Power is meant in three ways in terms of priority and posteriority: as absolute potency (*al-istiᶜdād al-muṭlaq*); as possible (*mumkinah*) or possessive (*malakah*); and as perfection (*kamāl*). Absolute potency is the state of being mere potentiality capable of receiving effects; it is pure power without the act, like the power in the child to write. As the child grows and develops into a youth, the power in the potentiality of receiving effects becomes gradually actualised by means of the instrument of actualisation to that extent which is possible for him to receive at this stage without need of the mediacy of any physical instrument.[27] He now knows how to use the ink and the pen; and understands the simple letters, thus possessing the capacity to write them. Then when he becomes an adult, the power becomes actualised completely by means of the instrument of actualisation, such that he can act whenever he pleases without need of acquisition, but that it is sufficient for him merely to intend the act and he acts, like the power in the writer who has reached consummation in his skill and knowledge when he is not writing. Indeed, it is the intellect that is the agent or instrument of actualisation of the power that lies in potentiality in the various stages of human development from infancy to maturity.[28]

The relations and operations of the speculative power of the cognitive intellect involve four aspects of the intellect governing the stages of human intellectual development from mere potency to perfect actualisation. The first aspect is called the material intellect (*al-ᶜaql al-hayulān,*). It is so called by way of analogy with the Greek concept of primary matter (*al-hayulā: Greek hylê*), which is pure matter without form, but capable of receiving all forms. There is, however, a difference between the Greek concept of primary matter and the material intellect we speak of here, and that is that while primary matter is capable of receiving all forms, the material intellect is capable of receiving only forms that its particular potentiality or power is capable of receiving and this latent capacity is not the same for every individual.[29] The second aspect is the possible intellect (*al-ᶜaql al-mumkin*) or the possessive intellect (*al-ᶜaql bi al-malakah*), which is able, by means of the power that has become activated in it, to receive from the primary intelligibles the first principles established by premises upon which rest self-evident truths, that is, those obtained not by means of deduction nor by verification, but necessarily— such as apprehension of the truth in the statement that the whole of something is greater than the parts, or that things equal to one and the same thing are equal to one another. Related to the material intellect, this intellect is active, for while the former has only the power without the act such that nothing can issue forth from it, nor has the instrument of actualisation ever been achieved by it, it is the latter intellect that is the agent for bringing forth what is potential in the former in accordance with the power to produce that is possible in itself at this stage. Related to the possessive intellect, this intellect that is in action makes possible for the former the reception of speculative forms from the primary intelligibles, by means of which it becomes possible for the former to arrive at the secondary intelligibles. The possessive intellect does not appraise these forms or give insights into their true natures, but merely acts as their repository. In this respect the intellect is possessive because it is able to possess and conserve the forms for further action by what comes after it. At this level, it is again the intellect-in-action that appraises the speculative forms by its act; it performs intellection of them and perceives that it performs the intellection. It is called the intellect-in-action (*al-ᶜaql bi al-fi'l*) because it is the agent for bringing forth by act, and it performs intellection whenever it pleases without need of the effort of acquisition. In relation to what comes after it, the intellect-inaction may be called the potential intellect (*al-ᶜaql bi al-quwwah*); for the active nature of the intellect, in relation to its capacity to act absolutely, appraises further the forms present in it by means of act, and by the same means it performs intellection of them and further performs intellection of its intellection. At this stage of its actualisation it is called the acquired intellect (*al-ᶜaql al-mustafād*). It is called 'acquired' because it perceives clearly that when the potential intellect passes over into absolute actuality, it does so by virtue of an intellect that is always in act, and that when this intellect that is always in act makes a specific contact with the potential intellect, it imprints into the latter a specific form, so that the intellect acquires these forms from outside itself.[30]

From the foregoing it becomes clear that there are three stages through which the human intellect passes in its intellectual development from pure potentiality to actuality. The first stage is that of the material intellect, which is nothing but a pure potency of receiving intelligible forms. When its dormant state is activated by intelligible impressions coming from the intellect-in-action, it becomes possible for it to possess the intelligible forms without actually thinking upon them. At this stage the material intellect has imprinted upon it the intelligible forms and becomes their conserver. It is no longer in a state of absolute potentiality; it is now a possible intellect possessing principles of knowledge. This is the second stage. Then when at this stage of the possible intellect, it is again activated by the intellect-in-action, it appraises the intelligible forms imprinted upon it. When it has all the speculative forms and acquisition ceases, the possible intellect passes into a state of settled tendency to think upon them. Its former state of relative potentiality has now become perfected potentiality. At this stage the possible intellect as intellect-in-action becomes capable of performing the act of thinking by itself, and the tendency to do so has become habitual to it. This is the third stage wherein the possible intellect becomes the possessive intellect. These developmental stages are common in all mankind, but in some cases there is indeed a fourth stage. When the possessive intellect actually reflects upon its own contents, that is, when it thinks, and thinks the thought it is thinking, it has reached the stage of absolute actuality and becomes the acquired intellect.

Since the potential intellect cannot by itself become actual, the actualisation of the human intellect from absolute potentiality to absolute actuality presupposes the existence of an external intelligence which is always in act, and which transforms the human intellect from the state of pure latency to that of perfect actuality. This external intelligence is the Active Intelligence (*al-ᶜaql al-faᶜāl*) identified as the Holy Spirit (*al-rūḥ al-qudus*),[31] and ultimately as God. In relation to the human intellect, the Active Intelligence is the intellect-in-action which rouses the potential material intellect from its state of dormancy by activating it in the thought of universal forms and eternal truths thereby transforming it into the possible intellect. Then, becoming more and more actualised (i.e., as the possessive intellect) by means of the illumination which it receives from the intellect-in-action, the human intellect becomes capable of self-intellection (i.e., the stage of the acquired intellect) and resembles the Active Intelligence. In relation to the Active Intelligence, the acquired intellect is like the potential material intellect, becoming transformed into a higher form when it receives illumination from the former. Thus, the human intellect may be classified as follow:

CLASSIFICATION OF THE INTELLECT

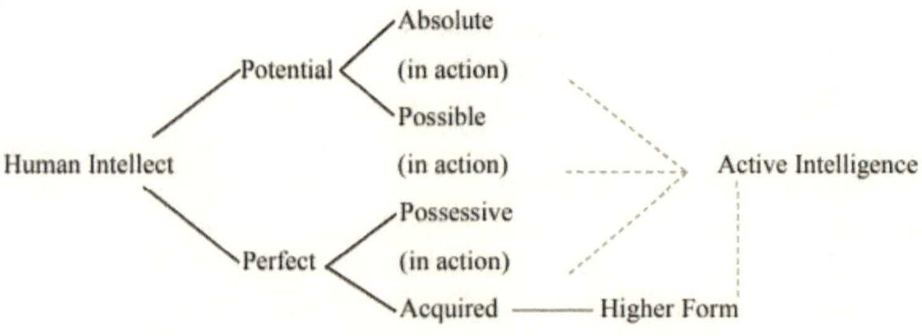

These, then, are the various degrees of power in the relations and operations of the speculative nature of the cognitive intellect. In this we see that the consummation of the animal genus and the human species is accomplished in the acquired intellect. Now this acquired intellect attains to higher forms of intellect graded in various degrees of excellence. In relation to the higher planes of existence, the acquired intellect is none other than the holy intellect (*al-ᶜaql al-qudsi*), which characterises the intellects of the prophets, the saints, and the learned who are established in knowledge, each according to their various degrees of excellence. Although the human soul is common in mankind, it differs in potency (2:286; 7:42; 23:62) and it differs in individuals due to differences in the accidents that make up every personality; and the potential power in the material intellect is therefore not equal in capacity for everyone. The potency in the intellect is ordered according to nobility of soul, the highest being, that of the Holy Prophet.[32] The intellect is essentially a spiritual substance; it is non-material and separate from matter and only its act is connected with matter. A material or physical entity such as a body can neither receive nor contain intelligibles; nor can intelligibles reside in a body because a physical entity is divisible, and whatever resides in it is also divisible. Since the intelligible is a single, universal form it is indivisible, and it is impossible for it to reside in bodily entities.[33] Intelligible forms, and even forms of the cognitive imagination, have no physical repository. The internal senses in the body receive only sensible, particular forms whose images and meanings are conserved in the representative and the retentive or recollective faculties which serve the imaginative powers. If the soul, which does not retain such forms, wishes to review rational concepts pertaining to them, necessitating a reconsideration of the forms through the medium of these faculties, it merely has to recall them as they exist in their repositories. If, however, they no longer exist in their repositories, then their reappraisal by the rational soul necessitates a process of reacquisition. As for the intelligible forms, the intellect utilises their meanings after they have been imprinted in it. It does not possess the actual intelligible realities themselves, as they are contained neither in the body nor in any physical entity as we have already stated, nor in the soul because if they were, the soul would have been aware of them; and its being aware of them simply means the act of intellection by the rational soul or intellect: and this refers to their forms or meanings as imprinted in it, not to the intelligible realities themselves. Since these intelligible realities are neither in the body nor in the soul, they must be external to them. Their separate existence external to them means either their being self-subsistent entities, or entities inhering in a substance whence they originate and whose predisposition is to imprint intelligible forms in the human soul. It is not possible for them to be self-subsistent, for intelligible realities inhere in a substance; and thus, it follows that their repository and source of origin is that substance we call the Active Intelligence.[34]

The relation of the Active Intelligence to the soul is like that of the sun to the eye.[35] Without light coming from the sun, the eyes in darkness remain as potential organs of vision; and the objects of sight remain potentially visible. Only when the sun sheds its light do the eyes become actually seeing, and their objects become actually visible. So in like manner does the potential intellect become actual intellect, and the potential intelligibles become actual intelligibles by means of the light that is shed by the Active Intelligence upon the soul. When the intellective power of the soul—that is, the potential intellect-appraises the particulars in the imagination, this act of appraisal puts it in a state of readiness to receive the universal intelligible from the Active Intelligence by way of illumination. The arrival at the meanings of the particular images whose material attachments have all been abstracted by the illumination of the Active Intelligence is due to an immediate apprehension in the soul or intellect caused by the illumination that comes directly from the Active Intelligence. The elements of meanings that are in the images are then not the cause of the production of their like in the intellect. The action of the Active Intelligence upon the potential intellect, causing the latter's immediate apprehension which transforms it into an actual intellect, is very much like the immediate apprehension arrived at by the intellect of the necessary connection between the premises and the conclusion in a syllogism. The activity of the soul in the appraisal of the particulars is then simply to bring itself to a state of readiness to receive the intelligibles from the Active Intelligence.[36]

In relation to the soul, the intellect is a faculty or power of the soul that becomes manifest in man as the rational soul. This intellective power is something different from the rational soul, since the active agent is the soul, and the intellect is in this respect its instrument, like the knife and the cutting. But in reality, intellect, soul, and mind point to the same entity, being called intellect because the entity is perceptive; being called soul because the entity governs the body; being called mind because the entity is predisposed to the apprehension of realities.

The human soul, though independent of the body, yet requires the body in this physical world in order to acquire principles of ideas and beliefs. By means of its relationship with the body, the rational soul makes use of the animal powers to gain, among the data supplied to it by the senses, the particulars. Through the particulars it acquires, among other things, four informing matters:

1. The isolation of single universals from particulars by way of abstraction of their meanings from matter and from material connections and connective relations; and consideration of the common and differentiating factors in their essential and accidental existence. Through this process the soul acquires the principles of ideas by utilising the imagination and the estimation,

such as the genus and the differentia, the general and the particular accident.[37]

2.   The establishment of comparative relations and ratios between the single universals in the manner of negation and affirmation.

3.   The acquisition of empirical premises, which are obtained by means of the senses through sensible experience, and by means of the process of reasoning from parallel cases, or analogy, through repeated observation.

4.   Reports that are successively transmitted on which rest true beliefs.[38]

We have thus far been explaining in a brief and general way the soul's intellective activity in the course of its cognitive involvement in the material and intelligible domains of existence, the world of gross matter and the world of pure ideas. We pointed out that this activity consists in the abstraction of matter and its attendant attachments by means of its external and internal senses and of the intellect. Since we said that the soul is a spiritual substance independent of the body, and since this explanation of the soul's intellective activity and cognitive involvement pertains to the worlds of matter and intellect, and of body and mind, it may be erroneously construed that when the body no longer lives the soul simply reverts to a purely intellectual world of utter abstraction.[39] But the soul's consciousness of itself is not only something intellectual in nature, it is something imaginal as well; and this means that not only the intellective power of the soul, hut the imaginative power also survive physical death. Imagination is a cognitive power of the soul. We are not here referring to that aspect of the imagination that is called phantasy, but to a spiritual, or intelligential 'creative' imagination reflective of a real world of images (*ᶜalam al-mithāl*) ontologically existing independently between the world of gross matter and the world of pure ideas. This intermediary world reflects realities in the world of pure intelligibles, which are in turn projected by it in the form of imperfect reflections in the world of sense and sensible experience.[40] The things in the world of images, which are reflections of realities in the intelligible world, exist in reality, their nature as images being neither purely intelligible nor grossly material. Images like those in the dream state have form and extension and quantity, and yet they are not material; they partake of both aspects of reality, the material and the intelligible, but are in nature neither one nor the other. They are thus unlike the Platonic Ideas which are pure abstractions of the intellect.[41] Thus, when we speak of the intellect's abstraction of matter and its accidental attachments, it should not be understood thereby to mean that the soul affects a complete denudation of forms in the intelligibles; it is the materiality in matter that is abstracted by the intellect, and not the imaginality as well, for images are not matter and materiality does not pertain to them. The imagination that we mean, which is a cognitive faculty or power of the soul, like intellect, is immaterial, and therefore does not 'contain' the images. When we speak of intellegible forms being 'in' the mind, or images being 'in' the cognitive imagination, we do not mean that these forms or images are 'contained' in them; it is rather that they are constructions of the intellect or mind during the course of its intellection of them such that they are 'present' to the intellect, and hence referred to as being 'in' the mind; and productions of the cognitive imagination as it involves itself in projecting the sensible world.

In our present state, the intellect's inability to conceive or perceive abstract entities is not due to its essential nature, nor is it due to the nature of the abstract entities, but rather it is due to its own preoccupation with the body which is needed by it as we have mentioned. This being engrossed with the affairs of the body prevents it from perceiving the abstract realities in their original nature because the body acts as an obstruction. When, however, consciousness of the body and of the subjective self or ego is subdued, the intellect will be able to make contact with the Active Intelligence and will then be capable of perceiving the abstract realities as they are.[42]

Unlike the intellect, which undergoes a transformation from a state of potentiality to that of actuality, the imagination is from the beginning active. That aspect of the imagination whose powers are directed towards the world of sense and sensible experience is the sensitive imagination or phantasy. It serves the practical intellect by providing it with the forms or images and meanings of particular objects of knowledge. It is also the source of fictitious productions. In contrast to the sensitive imagination, that aspect of the imagination whose powers are directed towards the realms of the intellect and the spiritual realities is the cognitive imagination, which is capable of reflecting the forms of the real world of images. However, because of the intermediary position of the world of images, and due to the dual function of the imagination that is aligned to it, being involved in the operation of its powers both with the sensible and intelligible realms, the imagination cannot preoccupy itself with its own world of real images without distraction.[43]

We said in a note that the heart (*qalb*) is a subtle organ of cognition connected with the imaginative faculty of the soul. It is like a mirror that is ever turning in different directions. When forms appear in front of it, their images are reflected therein. The forms themselves remain always in their places outside the mirror, so that they are not transferred therein to the extent that the mirror may contain them. Only their images are reflected in the mirror. In like manner also, only when the mirror of the heart is turned towards the right direction without being distracted towards any other, and if it is not deficient in its reflective power and has achieved pellucid quality will the human soul be able to perceive clearly the real and true forms of the intelligential and spiritual realm.[44] Imagine yourself to be inside an opaque sphere. This sphere is within another such sphere, and that other within yet another one, all having each a single aperture. Now all these spheres are turning, rotating in different directions. Only when you have the power to make the spheres turn and rotate in such a way that their apertures would come in a line of conjunction with each other will the light from outside shine through, enabling you to see both what is within and without.

The power of imagination is not equal in men and differs according to their degrees of intellectual excellence and nobility of soul. In some it is stronger than in others, so that some may be able to see true visions of that intermediary world and others may not. We who affirm prophecy cannot deny the possibility that the forms of the world of images that are reflected in the cognitive imagination may get imprinted in the sensitive imagination or phantasy to the extent that the perceiver of these forms may actually see them in their sensible guise. Indeed, in the case of the Holy Prophet, for example, his cognitive imagination was so powerful that he was able to perceive intelligible realities in their sensible forms (e.g., the Angel in the form of a man); and sensible realities in their intelligible forms (e.g. the dead as alive in the other world).[45]

The function of the imagination is then to create sensible things, or rather it is the soul itself that creates sensible things and perceptible forms from within itself as well as images of unperceived objects. The thinking and feeling entity to which perception, whether sensitive, imaginative, and intellective, is attributed is then in reality not the external and internal senses, but the soul itself exercising its cognitive powers of intelligence and imagination. The soul is therefore not something passive; it is creative, and through perception, imagination, and intelligence it participates in the 'creation' and interpretation of the worlds of sense and sensible experience, of images, and of intelligible forms or ideas.

The soul, according to a tradition of the Holy Prophet, is created before the body,[46] meaning it existed long before the body. Some commentators think that the word for 'body' (sing. *jasād*) applied in the tradition, does not refer to organic bodies such as the human body, but rather to celestial or physical bodies. As for the word for 'spirit' (sing. *rūḥ*) occurring in the same tradition and understood as referring to the soul, they say that it refers to angelic entities. Their view in this matter reflects their position which amounts to a denial of the pre-existence of the soul and seems to have originated from the position taken by ibn Sīnā, who argued according to the principles of physics, that it is impossible for the soul to exist before the body. Its pre-existence according to those principles entails either it being a simple unity or a plurality, both of which are impossible. Moreover, ibn Sīnā's argument against the pre-existence of the soul is directed against the doctrine of metempsychosis (*al-tanāsukh*).[47] Some Muslim thinkers and writers seem to have taken such arguments as conclusive and deny the pre-existence of the soul. As for the passage in the Holy Qur'ān referring to the creation of man where God says that after having fashioned him (i.e., formed him as body), He breathed into him of His spirit (15:29), this does not demonstrate conclusively that the existence of the body is prior to that of the soul. It can also be interpreted that the spirit that was breathed into the body already implied the soul's pre-existence. Moreover, in another passage in the Holy Qur'ān God says; 'It is We Who created you (i.e., the spirits or souls) and then We formed you (i.e. the bodies). (7:11; More specific, 87:2). With regard to the interpretation of the term jasād being meant, in the tradition referred to above, to denote not the organic or human body, but the physical or celestial body, the testimony of linguistic usage demonstrates that jasād is synonymous with badan, which invariably refers to the organic and the human body; whereas a physical or celestial body is usually denoted by the term jisim, even though jisim too may be employed synonymously with jasād. The usual distinction between jisim and jasād is, however, that the former refers to body in the genus of quantity, whereas the latter refers to body in the genus of animal.[48]

But we do not agree with their position on the soul. Their adherence to the principles of physics in denying the pre-existence of the soul reflects the position of the essentialists or those who affirm the primacy of quiddity over existence. We maintain that their position on the soul is confused, and indeed ibn Sīnā himself seems to have contradicted his own position on the pre-existence of the soul in his psychology and his oriental philosophy, where the soul's prior existence is implied.[49] We do not admit that the principles of physics must necessarily be brought to bear insofar as the nature of the soul is concerned. Moreover, we do not concede that our affirmation of pre-existence of the soul has anything to do with the doctrine of metempsychosis, which—insofar as it pertains to the world—we likewise reject.[50] Nor do we admit, in affirming the soul's preexistence in relation to the body, that we believe the soul to be necessarily eternal, for we affirm that it is created. Furthermore, in line with those who affirm the primacy of existence over quiddity, our position on the pre-existence of the soul may not simply be equated with Platonism or Neoplatonism. We say, with al-Junāyd and others,[51] that the soul's pre-existence refers to a state of being unlike that of existence that is known to us, but to an existence in the interior condition of Being, in the consciousness of God. To this state of existence refer God's words in the Holy Qur'ān when He called to the souls: 'Am I not your Lord?', and they answered: 'Yes indeed!' (7:172) By virtue of the power that God gave them to respond to

His call, we infer that the soul knows God as its Lord; it knows itself as His creature; it knows other souls as distinct from itself; and it possesses power to apprehend what knowledge communicates. For this reason—that is, the soul's possession of a cognitive power enabling it to identify its Lord and Creator, itself, and others like itself, and to make distinctions as well as to formulate and communicate meaningful signs by means of an innate power of speech (i.e. *nuṭiq* with reference to the term *qawl*)—the soul is called the 'rational' soul.[52] This also means that the soul already has some form of knowledge of the realms spiritual before its attachment to the body. The human body and the world of sense and sensible experience provide the soul with a school for its training to know God also, this time through the veils of His Creation.

NOTES

1. See my *Islam: The Concept of Religion and the foundation of Ethics and Morality,* (Kuala Lumpur, 1976).

2. Ismāᶜil bin Muhammad al-Jarrāhī, *Kashf al-Khafā'li Muz,1 al-Ilbās*, in *Ahmad Qalash*, ed., (Beirut: Mu'assasah al-Risālah, 1985), 4th pr, 419, no. 2806. Al-Ṭābarānī, al-Tirmizī ibn Abī Shaybah, from ibn ᶜAbbas.

3. Jamāl al-Dīn Muhammad ibn Manzūr, Lisān al-ᶜArab (Beirut: Dār Sādir and Dār Beyrut, 1388/1968), vol. 6: 11, col. 1.

4. Contrary to the invariable translation by most people of the word *ikhtiyār* by 'choice', we maintain that *ikhtiyār* does not simply mean 'choice'. The word khayr, meaning 'good' which is bound in meaning with *ikhtiyār* and being derived from the same root, determines that the choice meant is towards what is good. This point is most important when aligned to the philosophical question of freedom. A so-called 'choice' towards what is bad is therefore not a choice. Since we affirm that freedom is to act as our real and true nature demands, only the exercise of that choice which is good can properly be called a 'free choice'. A choice for the better is an exercise of freedom. It presupposes knowledge of good and evil. A 'choice' for the worse is not a choice, as it is based upon ignorance and on the instigation of the soul that inclines towards the blameworthy aspects of the animal powers.

5. Abū Hāmid Muhammad al-Ghazālī, *Mishkāt al-Anwār*, ed. Abū al ᶜAla Afi (Cairo, 1964), p. 47.

6. Abū Hāmid Muhammad al-Ghazālī, *Ihyā'ᶜUlum* al-Dīn (Cairo, 1939), vol. 3: 3; al-Ghazālī, *Maᶜārij*, (Beirut, 1978), pp. 5 fol.

7. Bayhaqī, Zuhd, from Jābir. Ibn Hajar says this Hadīth is well known. *Kashf al-Khafā'*, vol. 1, p. 511, no. 1362.

8. Abū Hāmid Muhammad al-Ghazālī, *Maᶜārij al Quds fi Madārij Macrifat al-Nafs* (Beirut, 1978), pp. 15-18.

9. Al-Ghazālī, *Maᶜārij*, pp. 21-22; Abu ᶜAlī al-Husayn ibn Sīnā\, *Kitāb al-Shifā'*, eds. G. Qanawāt,and Sacīd Zāyid (Cairo: Al-Maktabah al-ᶜArabiyyah), pp. 9-10; Najāt, p. 197.

10. Al-Ghazālī, *Maʿārij*, p. 37 fol; ibn Sīnā, *Shifāʾ*, p. 33; Kitāb al-Najāt, eds. G. Qanawāt–, Ma Hmud al-Khudayrī and Fuʾād al-Ahwanī (Cairo, 1953), pp. 197-198.

11. Al-Ghazālī, *Maʿārij*, p. 41; ibn Sīnā, *Shifāʾ*, pp. 33-34; Najāt, p. 198.

12. Al-Ghazālī, *Maʿārij*, pp. 44-45; ibn Sīnā, Najāt, pp. 200-201.

13. The term wijdān is used by al-Ghazālī in the *Maʿārij*, p. 45. Here it is understood in its general sense as intuition based on introspection.

14. I.e., an internal sense common to all the five external senses. It unites the sensations of all the senses in a general sensation or perception. On *al-hiss al-mushtarak*, see al-Shifāʾ, pp. 145 fol. The Latin translation is communis sensus, from which the term 'common sense' is derived. Here, then, common sense is used as a technical term, and not in its general everyday usage as something quite evident or obvious.

15. Al-Ghazālī, *Mishkāt al-Anwār*, p. 47.

16. Al-Ghazālī, *Maʿārij*, p. 46.

17. Ibid., p. 47.

18. Ibid., pp. 45-47

19. Al-Ghazālī, *Maʿārij*, pp. 47-48; ibn Sīnā, *Shifāʾ*, pp. 143-150.

20. Al-Ghazālī, *Maʿārij*, pp. 49-50; ibn Sīnā, *Shifāʾ*, p. 185; Najāt, pp. 202-203.

21. I.e., effects that are good or those that are bad. See the three degrees of the soul mentioned above.

22. I.e., like the concept 'rational animal' as derived from another concept 'man'.

23. I.e., like the concept 'man' as corresponding to a particular, existent human being.

24. See Al-Ghazālī, *Maʿārij*, pp. 61-62; ibn Sīnā, *Shifāʾ*, pp.50-51 fol; Najāt, pp. 207-210.

25. Ibn Sīnā, *Shifāʾ*, pp. 208-211; Al-Ghazālī, *Maʿārij*, p.126.

26. Al-Ghazālī, *Maʿārij*, p. 51; ibn Sīnā\, *Shifāʾ*, p. 39; Najāt, p. 204.

27. Without need of the mediacy of any physical instrument because the real instrument of actualisation is the intellect, as we state presently.

28. Al-Ghazālī, *Maʿārij*, p. 91; ibn Sīnā, *Shifāʾ*, pp. 39-40; Najāt, p. 204.

29. See below, and also (2:286), (7:42) and (23:62).

30. Al-Ghazālī, *Maʿārij*, p. 52; ibn Sīnā, *Shifāʾ*, pp. 39-40; Najāt, p. 205.

31. Al-Ghazālī, *Maʿārij*, p. 124. Al-Ghazālī adduces as proof of the identity of the Active Intelligence the Sacred Texts 53:5-6; 42:51; and 81:19-20; *Maʿārij*, p. 123.

32. Al-Ghazālī, *Maʿārij*, p. 53; ibn Sīnā, *Shifāʾ*, pp. 212-220.

33. Ibn Sīnā, *Shifāʾ*, p. 123; Najāt, pp. 213-216.

34. Al-Ghazālī, *Maʿārij*, p. 124.

35. Al-Ghazālī, *Maʿārij*, p. 125; ibn Sīnā, *Shifāʾ*, p.208; Najāt, p. 231. See also above.

36. Al-Ghazālī, *Maʿārij*, p. 125; ibn Sīnā, *Shifāʾ*, p.208.

37. A genus is a class of objects of knowledge more extensive than the species; for example, 'animal'. A differentia is a property distinguishing a species from

other species of the same genus; for example, 'rational' from the genus 'animal'. An accident is an occurrence, a happening, an event, an essential property of substance that is continually being replaced by similars. A particular accident is an inseparable accident of a class of objects, such as the 'blackness' of crows. A general accident is a separable accident which allows some members of a class to differ from other members of the same class, such as the 'white' or 'fat' horses from the 'black' or 'lean' horses; it equally allows a thing to differ from itself at different times, as it happens in all cases of things that grow and decay.

38. Al-Ghazālī, *Macārij*, pp. 101-102; ibn Sīnā, *Shifā'*, p. 197; Najāt, pp. 220-221.

39. The psychology of the human soul sketched in the foregoing pages, which we have paraphrased from the Macārij of al-Ghazālī, has largely been derived by al-Ghazālī from the Shifā' and the Najā of ibn Sīnā as indicated in the reference notes. However, al-Ghazālī has added important modifications of his own. He has in fact also given a resume of the theory of the philosophers on the animal and rational powers of the soul in his *Tahāfut* (Cairo, 1321H), pp. 70-71, saying that what they affirmed does not contradict religion -on the contrary, religion lends its support to their theory in this matter. Only their claim with regard to the primacy of the intellect as the sole guide to knowledge of the ultimate nature of reality is disputed (*Tahāfut*, p. 71). Religion, apart from stressing the cognitive role of the intellect (*ʿaql*} emphasises no less the role of the heart (*qalb*) as a spiritual organ of cognition. The heart, also called *fuʿād*, is the organ of spiritual perception (see for example in the Holy Qur'ān 53:11. This spiritual perception, which is of the nature of perceptive experience and tasting, is connected, with the imaginative faculty of the soul. See the schema of the soul on the final page of this article.

40. The world of images or *ʿalam al-mithāl* corresponds in theological terms to the *barzakh*, that is, an intermediary world into which he who dies enters and remains for a period from the time of death to resurrection.

41. The idea of a real world of images (*ʿalam al-mithāl*) and the science of symbolism pertaining to the interpretation of the reflections of that world in our world of sense and sensible experience, have their roots in Ghazālī and perhaps also in ibn Sīnā. In the *Maʿārij*, Ghazālī has given an elaborate though concise explanation of the powers of the imagination (pp. 135-145; see also 125-134). This was developed in Muslim metaphysical thinking especially by ibn ʿArabī, who derived many of his interpretations on the nature of reality from the writings of al-Ghazālī. See further the *Mishkāt* of al-Ghazālī, which is a profound commentary on the Verse of Light in the Sacred Text, and the conclusion to ʿAfīfī's general introduction to the *Mishkāt*, pp. 34-35. See also Muhīyī al-Dīn ibn ʿArabī, Fus ūs al-Hikam, ed. Abū l- ʿAlā ʿAfīfī' Cairo, 1365/1946), pp. 99-104; and ʿAfīfī's *ta'liqat* to the *Fusūs*, pp. 74-76; 105-118.

42. Al-Ghazālī, *Maʿārij*, p. 127; see also ibn Sīnā, Najāt, pp. 219-220.

43. Al-Ghazālī, *Maʿārij*, p. 137.

44. Ibid., p. 93.

45. Ibid., p. 78.

46. This is a well-known *Ḥadīth* also reported in *Macārij*, p. 111. Al-Ghazālī, however, has given an interpretation of it aligned with the position of the philosophers who, following Aristotle, maintained that every soul is created to suit a particular body, thereby denying the pre-existence of the soul. But this position, as we will state presently, appears to have no real cogency and, if so, must be regarded as untenable.

47. Ibn Sīnā, *Shifā'*, pp. 198-201; 202 fol; *Najāt*, pp. 222-230. See also Al-Ghazālī, *Maʿārij*, pp. 105-115.

48. See my Commentary on the Hujjat al-Siddīq (Kuala Lumpur: Ministry of Culture, 1986), p. 330, note 463. Cf. Lisān al-ʿArab, vol. 3, p. 120, cols. 1 & 2; vol. 12, p. 99, col. 1.

49. E.g., al-Najāt, p. 223; and Fazlur Rahman's commentary in *Avicenna's Psychology* (London: Oxford University Press, 1952), p.107, with reference to Ch.XII, p. 57. See also ibn Sīnā,'s poem on the soul called Al-Qasīdatu al-cAyaniyyah, trans. A.J. Arberry in Avicenna's Theology, (London, 1951), pp. 77-78.

50. See al-Ghazālī, *Tahāfut,* pp. 86-87.

51. Abū al-Qāsim Junāyd, *Kitāb al-Mithāq*, pp. 40-43; Abū Bakr Muhammad alKalābādhī, Kitāb al *Taʿārruf* in ʿAbd al-Halim Mahmūd, ed., (Beirut, 1400/1980), p.68.

52. I.e., *al-nafs al-nātīqah. Natīq* signifies the reasoning powers, the rational faculty, and corresponds to the Greek logos and the Latin *ratio*. It points to an inner faculty that apprehends realities and formulates meaning involving judgement, discrimination, and clarification. It is derived from the same Arabic root that conveys the basic meaning of 'speech' signifying a certain power and capacity to articulate words or symbolic forms in meaningful pattern. *Mantīq*, the Arabic word for logic, is derived from the same root and includes within its semantic structure what is conveyed by ma *ʿqūl*, which is the intelligible character of a thing as grasped by the mind. In this sense, ratio can be understood as being synonymous with *ma ʿqūl*, which in Latin is *intentio*. According to al-Ghazālī, this entity that we call the 'rational soul' and which we identify with that which is referred to in the Quranic passage mentioned above, signifies the second aspect of the heart (*qalb*) referred to in page 5 above. This entity is also identified by him as the spirit of man (*rūḥ*) that carries the trust (*amānah*) granted by God, and that is by nature created with the power and capacity to be the abiding center of knowledge. It is by its saying 'Yes indeed! (*balā*) that, which affirms the Divine unity. It is also the original root (*asīl*) of mankind to which ultimate state of existence it will return in the world to come. See al-Ghazālī, *Maʿārij*, p. 17.

8

The Heart and Personality Development

MANZURUL HUQ

Ever since psychology broke away from its ancestral moorings by giving up its original definition of being a science of the soul, it has kept shifting its position and connotation to keep up with the current mode and practices of the contemporary scientific world. In one phase of this shifting process, it not only lost its spiritual substance, but it was emptied of its mental contents at the hands of a group of behaviorists who redefined psychology as a science of behaviour. Consequently, concepts of the mind and mental processes remained banished from the domain of psychology for a considerable length of time.

However, with the success of modern computer technology in simulating many aspects of the human information processing system, several cognitive psychologists have rehabilitated and rekindled interest in mental processes in the discipline of psychology. Mainly due to their highly promising experimental investigations in exploring the inner mental structures and processes underlying the surface of explicit behaviour, psychology has begun to be defined nowadays as the science of behaviour and mental process.[1]

The cognitive psychologists salvaged the behaviouristic man from merely being an automaton—a passive and reactive man, pulled and pushed by a myriad of stimuli in the environment—and transformed him into a highly autonomous and proactive man by asserting the principle of active mediation of inner mental processes for the occurrence of behaviour. But since cognitive psychology is committed to a rigorous adherence to a framework of scientific operationism and empirical-experimental canons of modern science, the mental concepts formulated by it are still conspicuously inadequate to sense and tap the supra-sensuous elements and processes in man, which mark him as distinctly human and make him immensely versatile, creative, and capable of scaling the most sublime

143

heights of personality development.

If human nature is believed to be spiritual at its core, it is obvious that the reality of human nature will ever elude the grip of psychology should a tradition of hard-bound empiricism continue to be followed. The inability of modern psychology to take into cognizance the spiritual base of human personality appears to be rooted in its characteristic trend to take flight in the artificial bounds of the laboratory, shutting all its doors towards supersensory phenomena, and relying solely on observation and human reason to the total exclusion of the divine source of revealed knowledge.

The scientific tools used by modern science are no doubt good in achieving the goals for which they were originally designed i.e., to explore and understand the properties and relationships of objects and aspects of natural phenomena, and they have served their purpose with a highly impressive degree of success. But when these same tools are applied to explore the nature of human beings on the assumption that they too are nothing but a complex system of physio-chemical elements forming a part of the natural phenomena, the results produce a highly frustrating and humiliating image of man as engaged in continuous struggle to fulfill such needs and desires that are largely shared by animals in general.

The superiority of man to other animals seem to lie, according to this conceptual framework, only in the sophistication of means he adopts to fulfill his basically animalistic needs. Though some psychologists often make mention of some higher order needs in man, they are not usually conceived to occupy positions of primary importance and potency in the hierarchy of human needs. Of course, the more humanistically oriented among the modern psychologists put special emphasis upon those features of human nature which dignify man over other animals and distinguish him from them. However, their conception of the essence of human nature, barring a few exceptions, are not essentially spiritual. To reiterate, such inability to realize the inner spiritual core of human nature seems to stem from the inherent limitations of the sensory–empirical tools of modern science to have access to the supersensory realities of human beings.

However, the Muslims, who believe that humanity has been created by Allah (SWT) and has been sent by Him to this world as His vicegerent endowed with a divine "spirit" with inherent divine potentials, cannot exclusively trust and depend on such scientific tools which are unable to sense and unfold the spiritual basis of human existence, and which consequently fail to provide any knowledge and direction for the promotion and development of the real human self. As the divine representative, man must turn to Allah (SWT), the ultimate source of his existence on this earth, to attain genuine knowledge of his true self and to have infallible guidance for its full-scale promotion and development. Such knowledge has always been provided through the divine revelations communicated to mankind through the divine messengers. As the final revealed scripture, the Qur'ān is the perfect embodiment of revealed knowledge, and the life and traditions of the final Prophet of Islam (SAS) is the complete operational demonstration of the entire corpus of this divine knowledge.

Scientific method and tools can, however, act as useful aids and secondary source of knowledge to further elucidate certain aspects of human personality when guided by the directions provided in the revealed knowledge. To have a stable and secure foundation for raising human personality to its towering heights by harnessing all its inherent endowments, we must therefore, have recourse to the divine source of knowledge. In the following discourse, we will highlight some basic and major features of human personality and its potentials in the light of the Qur'ān and the sunnah [the traditions of the Holy Prophet (SAS)], the practical elucidation of the Qur'ān along with their interpretations by the righteous scholars of Islam.

ISLAMIC VIEWS

In contrast to the soulless, lopsided, and truncated views of human personality and behaviour by most of the modern psychologists, the Islamic tradition presents a spirtual, kaleidoscopic, and holistic image of human personality that depicts the highest peak of its development as well as the lowest abyss of its degradation. Most importantly, the Islamic views provide precise guidelines for ascending the targeted development of personality and averting the disastrous course of its degeneration. Based on the divine revelation, and prophetic traditions, Muslim scholars and savants have worked out an adequately clear picture of various dimensions of human nature, properties, and functions of different aspects of human self along with their interrelationship with each other. Since in the Islamic tradition, the *qalb* (heart) is both the core and architect of human personality,[2] the focus of our discussion in the following passages will be the nature and role of the heart or *qalb* in relation to man's behaviour and personality development.

The prevailing concepts of psychology tend to privilege the brain as the central organ which receives stimuli-inputs, analyzes them, and takes decision for necessary actions. However, Muslim scholars, while acknowledging the input receiving function and some interpretative processes of the human brain, do not ascribe to it the decision-making functions. Barring some analytical decision-making function of reflexive nature, all other behavioural responses are ultimately controlled by the heart and not by the brain. This view, however, does not totally negate the brain centered concepts of modern psychology which have identified certain regions of the brain as centers for regulating specific psychological functions. In fact, Imam al-Ghazālī, the illustrious Muslim philosopher and savant of the 11th century A.C., has specified separate regions for different such functions. For example, the memory has been located in the hinder lobe of the brain; the imaginative faculty has been located in the frontal lobe of the brain, while the middle folds of the brain have been specified for the power of reflection.[3] But these seats of the brain, the whole of the brain or even the total nervous system, control and regulate the bodily functions and behaviour only as a mediating role system and not as primary agents. According to Islamic tradition, it is the *qalb* or the heart which occupying the supreme autonomous status in the personality system, controls, and rules over all the regions of the brain and the whole nervous system. The heart has been said to be the master and the key entity that regulates all sorts of behavioural functions and drives the entire course of personality development, both in its progressive and regressive directions.[4] Therefore, the construction and development of personality to its fullest range or the corruption and degeneration of it, all depends on the state and condition of the human heart. It is the heart, which if sound and healthy, drives and channels human potentials into positive directions of growth and progress. On the other hand, if the heart becomes sick and corrupt, the growth of all human potentials is blocked, and the personality turns towards a regressive course of ruination and self-debasement.

The above assertions and contents have been very succinctly and comprehensibly expressed in the following Ḥadīth of the Holy Prophet (SAS):

> There is a piece of flesh in the body. If it is healthy, the whole body is healthy. If it becomes unhealthy, the whole body gets unhealthy— beware! that is the heart.[5]

Based on this Ḥadīth, the Muslim scholars have likened the heart to a king to which all the organs, faculties and the senses have been subordinated for their uses.

THE MEANING OF THE TERM HEART, OR QALB

The heart or *qalb*, also referred to as *rūḥ* (soul), *nafs* (nature) and *ᶜaql* (intellect), has been interpreted by the commentators of Ḥadīth as that transcendental supersensory entity which is related physiologically to the cone shaped piece of flesh located in the left part of the chest. The spiritual heart commands the physical heart, and thus the whole body, through two stages. In the first stage, decision-carrying impulses ascend from the heart to the brain and then from the brain descend to the muscles of the body. According to the Islamic doctrine, the behaviour and inner-physiological processes are manifestations of psycho-spiritual events and processes occurring in the heart as opposed to the Western View that holds psycho-spiritual phenomena as a shadow process. Allah (SWT) has made the heart responsible of all human deeds, since from it spring all motives and actions.

> ...for he brings down the Revelation to thy heart by Allah's will, a confirmation of what went before. And guidance and glad tidings for those who believe. (2:97)

Al-Imām al-Rāzī mentions that the heart is responsible for behavioural consequences since *tanzil* and *waḥy* come to it.[6] Imam al-Ghazālī identified the heart as the essence of man, signifying it as the core of human personality and behaviour. For understanding the role of *qalb*, we should take into consideration that man, as the vicegerent of Allah (SWT), has been endowed with a combination of innate qualities.

ATTRIBUTES OF THE HEART

The qalb has been endowed with the capacity to perceive the attributes of Allah (SWT), and the realities of all other created phenomena and their relationship with the creator. Therefore, all senses and faculties of human being have been subordinated to the *qalb*. However, full knowledge of the reality of *qalb* is beyond human perception, because the soul proceeds *amr* (direction), about which man has limited knowledge. (17:85)

Survival or bodily needs, which are necessary for attaining the goal of divine vicegerency, are fulfilled through the motor and sensory powers. Motor powers constitute propensities and impulses like hunger, thirst, sex, etc. Sensory powers (*mudrika*) constitute either outer physical senses or inner senses like common sense, imagination, *quwwat al waḥm*, etc.

All these powers are subordinated to the *qalb*, the original dynamic force that directs impulses and actions, perceives, and sets goals, and finally makes the choice for a particular response pattern or behaviour. The *qalb's* overall function thus matches the "central processor," the decision-making structure controlling everything else in the whole information processing system.[7]

Any information processed in the working memory is stored finally in the heart as "knowledge," as implied in part of the following Ḥadīth which says,

> Whoever reads the Qur'ān secures the knowledge of prophethood within his ribs [heart], though Divine revelation is not sent to him.[8]

It is this permanent memory belonging to the heart that is used to evaluate and process incoming information by the working memory.

HEART: *ʿAQL* AND *'IRADAH*

Besides regulating and controlling bodily functions, the *qalb* possesses two qualities that distinguish humans from other animals—the *ʿaql* (intellect) and *'irādah* (will). *Qalb*, through *ʿaql*, can comprehend the real significance of things as well as recognise the ultimate Truth and Reality i.e., Allah (SWT) and His attributes. The human intellect has the ability to generalise and form hierarchical patterns of concepts of higher order unlike the limited forms of concept formation in some animals, e.g., chimpanzees. The innate consciousness of their Creator in animals is limited to bare awareness of the Creator as their Master and Sustainer,[9] and is not comparable to man's consciousness of Allah (SWT) due to his *qalb*.

> *The seven heavens and the earth and all that is therein praise Him, and there is not a thing hymneth not His praise; but ye understand not their praise... (24:41).*

This transcendental consciousness has been alluded to in the following *Ḥadīth al qudsī*,

> The heavens and the earth cannot contain Me, but the heart of My believing slave hath room for Me.[10]

Reason, or *al-ʿaql al-juzi*, as used by M. Hassan al Askari, distributes the light of intellect to the faculties of imagination and emotion, and the faculty of senses knits their functions together while keeping them normally under control.[11] *'Irādah* is the desire or yearning to reach a goal. Will, conditioned by the intellect, has an awareness of the ultimate reality and goal of life, though it might initially be triggered by appetite or hunger.

PERSONALITY STEMS FROM THE HEART'S PERCEPTION OF REALITY

The whole behaviour pattern or human personality is inextricably anchored to the heart and stems from its perception of reality since intellect and will operate in combination to form judgements, decisions, courses of action that lead to a final goal. Through the inner and outer apprehensive senses, the *ʿaql* provides the foundations from which the heart constructs its structure of values and goals. These values and goals, in turn, generate desires and wills, which are finally actualised as behaviour outputs by the "will" of the heart It seems relevant here to clarify the question of freedom of will. Because man is free to form his beliefs and behaviour, he is held responsible for the consequences of his behaviour. As al-Ghazālī points out, if humans were not free, then the instructions and exhortations in the Qur'ān and Sunnah would cease to have any meaning.[12] In this respect, the Qur'ān says

> Say, the Truth is from your Lord. Let him who will, believe, and let him who will reject (it)… (118:29).

However, this freedom of will is not absolute, and Divine Laws and the Divine Will determine its limits.[13]

ᶜAQL AND *SHAYITĀNIYYAH* WORKING THROUGH *SHAHWAH* AND *GHAḌAB* FOR CONSTRUCTIVE OR DESTRUCTIVE PURPOSES

ᶜAql and *shayītāniyyah* occupy positions at opposite poles in the human self and both struggle to control *shahwah* (appetite) and *ghaḍab* (anger) so as to work through them for constructive or destructive ends respectively. *ᶜAql*, the divine element tries to control and regulate these forces and divert them to constructive channels for the growth and development of the self. If it succeeds in subordinating them to make them useful to the self, the devil in him also becomes subdued and its malignant forces are rendered ineffective. Once the mischievous tendency of devilish element has been neutralized and the animal forces are made to work in harmony with the *ᶜaql*, its struggle comes to an end. This state of constant harmony enables the self to make unimpeded progress towards actualizing its inherent potentials to qualify him for the status of divine vicegerency. In the Qur'ānic phrase, this state of the self where harmony has been stabilized is referred to as *al-nafs-al-muṭma'innah*, or the tranquil soul (89:27).

On the other hand, if these animal forces overpower the divine element at the instigation of al-shayītāniyyah, the evil tendencies dominate and reign over the self. *ᶜAql* gets weakened and its functions are blocked and paralyzed. As a result, all the other faculties of the self become subservient to animal forces and eventually, *ᶜaql* may also become their captive. All these faculties are then used to fulfill the impulses of passions, anger, and lust, and eventually reason is also made to serve them by making plans and schemes for the gratification of these impulses. In the end, veiled over by animal passions and desires, the heart becomes totally blind, so that in gratifying animal desires and lusts the individual loses sight of the real and ultimate good of his own human self. Since all these take place at the constant instigation of the evil tendency as the active principle behind them, this state has been called as *al-nafs al-ammārah bi al sū'*, i.e., the instigating soul, in the Qur'ān (12:53).

There is, however, an intermediate state between the above two.

It seldom occurs that the divine element is completely smothered to death and gives up its struggle against the evil tendencies. Often, the divine element remains engaged in sustained struggle against satanic instigation and animal impulses. The Qur'ān has denoted this state as *al-nafs al-lawwāmah*, the admonishing soul (75:2).

At any period or stage of human life, human behaviour and personality can be said to be a reflection or manifestation of one of these three states currently prevailing in the self. Obviously, the progress of human self is characterized by its upward movement from the lowest state of *al-nafs al-ammārah bi al sū'* (the instigating soul) through the state of reproaching self, to that of *al-nafs-al-muṭma'innah*, or the tranquil self. The tranquil self represents the optimum state of power distribution among the basic aspects associated to the self, i.e., divine, animal, and demonic, where the heart, as the king, holds the reins of control guided by the wise counsel of intellect. In this state, the rebellious tendency of the demonic element remains curbed at an innocuous level, and both the animal instincts of appetite and anger are fully made to align themselves with the natural disposition and functions of the heart. Here the heart achieves its ideal through the mediation of intellect, and a state of equilibrium prevails in the self, which is most conducive for the growth and actualization of the innate divine attributes of the soul or heart.

As according to the Qur'ān, man has been destined to function as vicegerent of Allah (SWT), and so it can be conceived that within their inner nature men and women have a reserve, essentially in finite measures, of the qualities and virtues mirroring the attributes of Allah (SWT), the Sovereign Sustainer, whom he or she represents. A Ḥadīth mentioned by Imam Ghazālī in his *Kimiyā as-Saʿādat* seems to confirm this. The Ḥadīth says to the effect that Allah (SWT) has created man after His attributes.[14] Commentators have interpreted the Ḥadīth to mean that man has been created by Allah (SWT) with the qualities resembling the Attributes of Allah (SWT) Himself. In another Ḥadīth reported in *Mishkāt*, man has been likened to mines.[15] This also implies that beneath the surface of animal structure, man possesses at the depth of his nature an immense reserve of untapped potentials. If we take these Aḥadīth into consideration, these potentials may be reasonably construed to be the humanized version of the divine attributes that may be harnessed by appropriate measures.

DOMINATION OF ANIMAL OR DEMONIC QUALITIES IN PERSONALITY

Now which one of these qualities—animal, divine or demonic—will be harnessed and will come to dominate human personality and behaviour depends on the nature and content of an individual's perception of his own self, the external world, and the ultimate Reality. A person has to enter into interactions with his or her environment to fulfill various kinds of needs—physical, psychological, and spiritual. The mode of behaviour and personality style leading to the fulfillment of these needs varies based on the perception of his nature of self and the world around him. For example, if somebody perceives himself to be composed of only biological elements, he will pay attention solely to the prompting of his biological needs and will remain insensitive to the inner voice of his heart demanding satisfaction of the spiritual needs. Aware only of his animal needs, he will be driven to gratify these needs through his interaction with the environment. Since the voice of the heart remains unattended, intellect, the heart's essential property, also remains ineffective, and the layers of sensuous deposits gathered by the heart through the gratification of animal passions and desires blind the heart to the abiding transcendental principles and system underlying the events and the phenomena of the world. With the eyes of the heart veiled by passions and desires, the person is hindered from seeing the signs and manifestations of *tawḥīd*, the ultimate Unity and Reality governing the events and affairs of the universe. Bereft of the wisdom and insight of the heart, the individual's vision and realization remains blocked and locked into a world composed of sensory events and reality, and his behaviour is confined to gratifying the bio-physical needs in a restricted territory of a spatially and temporally bounded phenomenal world. Because of the lack of insight by the heart, he fails to learn from the past and is not able to foresee the ultimate consequences of his impulsive actions and deeds.

Such a narrow and distorted perception of life and reality gives rise to a corresponding set of delusional goals and utterly distorted and detrimental sense of values. Guided solely by sensory perception and deprived of the inner vision of the heart, such people see their pleasure, happiness and success in material objects and positions of this phenomenal world. Their only goal in life remains to achieve these gross and tangible material benefits without any regard to the ways and means of their acquisition. Practical expediency is their only guide, and all other values of truth, honesty or humanity can be sacrificed at the altar of these delusional material goals that have virtually turned to gods in their perception. Often at the instance of the lower self, such people have to develop fully the art of guile and treachery to succeed and secure more and more of these earthly gods.

The Qur'ān refers to such a state of the self in the following verse:

> *They have hearts wherewith they understand not, eyes wherewith they see not, and ears wherewith they hear not. They are like cattle—nay even more misguided for they are heedless (of the warning). (7:179).*

And further,

> *Do they not travel through the land, so that their hearts may thus learn wisdom and their ears may thus learn to hear? Truly it is not their eyes, rather it is their hearts which are in their breasts that are blind. (22:46).*

So those who base their behaviour on the perception of their animal selves and respond to the immediate and apparent meanings of the sensory inputs only and prefer to remain insensitive to the wisdom of the heart will not see the signs of Allah's (SWT) unity, providence or wrath manifested in nature, and the history of humanity. Consequently, they often reject the truth and the message revealed by God through His messengers. Fed by unchecked gratification of passions and lusts, deprived of the wisdom of the heart and instigated by the demonic element of the self, the animal self comes to dominate the personality. Thus, if the animal component *shahwah*, or appetite, gains dominance, bestial characteristics such as gluttony, greed, wickedness, hypocrisy, jealousy etc. are bred in the self.

On the other hand, if the animal component *ghaḍab*, or anger, comes to predominate, the characteristics of ferocious animals such as enmity, hatred, contempt, pride, love of aggrandizement emerge. If both *shahwah* and *ghaḍab* combine to predominate, devilish characteristics such as treachery, deceit, cunning, enmity etc. come to appear in the character. In fact, it is the shayīṭāniyyah, the demonic tendency, which gains ascendancy at this stage and all the other faculties are subordinated to it. Even reason becomes so subdued that it starts serving this pseudo-master by making plans for realizing its evil designs. However, the above bestial characteristics are often manifested in disguise in order to avoid the censure of the residual voice of the intellect that survives in the heart, as well as to make them appear acceptable to the society at large.

Maulānā Rumī, the illustrious Ṣūfī theologian of 13th century C.E., precisely depicts this typical behaviour as manifestations of animal lusts and passions in the state of full domination of *al-nafs al-ammārah bi al sū'*, or the instigating soul.[16] Devoid of the perception of God as the Absolute Sovereign Sustainer, the self assumes as its gods a multiple of things which appear capable of catering to its lusts, and it turns into a virtual worshipper of such things as wealth, women, position and power. Often power becomes the most potent idol sought. To satisfy the undying passions of such a power seeking self, some rulers commit utterly inhuman kinds of atrocities to their fellowmen. Innocent lives are sacrificed at the altar of their power god to stabilize and secure their positions. But continued recklessness in the use of power breeds enmity and hatred against them and ultimately gives rise to feelings of insecurity in their minds. To seek relief in such a situation, a man might feel driven to compel unquestioning obedience in others through intimidating threats.

While in power, such a man may even pretend to champion the ends of the people and guide their religious actions. If he succeeds in winning the trust of the ignorant people, he will eventually design plots to divide people and create rivalries among leaders with a view towards eliminating them. However, through these self-defeating measures, such people increasingly alienate themselves from others, their inner divine selves, and finally from Allah (SWT), the absolute divine Self and Reality.

The above narrative, however, should not give the impression that the human heart is a helpless victim compulsively overpowered by the animal and demonic elements. The heart is always free to choose and opt for a progressive or regressive line of personality development, and at any stage of its development it can change and make necessary reversals in its developmental programs. Such changes, of course, may be relatively easy or difficult, depending on favorable or unfavorable conditions currently prevailing within the human self and outside it.

OPENING OF THE HEART'S EYES

According to the Qur'ān, the ultimate object of all sensory observations is to open the eyes of the heart to enable it to perceive the Reality beyond all doubt. This critical function of the heart has been mentioned in many Qur'ānic verses. For example, Allah (SWT) says:

They have hearts wherewith they understand not, eyes wherewith they see not, and ears wherewith they hear not. They are like cattle—nay even more misguided. For they are heedless (of the warning). (7:179)

Have they, then, never journeyed about the earth, letting their hearts gather wisdom, and causing their ears to hear. Yet, verily, it is not their eyes that have become blind—but blind has become the hearts that are in their breasts. (22:46)

These verses imply that though the sense organs function physically, their purpose is not achieved unless the heart's eyes are opened. This interpretation appears confirmed by Allah's (SWT) statement:

Lo! The hearing, and the sight and the heart of each of these will be asked. (17:36)

In the context of the above verse, Imam Rāzī notes that since the ears and the eyes have no other function but to make their contents reach the heart, any question put to them is in reality a question put to the heart—the heart being the judge and governor concerning all that is delivered to it by the ears and the eyes.[17] Therefore, it is the heart which is ultimately responsible for the interpretation and meaning it ascribes to the sensory information received. Thus, the Qur'ān emphasizes this crucial function of the heart: interpreting the meaning and messages contained in the natural phenomena as well as the events of human history.

ISLAMIC CONCEPTS OF PSYCHO-SPIRITUAL PROCESSES OF THE HEART'S COGNITION OF ALLAH'S (SWT) UNITY (MA'RIFA)

It is pertinent to present at this point an outline of the Islamic concept of the psycho-spiritual processes through which the heart is gradually awakened and illumined to the cognition of the Transcendental Reality as interpreted by Ghazālī from the following translation of a Qur'ānic verse:

> *Allah is the light of the heavens and the earth. The parable of His light is as if there were a Niche and within it a Lamp. The Lamp enclosed by glass. The glass as it was a brilliant star: lit from a blessed tree, an olive, neither of East nor of the West, whose oil is well-nigh luminous, though fire scarce touched it. Light upon Light! God doth guide whom He will to His Light. God doth know all things (24:35).*

In his excellent elucidation of this "Light Verse", al-Ghazālī has mentioned five phases of the qalb's illuminative faculty for perceiving Reality through different levels of its manifestation, from the sensory at the surface, to the transcendental at the innermost core. These five faculties or spirits have been symbolized as the Niche, Glass, Lamp, Tree and Oil in the above verse. The Niche is the sensuous faculty, whose light comes through the sense organs. The Glass, Lamp, Tree and Oil stand successively for imagination, intelligential spirit, ratiocinative spirit and finally transcendental spirit. Sense data processed and elucidated through these five grades of light results at the end in the perception of the Ultimate Transcendental Reality.[18]

Only when the self recognizes the ultimate Transcendental Reality as the Divine Unity encompassing and sustaining the whole universe with absolute sovereignty and omnipotence, can the human personality overcome and free itself from all kinds of influences alien to the real human self, be they within or without his being or personality. At this stage of the realization of tawḥīd, ones' personality begins to absorb the divine colour into its self, and the untapped treasure of the divine attributes start to surge up from the submerged region of the heart's unconscious layers to manifest themselves in overt behaviour. Consequently, human personality starts to reflect the behaviour of Allah (SWT), the universal Sustainer, Whom it is destined to represent as His vicegerent.

TAWHID ENERGIZES THE HEART

As īmān settles down into the depth of the heart, it frees the mind and all its psychic functions from all sorts of cognitive bondage which arrest and cripple the growth and development of the heart's treasure of divine potentials. Intellect, the pivotal divine property of the heart, illumined by the transcendental light of tawḥīd, grows to ascendancy over all other components of the self and effectively subordinates all animal drives and passions to make them consistent with the divine nature of the real human self. Instead of being guided by senses, the heart, the king of human personality, takes into trust the counsel of ᶜaql, or intellect, that has been illumined and nurtured to maturity. Realizing Allah (SWT) as the absolute source of all success, ᶜaql turns to the knowledge revealed from Him for furnishing the heart with the infallible guidance to make personality and behaviour conform to divine will. As one acts upon the truths and instructions divulged through the divine scripture, the Qur'ān, dimensions of the real human self and its relationship with the Ultimate Reality and the universe that remained so long unattended, are revealed to one's heart. The self enters into an active interaction and communion with the being of Allah (SWT), the Ultimate Reality, leading to a continuous exploration of the heart's latent divine qualities for adorning the personality with them.

These are the human versions of the qualities that reflect the attributes of Allah (SWT), which, according to some scholars, have been referred to in the Ḥadīth, as quoted by Ghazālī in his *Kimiyā as-Saᶜādat*:[19] its meaning is to the effect that man has been created after the attributes of Allah (SWT). For most people these divine virtues lie dormant in the unconscious vault of the self, awaiting to be tapped and brought to the surface by some supersensory consciousness. It is because of this hidden treasure that human beings have been termed mines in a Ḥadīth mentioned in *Mishkāt*.[20] Through gradual maturation of the perception of *tawḥīd* and other essentials of *īmān*, the identity of human self as supra-animal endowed with divine qualities representing the absolute divine being in this world gets crystallized in human consciousness. Equipped with this novel identity and the perception of the unique relationship with God and the universe, the personality becomes poised to develop and behave in a manner harmonious with its newly emerged identity and relationship.

As *īmān* continues to spread its sway to wider spheres of the heart, it increasingly captures the domain of emotions and uses them to facilitate the growth of inner personality endowments and protects them from the corrupting effects of lower drives and passions by restricting their satisfaction to divinely restricted limits. For instance, cognition and belief in Allah's (SWT) Omnipotence and Absolute discretion in providing sustenance, giving success and rewards, and inflicting miseries and punishments generates deep emotions of love and fear of Allah (SWT). When these two major emotions get deeply associated with Allah, they completely reorganize the universe of the values of the believers. Love of Allah (SWT) attributes positive value to all those virtues and deeds which are approved and appreciated by Allah (SWT), and the fear of Allah (SWT) attributes negative values to all traits and behaviour that are disliked and condemned by Allah (SWT). Together, these two emotions become highly potent factors in directing the innate divine qualities to their maximum growth.

For example, believers will restrain themselves from taking haram (forbidden) drinks like alcohol and thereby protect themselves from losing their sanity and behaving in an immodest manner. At other times, in consonance with divine pleasure, the conscience will induce them to serve the hungry ones with food even if they themselves have to remain without food, and thereby develop the divine virtue of generosity and benevolence. In fact, the growing potency of *īmān* ultimately culminates in integrating all emotions and drives into an all-comprehensive enduring yearning to achieve the pleasure of Allah (SWT). This yearning assumes the status of a master motive arching over all other drives and motives.

Once this motive to attain Allah's (SWT) pleasure gains stability through the maturity of cognition and faith in *tawḥīd*, it can effectively make the heart take unshakable decisions to act and develop in line with the primordial spiritual nature of personality by unstintingly following the divine instructions. Maturity of *īmān* also equips the personality with an irresistible determination to boldly overcome all resistance from within and without in the way of his fullest growth and development. This arch-motive exerts its prime effect upon the heart's decision-making functions. This motive effectively induces the heart to make all its behavioural decisions to reflect the divine will and pleasure. To make the decisions conform to God's will, the believers turn to divine revelation and its practical elucidation in the sunnah [the traditions of the Prophet (SAS)].

A special reference should be made here to the development of the divine virtue of altruism. The burgeoning spark of divine altruism was regularly nurtured through cultivating the plant of *īmān* in the hearts of the early Muslims. The later stages of the growing Ummah facilitated the steady growth of this *īmān* -plant to its final fruition into personalities worthy to be called divine vicegerents. The progress of inner cognition of *tawḥīd* through da'wah and its allied strivings, and the consequent increase in the heart's potency and mastery over all the aspects of the self, energized the votaries of the new faith to explore deeper into the layers of their hearts through the all-pervading light of *tawḥīd*. This in turn enabled them to tap and bring more of the divine virtues to surface, ready to manifest themselves through appropriate behaviour. As a result, the egoistic animal instincts were effectively regulated or suppressed to harmonize themselves with the emergent divine qualities gushing out from the deeper beds of the hearts.

As the *ma'rifa* (cognition) of Allah (SWT) took firm root in the hearts of the believers through appropriate strivings in the Makkan period, their personality started to bear the most succulent fruits of altruism in the Madinan period. The degree of altruism as expressed in helping others increased even to much higher levels later in Madinan years as the hearts of the Muslims continued to attain higher states of maturity in the conviction and cognition of *tawḥīd*. There are several instances in which the Madinan Muslims helped and serve others while they themselves were in states of dire necessity. Recognition of such characteristic behaviour is found in the following verse:

> *They prefer others above themselves, though poverty became their lot (49:9; 4th year A.H.).*

This spirit of self-sacrifice became a conspicuously dominant trait of the entire Muslim community. This was developed to such excellence that several events of sacrificing even the last drinks of water by the dying warriors in favor of their fellow brothers have been reported in the books of sīrah i.e., biographical accounts.[21]

At the peak of its development, the deep-rooted concern, and the burning zeal to strive for the welfare of the whole of mankind turned into a cardinal virtue that reigned supreme over all other divine traits of the Ummah's personality. Though the development of this virtue was triggered by the spirit of da'wah among each individual of this Ummah, its ascension to the top echelon of personality organization required constant subordination of all egoistic passions and concerns to the supreme drive of striving for the welfare of mankind. As a result of sustained and relentless struggle against all inner ego-resistance and various external ordeals in the earlier period of Islam, the hearts of the Muslims attained the state of an effective mastery over their lower egoistic drives and passions, and the drive for striving for the welfare and salvation of mankind assumed an irrevocable stability and an all-pervasive magnitude in their personality. In appreciation of this reigning personality trait, Allah (SWT) declared this ummah of Madina that had passed through the formative period in their Makkan years, as "the best of people":

> *Ye are the best of the people that hath been raised up for (the welfare of) mankind... (3:104, 3rd/4rth yr. A.H.).*

The history of the Ummah bears out the fact that the early Muslims proved themselves wholly worthy of this divine laurel by harnessing all the surging divine traits of their hearts for the welfare of mankind.

THE HEART'S DISBELIEF: SOURCE OF ALL CORRUPT AND PERVERTED PERSONALITY TRAITS

In contrast to the foregoing course of personality development in the constructive direction, the Qur'ān also depicts an opposite course of personality regression ascribing its source to the disease of hearts. This disease of their hearts, according to the Qur'ān, induces them to the rejection of truth which often makes them fall into a vicious circle from which it becomes difficult to escape. Referring to them Allah (SWT) says:

> *In their hearts is a disease, and Allah increaseth their disease. A painful doom is theirs because they lie (2:10).*

> *But as for those in whose hearts is disease, it (revelation) only addeth wickedness to their wickedness, and they die while they are disbelievers (9:125).*

The syndromes of the disease includes lying, arrogance, zealotry, hatred, vacillation, breach of trust, withholding from spending for the sake of Allah (SWT) for the public good, treachery, deceiving others etc. Of these, lying and arrogance may be considered to be the source traits from which all the other symptoms stem. While the fundamental deceit of the disbelievers (*kāfirūn*) consists in rejecting the truth of tawḥīd and matters associated with it, the lying of the hypocrites (*munāfiqūn*) consists in a double-folded falsifying of the truth: they reject the truth in their hearts and also seek to hide this rejection by false profession of belief as mentioned in the following verse:

> *And of mankind are some who say, we believe in Allah and the Last Day, when they believe not. (2:8)*

Such lies only aggravate the inner disease that expresses itself in other symptomatic off-shoot perversions such as habitual lying in usual conversations, breach of promises, and breach of trust, as has been mentioned in a Ḥadīth in *Mishkāt*.[22] A little thought will reveal that all these practices are actually different forms of lying. The seat of disbelief i.e., the falsification of truth, is the heart. Therefore, by harboring disbelief, the heart turns into a base for all corrupt and perverted personality traits stemming from disbelief.

Special mention should also be made of pride, a highly destructive trait which works insidiously in the heart to distort the perception of reality and pushes the personality to a level of degeneration from where it is often impossible to recover. Characterizing its devastating influence, some Muslim savants have even diagnosed it as the mother of all diseases.[23] This is the trait which led Satan to rebel and disbelieve as is said in the Qur'ān: *"He demurred through pride, and so became a disbeliever"* (2:34).

Due to their close relationship, the Qur'ān has mentioned these two vices as concomitant traits "Nay! Those who disbelieve are in false pride and schism" (38:2).

Indeed, these two traits seem to function reciprocally, augmenting each other's strength to aggravate the heart's diseases and perversion of personality. Self–pride veils the heart's awareness of Allah's (SWT) awe and majesty and confines one's vision of the self and the world to an ego-centric one. Thus blocked, the inner eyes of the heart cannot transcend its self-imposed limits of perceptual field and therefore fail to realize the transcendental truth of Allah's (SWT) absolute sovereignty and unity.

Their physical organs of sight and hearing are unimpaired and are able to perceive the physical phenomena, but due to the blindness of their hearts, they do not perceive the intangible transcendental truth. The Qur'ān refers to this state tersely in the following verses:

> *They have hearts which perceive not, eyes which see not, and ears wherewith they hear not (7:179).*

> *Have they, then, never journeyed about the earth, letting their hearts gain wisdom, and causing their ears to hear. Yet verily it is not their eyes that have become blind—but blind has become the hearts that are in their breasts (22:46).*

Thus, the inevitable consequence of disbelief and pride is that the heart loses its innate capacity to realize the transcendental unity of Allah (SWT). By restricting the heart's domain of perception within the narrow bounds of the tangible world, disbelief paralyses the higher intellectual function of the heart and makes the self dissociate from the being of Allah (SWT). Dissociated from the absolute Being of Allah (SWT) and deprived of the guiding light of heart's intellect, the self falls an easy prey to the prompting of the passions of the animal self and the instigation of Satan, which make the self degenerate into the state of *al-nafs al-ammārah bi al sū'* (the instigating soul) with its concomitant vices. A brief description of the typical traits of this state has been given in the opening section of this discourse. In the foregoing passages, we have thus made a humble attempt to elucidate, at least partially, the theme contained in the following Ḥadīth that we mentioned in the beginning:

> There is a piece of flesh in the body. If it is healthy, the whole body is healthy. If it becomes unhealthy, the whole body gets unhealthy—

Beware! That is the heart.[24]

CONCLUSION

In the light of revealed knowledge, it is thus clear that the transcendental heart is the core and springboard from which all genuinely human virtues, representing the attributes of Allah (SWT), stem. Though the heart carries these divine imprints from the transcendental world, they remain untapped and wrapped up by layers of gross sensory perception of the phenomenal world. The sensory–phenomenal perception of the empirical world hinders the cognition of Allah's (SWT) transcendental unity as well as the inner divine potentials of man's own real self. The stimulation from the sensory empirical world keeps a spiritually insensitive person preoccupied in fulfilling the psycho-physiological needs and desires, blocking the emergence of his or her real spiritual self. This process turns a human to a creature resembling the lower animals and smothers the possibilities of the growth and emergence of one's real self.

It is only when the heart perceives the transcendental being of Allah (SWT) as its exclusive lord and sovereign sustainer is the heart freed from the overriding influence of all false gods appearing in the form of various phenomena of the sensory–material world. This light of transcendental cognition guides the human self firmly through the challenging expedition of exploring and harnessing the inherent divine properties to turn him from a gross animal to a divine vicegerent.

The implication of the foregoing is that to avert the process of degeneration of human beings to the state of animals and to raise them to the coveted status of divine vicegerents, all efforts should be made to liberate human hearts from the crippling and corrupting impacts of the various phenomenal forces: the myth of their power and lordship can be shattered through implanting and nourishing firm and perfect cognition of the transcendental unity and sovereignty of Allah (SWT) in the hearts of the people. With this cognition, people will be equipped with the master-key to unlock their inner reserves of divine treasures. To exploit and harness these untapped treasures for attaining peak personality development, we must follow precisely the guidance communicated in the revealed knowledge, some major features of which have been highlighted in various sections of the present discourse.

NOTES

1. See, among others, A.B. Crider, G.R. Goethals, R.D. Kavanaugh, and P.R. Solomon.
2. See Absar Ahmad. *Quranic Concepts of Human psyche*, in Zafar Afaq Ansari, ed., *Quranic Concepts of Human Psyche*, Lahore: 1992, 15-37;

Also, Manzurul Huq, *Heart: the Locus of Human Psyche* in Quranic Concepts of Human Psyche, pp. 56-67.

3. Umaruddin, The Ethical Philosophy of Al- Ghazālī (Alighar:1962), p.61.
4. Ibid.
5. *Bukhārī*, Vol.1, *Ḥadīth* No. 47.
6. Imam Razī, *Ilm al-Akhlāq*, trans. M. Saghīr Hasan Masumi (Islamabad: Islamic Research Institute, 1985), pp. 135-140.
7. D.H. Dodd and R.M. White, *Cognition* (Alyn & Bacon Inc: 1980), p. 14.
8. Sheikh al-Ḥadīth Maulānā Muhammad Zakariya, *"Virtues of the Holy Qur'ān"* Fadā'il al-Aᶜmāl, English tr. Azizuddin, (Lahore: Kutubkhana Faizi), pp. 77-78.
9. See Mufti Muhammad Shāfī, Ma'ariful Qur'ān, Abridged Bengali tr., Maulānā Muhiuddin Khan; (King Fahd Qur'ān Printing Project), pp.5-6.
10. Naumana Amjad, "Psyche in Islamic Gnostic and Philosophical Tradition"; in Z. A. Ansari, ed., *Quranic Concepts of Human Psyche*, 1992, pp. 39-56.
11. Ibid, p. 52.
12. Umaruddin, *The Ethical Philosophy of Al-Ghazālī*, p.69.
13. See M. Achoui's, Human Nature from a Comparative Psychological Perspective, in this Volume.
14. Al-Ghazālī, *Kimiyā as-Saᶜādat*, Bengali tr. Maulānā Nurur Rahmān, p.87.
15. Al-Ghazālī, *Mishkāt al Anwār*, Bengali tr. Maulānā Nur Muhammad ᶜAzmī, (Dhaka: Emdadia Library, 1967), vol.2, p. 6.
16. See A. R. Arasteh, *Rūmī (the Persian), the Ṣūfī* (Routledge & Keagan Paul,1965), pp. 92- 103.
17. Imam Rāzī, *Ilm al-Akhlāq*, trans. M. Saghīr Hasan Masumi, p. 123.
18. M. Huq, *Heart: the Locus of Human Psyche*, in Z.A. Ansari, ed., Quranic Concepts of Human Psyche, 1992, pp. 57-67
19. Al-Ghazālī, *Kimiyā as-Saᶜādat*, p.87
20. Al-Ghazālī, *Mishkāt al Anwār*, vol 2, p. 6.
21. Sheikh *al-Ḥadīth* Maulānā Muhammad Zakariya, *Fadā'il al-Sadaqat*, trans. Abdul Karim & Malik Haq Nawaz, Darul Isha'at, Karachi, p.658.
22. *Mishkat Sharif*, Benagali trans. By Maulānā Nur Muhammad ᶜAj"mi, – 1971; vol.1, p.97.
23. See Sheikh *al-Ḥadīth* Maulānā Muhammad Zakariya, Umm al-Amrād (Urdu); (Lahore Maktaba Diniyat), p. 8.
24. Bukhārī, Vol.1, Ḥadīth No.47.

9

Pathology of the Heart in the Qur'ān: A Metaphysico-Psychological Explanation

ABSAR AHMAD

In any meaningful account and assessment of the Muslims' contribution to studies of mental health, one should turn to the Holy Qur'ān and see how it has coloured and shaped Muslims' outlook towards human psychology and morals. The Qur'ān possesses a cohesive outlook on the universe and human life. It is a book that is squarely aimed at man; indeed, it calls itself "guidance for mankind." It is increasingly realised now that the challenge to modern civilization is largely spiritual and psychological rather than planning, organizing or technology. It is not planning and scientific development alone which will work the miracle and usher in the millennium that everyone dreams about. It is only by facing it on a spiritual-cum-psychological level that humanity can improve and reform this benighted world of ours. It is the individual with all his tensions, restlessness, craving for a deity, if permitted to exercise a free mind and an unshackled soul, can build the world which science and technology have fallen short of doing. The inescapable result has been the depression and deterioration of the human, the dismemberment of his personality and its subservience to animal passions.

Man, according to the Qur'ān, is Allah's creature just like any other created being; thus, he resembles any natural creation, for He fashioned Adam out of baked clay. But man is distinguished from the rest of natural creations by the fact that, after fashioning him, Allah "breathed His own spirit" into him. Thus, the Holy Qur'ān conceives of man as a theomorphic and not an anthropomorphic being. There is something of a divine nature (*malakūt*) in man; and it is in the light of this profound nature of man that Islam envisages him. That divine element in man is first an intellect, and a soul that can discern between the true and the false and is by its "primordial nature" (*fiṭrah*) led to Unity or *tawḥīd*. As such, the basic idea of Islam is that through the use of intellect and higher spiritual faculties, which discern between the absolute and the contingent or relative, one should come to surrender to the will of the Absolute. This, in fact, is the meaning of the word Muslim: one who has accepted through free choice to conform his will to the Divine Will made known in detail in the divinely revealed law of the Qur'ān. Thus, according to the Qur'ānic teachings, man is not a Homosapien, but rather Homo-cum-Deo and is a composite being consisting of two substances viz., a physical or material element and a spiritual one. While Islam is the epitome of the Divine cosmic order, man as a physical being, is also an epitome of the cosmos, a microcosmic representation, *al-ᶜālam al-ṣâghīr*, of the macrocosm, *ᶜālam al-kabīr*. Man is both soul and body; he is at once a physical being and a spiritual one, and his soul governs his body as Allah governs the universe.

In a paper published elsewhere,[1] I have taken pains to argue that the Qur'ān presents a dualistic, i.e., two-component views of man. To my mind, the assertion "breathed into him of My spirit" (15:29), is an explicit and categorical statement of a divine (i.e., spiritual) element or component in man. Taking it as merely a "faculty of God-like knowledge"[2] or "endowing man with life and consciousness"[3] is tantamount to a total negation of the two-component Qur'ānic conception of man and human personality. This very conception is further reaffirmed in most unambiguous terms in verses 12-14 of *sūrah al-Mu'minūn*, thus:

> *Now, indeed We created man out of the essence of clay, and then We caused him to remain as a drop of sperm in (the womb's) firm keeping, and then We created out of the drop of sperm a germ-cell, and then We clothed the bones with flesh—and then We brought (all this) into a new creation: hallowed, therefore, is Allah, the best of creators. (23:12-14)*

God's breathing of His spirit into man and "bringing this fetus into a new creation" are obviously of immense metaphysical significance.[4] Starting from *sulālah* up to the stage of a fully developed embryo, all the details have no doubt been given to stress man's humble origin. But what sets apart a human infant from an animal infant is the last episode in which it underwent not only a totally new shaping but rather assumed an altogether different status as a spiritual being imbued with a soul. So "bringing into a new creation" clearly signifies the addition of a new ontological element, the soul, into the living animal infant, making him *Homo Dei*, God's vicegerent on earth. The locution *insān*, according to the Qur'ān, is not to be attributed to man's animal and corporeal body, but to that divine spirit or soul, the presence of which makes man superior to angels. Out of a duality, one element of man—his spiritual psyche or soul—is the basis on which Allah has called the creation of human beings the "best of moulds" or "best conformation" in *surah al-Tin*. Verse 4 of this *surah* reads:

Verily, We have created man in the best of conformation (or in the best of moulds). (95:4)

And the very next verse refers to the carnal desires pertaining to his bodily component, undue indulgence of which abase him to the lowest of the low. To man God gave the purest and best nature in the form of divinely infused spirit or soul, and it is man's duty to preserve the pattern on which God has made him. By making man His vicegerent, God exalted him in posse even higher than the angels, for the angels had to make obeisance to man. But surely man's position as vicegerent also gives him free will and discretion and if he uses them wrongly, he falls even lower than the beasts. Abasement, and reduction to the lowest of the low is a consequence of man's betrayal, or corruption of his original, positive nature: that is to say, a consequence of man's own misdeeds and omissions. The spiritual element, the primordial and uncorrupted psyche, of man has a tendency towards its divine source and finds solace and fulfilment in God and His revelation, the Holy Qur'ān. The bodily and corporeal part, on the contrary, exists at the purely animal level and always presses for more sensual gratification, thus personifying a man described in the Qur'ān in these words:

...but he always clung to the earth or gravitated down to the earth and followed but his own desires. (7:176)

THE HEART IN THE QUR'ĀNIC METAPHYSICAL VIEW OF HUMANS

The notion of heart or *qalb, fuād* and *âql* (in Qur'ānic terminology) is foundational in the ontology and epistemic structure of the Qur'ān. The heart, in the Qur'ān, is symbolically the seat of the true self, the repository of soul, or the core and kernel of human personality of which we may be conscious or ignorant of, but which is our true existential, intellectual, and thus universal centre. The heart of man is, as it were, immersed in the immutability of Being. Contemplation is stressed here more than the sharpness of intelligence. In contemplation of the heart, things appear in their transparency. According to Islamic epistemic theory, the element that can unite the soul of man to God is love (*hubb* or *muhabba*), for love alone is desire of possession or of union, while discursive knowledge appears as a static element having no operative or unitive virtue. For securing a complete vision of Reality therefore, sense perception must be supplemented by the function or activation of what the Qur'ān describes as *fuād* or *qalb*, i.e., heart. "Love" is held to include all modes of spiritual union, an eminently concrete participation in the transcendent realities. Intellect divorced from "love" is a rebel (like Satan), while intellect wedded to "love" has divine attributes. But surely "loving" Allah presupposes being conscious of Him. To be conscious of Him is to fix the heart in the Real, in permanent remembering of the Divine. Remembering or dhikr must be understood as referring essentially to an aspiration of the contingent being towards the Universal with the object of obtaining an inner illumination. Thus, Allah reveals Himself to the rational soul which possesses organs of spiritual communication and cognition such as the heart (*al-qalb*), which knows Him; the spirit (*al-rūḥ*), which loves Him; and the secret or inner-most ground of the soul (*al-sirr*), which contemplates Him. It is in this context that the Qur'ān throws Allah's indispensability for man into bold relief. Just as Allah's "remembrance" and presence means the meaningfulness and purposefulness of life, the removal of Allah from human consciousness means the removal of meaning and purpose from human life.

The warning in *sūrah al-Ḥāshr*— "Do not be like those who forgot Allah and (eventually) He caused them to forget themselves—these are the unrighteous ones" (59:19)—is of cardinal importance in this context. Allah's "remembrance" ensures the cementing of personality, mental health, and composure, where all details of life and particulars of human activity are properly integrated and synthesized; "forgetting" Allah, on the other hand, means fragmented existence, diseased mind, "secularized" life, an unintegrated and eventually disintegrated personality, and (in Hegelian terminology) rootedness in the particularity of the moment. This is precisely what Muhammad Iqbal's distinction between Godliness and un-Godliness means:

The sign of a *Kāfir* is that he is lost in the horizons.
The sign of a *Mu'min* is that the horizons are lost in him.

CHARACTERISTICS OF THE HEART AS REVEALED IN THE QUR'ĀN

Having said this much about the notion of heart in the context of the Qur'ānic metaphysical view of the human individual, let us now briefly explore the diverse ways in which the holy Book characterises it.

According to many verses occurring in *sūrah al-A'rāf, al-¨Hajj* and *al-Isrā'*, the heart is the faculty or organ by means of which an individual grasps the truth of ultimate moral and metaphysical verities. The Qur'ān in this context uses the locutions *ta'qqul* and *tadabbur* with respect to the heart's cognitive processes. A heart that does not engage itself in deep and reflective thought is described as one that has "gone blind."

The heart is mentioned in the Qur'ān as the organ of volition and intention. All our actions follow from the heart-germinated and heart-inspired motivation. True, sincere and genuine faith and belief is in the interiority of one's self or heart, whereas verbal attestation of *Kalimah* only makes man a Muslim. Inner conviction and certitude are always in one's heart. A verse of *sūrah Hujarāt* makes it abundantly clear, "... and true belief has not yet entered their hearts."

In contrast to a "sick" heart, the Qur'ān employs numerous expressions:

e.g., *qalb muma'nun bi al-Īmān* (a heart pacified by īmān), *qalbim-munīb*, (a heart moving towards, and desiring the proximity of God [50:33]) and *qalbin salam* (a heart that is righteous and preserves the pristine purity of its positive primordial nature or *fiṭrah* [26:89]).

I shall now make a humble and modest attempt at analysing in detail the pathology of heart as explicated in the Qur'ān. There are recurrent Qur'ānic verses which speak about disease in people's hearts. The Qur'ān contains numerous allusions to "heart" in the context of hypocrisy or *nifāq*. Most of the Qur'ānic assertions of nifāq are in the political or communal contexts. Sūrah 63 of the Qur'ān has the title al *Munafiqūn* ("The Hypocrites"). It deals with the wiles, plots, and pretexts of the dissemblers, whom it likens to propped-up timbers. At other places the hypocrites are described as a menace to military discipline, quislings under pressure, and vacillators guessing at their shifting fortunes. Earlier, we noted that Islam represents a whole civilization, a complete culture, and a comprehensive world order. It provides moral guidance in all walks of life. Therefore Islamic values are not solely for the ascetic who renounces the world, but also for him who actively participates in different spheres of life and works within them. The moral values which people generally looked for in monasteries and cloisters were placed by Islam right in the mainstream of life, and the Prophet Muhammad (SAS) along with his companions struggled hard for more than two decades to transform the socio-political ideals of the Islamic faith into concrete reality. It is in the context of this struggle that the character-traits of hypocrites are dilated upon by the Qur'ān, the inner dimension of which is termed by Allah Almighty as a disease or malady of the heart. A hypocrite is the insincere person who thinks he can get the best of both worlds by compromising with good and evil. Thus, he only increases the disease of his heart because he is not true to himself. Even the good which comes to him, he can pervert to evil. What he lacks is firm commitment and dedication to Islam. Behind the outward disloyalties of the *munafiqūn* and their maneuverings lay the deeper questions of human soul-distress and heart's sickness. At four places in the Qur'ān, in opposition to *nifāq* (hypocrisy), is the phrase: "those in whose hearts there is sickness (*marad*)." I shall cite and try to understand them here in detail:

Verse 49 of *sūrah al-Anfāl*, which was revealed during and immediately after the battle of Badr, reads: "At the time when the hypocrites and those in whose hearts was disease were saying, 'their faith has deluded these (believers)'" i.e., into thinking that in spite of their numerical weakness and lack of arms, they could withstand the powerful Makkan army of the Quraish. "Those in whose heart was disease," is clearly a reference to the vacillating and faint-hearted among the Prophet's followers, who were afraid of meeting the Quraish in the battle.

Sūrah al-Ahzāb has three verses containing this phrase.

a. *Verse 12 reads: "And (remember how it was) when the hypocrites and those with diseased hearts said (to one another), 'God and His Prophet have promised us nothing but delusion" (33:12)*

This, as authentic traditions tell us, refers to the prophetic vision of Muhammad (SAS), at the time of digging the trench, of the future of Muslim conquest of the whole of Arabian Peninsula as well as of the Persian and Byzantine empires. Several traditions testify to the Prophet's announcement of this vision at the time in question.

b. In verse 32, the wives of the holy Prophet were asked to be truly conscious of God and their special position as wives of the Prophet and mothers of the believers and then advised, "... hence, be not over-soft in your speech, lest anyone whose heart is diseased should be moved to desire (you); but, withal, speak in a kindly way" (33:32). In this verse the disease of heart undoubtedly refers to carnal lust and sexual laxity.

c. Verse 60 of the *sūrah* describes the diseased heart with reference to perverse dealing, hostility towards Allah and the Prophet and moral defect or failing. Verse 52 of *sūrah al-Mā'idah* asserts that the hypocrites within the Muslim community vie with one another for the good-will of hostile Jews and Christians by trying to imitate their way of life. At other places the "disease" of heart is mentioned in the context of rancor or hate against the true Muslims, incredulity, and impiety. It is a shiftlessness whose symptoms are lip-service and dissimulation.

Just as the Holy Qur'ān speaks about the strengthening and increase of īmān or faith, similarly it speaks of the deepening of the disease of heart and its becoming more intense. The English translation of verse 125 of *sūrah al-Tawbah* reads:

> *But as for those in whose hearts is disease, each new message, adds but another (element of) disbelief to the disbelief which they already harbour. And they die while (still) refusing to acknowledge the truth.*

That is to say, to those spiritually diseased, Allah's grace is unwelcome, and they put forth more doubts to cover their disease. Thus, they die in their disease, and of their disease. Literally the verse means that each new revealed message adds another loathsome evil to their loathsome evil, i.e., makes them more stubborn in their denying the truth of Allah's message, because they are determined to deny everything that is incompatible with their worldly desires. This stubbornness in denial and disbelief has been characterized in the Qur'ān as the "hardening" of hearts, *thumma qasat qulūbuhum* (2:84). That is to say, the hypocrites or the half-hearted ones gradually lose their ability to discern between right and wrong and consequently incline towards unbelief and moral depravity.

Disease, if incurable, is hardly a realm of metaphor which fits with entire condemnation. The thought of a sickness in hypocrisy might be expected to check somewhat the vehemence of a denunciation that reckons only with guile. The Qur'ān clearly declares the heart's disease curable and offers itself as a cure or healing. Verse 57 of *sūrah Yūnus* speaks of "a healing ... for what is in the breast" (10:57). Verse 82 of *sūrah al-Isrā'* and verse 44 of *sūrah Fussilāt*, describe the Holy Book as containing all that gives health to the spirit. The phrase "what the breasts conceal," which is a frequent one, undoubtedly relates to the inner secrets and hidden springs of action, where *nifaq* develops. To think of these, even if only in part, within analogies of sickness, is to see them more realistically than a mere countering caution would allow. It is characteristic that Islam finds the remedy in revelation itself. For its confidence throughout in the problem of human moral evil and waywardness, is in true knowledge afforded by the Qur'ānic guidance. Since the guidance ought to be followed, even the "sickness" remains blameworthy and it should, quite reasonably be so, because of the logic of bodily disease is different from that of psychical disease or ailment. We do not generally blame a patient for his physical sickness, though even here an element of blame is not out of place if it comes through sheer negligence on the part of the individual. On the contrary, the disease of the heart is contracted through one's voluntary and willful moral depravity and lack of belief.

The religious doctrine of Islam, pace Christian or some other religions, does not invoke any irrational belief or blind dogma in this context. For example, Kenneth Cragg, the well-known English orientalist, quite unjustifiably laments that "... (in Islam) the sickness within sinfulness is not more gently, more patiently, treated."[5] He, however, rightly observes that if there is a *marad* in *nifāq*, the hypocrisy is more than a deliberate disloyalty to the community. It is a malady in the inner recesses of human heart and psyche. The sick are in truth those who spurn the remedy, the Qur'ān itself, the Divine Book that enkindles true belief in one's heart and provides a curative for spiritual and moral ailments. I fully agree with Cragg when he states that disease, in the final analysis, is not a political phenomenon.

And he rightly opines that scholars "should probe into those depths of human soul-distress, of the psychic wronging of the self, of bondage to fear and pride, which are the final reaches of the human tragedy."[6] He is, however, quite wrong in saying that the Qur'ānic religion relies on the efficacy of the political in the search for healthy and true human being. There is no denying the fact that Islam, being a divinely approved *dīn*—a complete code of life— cannot exclude from its purview the political and collective dimension of human life. Yet the category of the individual, his self-purification and salvation is its central aim. I wonder how a deep and perceptive scholar like Cragg can altogether ignore the magnificent mystic tradition in Islam catering for the health and invigoration of the spiritual core of man.

AETIOLOGY OF THE "SICKNESS" AND A FALLACY

A very brief mention of the etiology of the "sickness" of the heart is in order here. According to the Qur'ān, the fact that man carries within himself evil tendencies as well as good tendencies distinguishes him from angels, who are free from evil tendencies and are, so to say, "automatically good." In any case, there is a struggle between these two trends or dispositions in man. But the evil trend does become very strong through the objective fact of the existence of Satan, whose machinations have myriad forms (including creation in man of placidity, complacency, and self-satisfaction in his own virtue) and who, because of his (man's) innate tendency towards the easy and the immediate (compounded further by his dangerous capacity of self-deception) is able to dress up evil as good before him. Thus, Satan and evil tendency can all but destroy the capacity for inner vision and spiritual vigour described by the Qur'ān as taqwā i.e., God-consciousness. It is not the strength of Satan as such, but the failure of man himself to show strength against the Devil's blandishments and temptations, that constitute the real threat to man. This tinsel and dazzling exterior of the material world so catches and overpowers his heart and mind that he "gets lost" in the immediate and forgets the ākhirah, the real, solid, long-range and consequential ends, the highest purposes. He "gravitates down to the earth," as the Qur'ān idiomatically expressed it. As a result, his heart, the innermost part of his being, becomes sick and his personality becomes hollow and spineless. The Qur'ān likens such men to propped-up timbers which have no strength of their own.

It does little good, then, to heed the cavalier advice that nowadays comes so easily: "Do not think so much about yourself," "Get busy," "Take it easy." These suggestions do not seem adequate for what ails us inwardly. We should, on the other hand, begin to discover the plain truth that we are moral beings. We also have to make sense with our deeds and behaviour, with our purposes, motives and accomplishments. Instead of not thinking about ourselves and not having self-concern, it seems necessary, rather, to have a great deal of concern and to be very thoughtful about what one is making of oneself. The Qur'ānic "therapeutic" conception of human nature and psychic well-being is thus radically opposed to the view presented by some modern psychologists and therapists. For example, Albert Ellis thinks that what we normally call emotional disturbance, neurosis, or mental illness, largely consists of our demandingness.[7] Ellis accordingly teaches his clients, that the really important thing in life is to remain relatively undisturbed and to please oneself. Surviving and remaining reasonably happy while surviving, is the moral ideal of such psychologists. They advise us to abjure "musts", "oughts" and "shoulds," not to be rigid, but remain constantly open to changes, and to have new experiences. The result, as any thoughtful person can see, is individualism, egoism, narcissism, manipulation of people, superficiality, aimlessness, distrust, anxiety, and ruthlessness, to mention just a few mishaps and misfortunes of man's essential inner reality.

NOTES

1. Absar Ahmad, "Qur'ānic Concepts of Human Psyche" In Zafar Afaq Ansari (ed.) *Qur'ānic Concepts of Human Psyche* (Islamabad: International Institute of Islamic Thought, 1992), pp. 15-37.
2. Abdullah Yusuf Ali, *The Holy Qur'ān: English Translation of the Meaning and Commentary* (Al-Madinah: King Fahad Holy Qur'ān Printing Complex, 1414 H), Note 15: 1968.
3. Muhammad Asad, *The Message of the Qur'ān* (Gibraltar: Dar al-Andlus, 1980), Note 15:29.
4. Despite these clear Qur'ānic indications in favour of body-soul dualism, many Muslim scholars interpret the essential and the inner metaphysical core of man as merely life, and consciousness or "person." See for example F. Rahman's *Major Themes of the Qur'ān* (Chicago: Bibliotheca Islamica, 1980), p. 17.
5. Kenneth Cragg, The Mind of the Qur'ān: *Chapters in Reflection* (London: George Allen and Unwin, 1973), pp.103-104.
6. Ibid., p.104.

7. Reference here is to a system of psychotherapy, the Rational Emotive Therapy (RET) of Albert Ellis. See his *Handbook of Rational Emotive Therapy* (New York: Springer Publishing Co., 1977), p. 27, and other writings published in various journals.

10

Traditional Islamic Psychology

LALEH BAKHTIAR

There is a famous story about a contest that was held between Greek and Chinese artists as to which group had the better artists. Each was given a room which faced each other, separated by a door so that they could not see each other's work. The Greeks decorated the walls with beautiful flowers using rare colors and techniques. The Chinese, on the other hand, polished the surface of the walls in their room. When the door between them was removed, the beautiful art of the Greeks was reflected on the wall of the Chinese in all its original beauty and splendor. The Chinese won the contest because their creative solution most clearly represented the role of the human self in creation.[1]

In the traditional perspective, nature, aspects of which were re-created by the Greeks, and the self as mirror, re-created by the Chinese, are both reflections of the One God's self-disclosure in the Divine Name "Creator." The connection between nature and the self is seen to be not in matter or physical form, but in the creative process itself. This creative process is known as "nature in its mode of operation".

THE DIVINE REVEALED IN THE CREATIVE ACT

Nature in its mode of operation is how the divine presence in creation continues. Creation is not considered to have been a one time "big bang" from which God then retired from the universe, but an ongoing process of re-creation. With every expansion and contraction, with every breathing out and breathing in, all of nature, including the human self, dies and is reborn through the creative act. This death and rebirth occur through divine guidance, the second most important divine name for traditional psychology being al-hādi, the Guide.

This Divine Guidance which guides nature in its mode of operation has established a means of communications between the Creator and the self which consists of Signs.

We (God the Creator) shall show them (human beings) Our Signs upon the horizon (universe) and within themselves (the self) until it is clear to them (human beings) that He (God) is the Real (ḥaq). (41:53)

When the human being becomes conscious of self and then freely chooses to learn to read and to live by the Signs without and within, God's Will is done. Such a person will have completed the perfection of nature in its mode of operation within the self, and will be centered, having gained experiential knowledge of the oneness of God (monotheism, *tawḥīd*) reflected in nature and within themselves.

TRADITIONAL PSYCHOLOGY

Signs of God in nature, which includes the entire universe from the largest galaxy of stars and the planets to the smallest living organism on earth, are both external to the human being and internal. Knowledge of external signs forms the subject of the various natural sciences the human being has developed to understand the Divine Creation like cosmology, astronomy, philosophy, biology, chemistry and so forth, as well as the science of revelation, gaining knowledge about the Qur'ān where the 6000 some verses are each called a sign (*ayah*).

Understanding of the signs within developed through the Natural Sciences, particularly in medicine, and philosophy, particularly in Practical Philosophy. From the 13th century onwards, practical philosophy included the Science of Ethics, Economics and Politics. Traditional psychology is based on the Science of Ethics and can, therefore, most clearly be referred to as psychoethics. To develop a fair evaluation of psychoethics, in general, and its personality paradigm, in particular, it is necessary to understand its perspective of the human being's place in the universe, a perspective which is both holistic and integrative.

THE COVENANT BETWEEN SELF AND GOD

As the last creation of nature's creator, the human being occupies a special place in nature because out of all of nature, God breathes His Spirit within the human self alone. It is this infusion of the Divine Spirit which allows the human self to become conscious of self, an advantage no other aspect of nature has. Therefore, even though all of nature, the universe, and the cosmos are divinely created from the combination of natural elements and their qualities, only the human form has consciousness of self.

In the traditional perspective, this gift of consciousness was granted to the potential human spirit when it accepted the trust of the heavens and the earth

> *We offered the trust to the heavens and the earth and the mountains, but they refused to carry it and were afraid of it, and the human being carried it. (33:72)*

The acceptance of the trust includes the covenant with the Lord (Rabb) as the Qur'ān says,

> *And when your Lord took the seed of the children of Adam from their loins, and [asked], Am I not your Lord? and they bore witness, Yea, we do bear witness... so that they not respond on the Day of Judgment by saying, We were unaware of this. (7:173).*

Through this covenant, the human being becomes the trustee or representative of God on earth, accepts the trust of nature, and psychoethics is born.

SEEKING DIVINE ASSISTANCE

In order to carry out the duties of the trusteeship, divine assistance is sought. It is always available if sought as the Qur'ān verse says that God turns to those who turn to Him. (see 2:160). Al-Ghazālī (d. 1111)[2] goes so far as to say that without divine assistance, there is no conscious communication between the Creator and the trustee. In other words, without consciousness of self, communication of the regulations of the trust remains indirect and preconscious or even, perhaps, unconscious. Al-Ghazālī defines Divine Assistance as the harmony, agreement, or concord of the self's will and action with God's Will.[3] It appears as a sign, "That is the Grace of God, a free gift which He gives to Whom He Wills," (5:54)[4] and consists of four stages: Guidance from God (*hidāyah*), Direction (*rushd*), Leading (*tasdīd*), and Confirmation (*taʿyīd*). Guidance from God is of two types: guidance through nature (*takwīnī*) and guidance through nurture (*tashrīʿī*).

According to the traditional perspective, the verse stating [God] gave unto everything its nature and further gave it guidance, (20:50), proclaims God is the creator and the guide of all nature. Guidance is of two types, as previously stated. The first is *takwīnī* or primordial, universal guidance which all of nature receives, human or otherwise, as part of their *fiṭrah* or natural disposition. Universal guidance regulates whatever is created in nature through a natural, unreflective process, to implementing God's Will.

Human nature in the traditional perspective holds within itself all that came before it in creation, not in material terms, but in terms of nature in its mode of operation,[5] which is part of *takwīnī* guidance. Mineral, plant, animal, and human "souls" each contribute to a part of the development and perfection of nature's mode of operation. Minerals contribute to preserving the forms of the four elements of earth, air, fire, and water and their properties of cold and dry, hot and wet, hot and dry, and cold and wet, respectively. The plant soul contributes the ability to assimilate food, to grow, and to reproduce, while the animal soul contributes perception and motivation.

At the time of the evolution of the human soul or self, nature in its mode of operation was completed with what is known as the infusion of the divine spirit. Each of the other stages of nature's evolution received a gift, but the infusion of the divine spirit was an original gift; the gift of consciousness, which it shares with the Creator because of the covenant it made with God and the acceptance of the trust of nature.

The second type of both internal and external guidance is *tashrī͑ī* or acquired guidance, referring to guidance through the commands of revelation. It is rational in orientation and therefore the special guidance of the human being alone. If accepted as guidance in the perspective of submission to the will of God (Islam), acquired guidance becomes yet another gift to one who does submit to the will of God (Muslim). It is a particular kind of guidance, in a sense, because it speaks to human consciousness. It is to elucidate this kind of guidance that God sends Prophets[6] and the divine law as reinforcement against the forgetful and negligent human beings declaring on the Day of Judgment, "We were unaware of this." (7:173)

Guidance acquired through revelation as a stage of Divine Grace or assistance is a free gift from God because the giving was not obligatory on His part. However, the great theologian and philosopher, al-Ghazālī makes an important distinction here. God's communication through revelation, by which the self can acquire guidance, helps the self know the positive traits of its divinely bestowed natural disposition, but does not make the self-actualize them through practices. The self is free to make the choice to follow *tashrī͑ī* guidance or not to do so. If this guidance is not so chosen, the self will still be guided by *takwīnī* guidance, just as the rest of nature is. However, mineral, plant, and other animal forms have no choice, no free-will, so they submit completely to His will in completing their stage of perfection of nature in its mode of operation.

A natural being that has consciousness, which relies solely on *takwīnī* guidance, will not succeed in submitting to the will of God and completing the perfection of nature in its mode of operation because without the *tashrī͑ī* guidance of revelation, there will be no strengthening of free-will through the divine assistance of Direction, Leading, and Confirmation. These forms of divine assistance, along with guidance from God, strengthen the will of the self so that it gains greater conformity to

God's will. Without Divine Assistance, choices will be made whereby one's mineral, plant, and animal nature will be strengthened as opposed to free-will following the advice of reason. In other words, without the guidance of the Prophets and the Divine Law, which are part of revelation, the self will live by guidance through creation alone, never learning to be able to achieve its full potential and never completing the perfection of nature in its mode of operation which God so willed when He infused the spirit into the human form. *Tashrīʿī* guidance enhances the natural disposition of human Conscience and power of discernment to know the difference between positive and negative dispositions. It also helps the human being regulate the states of the self at every level of change and transformation towards completing the perfection of nature in its mode of operation at its highest level. Al-Ghazālī refers to the ayah, "But to those who follow guidance (*tashrīʿī*), He increases their guidance and bestows on them piety."[7] (47:17)

Nasīr al-Dīn Tūsī (d. 1201) explains how guidance comes either through nature or discipline. An example of nature is the principle which moves the passage of the sperm through the degrees of transformations to the point where it reaches the perfection of an animal; an example of discipline is the principle which moves wood, by means of tools and instruments, to the point where it reaches the perfection of a divan. Since the perfection of anything lies in the assimilation of that thing to its own principle, the perfection of discipline (regulated by *tashrīʿī* guidance) lies in its assimilation to nature (*takwīnī* guidance). Its assimilation to nature means that it follows nature in the advancement or the relegation of causes, in putting everything in its place, and in the observance of gradation and classification so that the perfection towards which Divine Omnipotence has directed nature, by way of subjection, may be realized from discipline by way of regulation.[8]

In addition to guidance from God in both its *takwīnī* and *tashrīʿī* forms, divine assistance contains three other stages previously alluded to, namely Direction (*rushd*), Leading (*tasdīd*), and Confirmation (*taʿyīd*). Direction (*rushd*) corresponds to the divine name "Rāshid", which means one who gives direction to all people in proportion to their acceptance of (*tashrīʿī*) guidance.[9] The *ayah*, "And We verily gave Abraham of old his direction and were aware of him" (21:51), illustrates this stage of divine assistance which is present when the self-senses it is being directed towards guidance (tashrīʿī). When the self is aware of the fact that it's will and actions together are directed to the right goal, its actions are made easier so that it achieves its goal in the shortest time possible and this is the third stage referred to by al-Ghazālī as Leading (*tasdīd*). The final stage of divine assistance is Confirmation (*taʿyīd*), which is referred to by the ayah, "How I confirmed you with the Spirit", (5:110), which is present in the self when insight is strengthened inwardly while outwardly suitable conditions are provided within the means available to attain the goal.

The self is guided through *tashrīʿī* guidance to various methods available to it to prepare itself as part of its trust to receive Divine Assistance. The methods are among the signs in the form of commands that are classified by al-Ghazālī according to the type of relationship the command refers to. Al-Ghazālī mentions two types of relationships for the vicegerent of God on earth, and thus the trustee of nature, to establish: first, the relationship between the self and its Creator-Guide; second, the relationship between the self and one's fellow human beings.

ESTABLISHING THE RELATIONSHIP BETWEEN THE SELF AND ITS CREATOR-GUIDE

This relationship is established, according to al-Ghazālī, through the commands of worship (*ʿibādah*), the most fundamental means of communication between the self and God, which is of two types: knowledge and actions. One who submits to the will of God seeks knowledge of *tashrīʿī* guidance through revelation and then puts the knowledge so gained into actions.

Knowledge

According to al-Ghazālī, knowledge should be used to come to understand the articles of belief rather than accepting them on faith alone. The articles of belief include: the belief that God is One; the belief that God sent prophets to guide mankind to Him and that Muhammad (sws) is the messenger and last prophet who will be sent until the end of time, when Jesus (as) will return; that the Qur'ān is the last revelation; and that after death the human being will be resurrected in the Hereafter and judged by God, who will reward or punish the person depending upon deeds performed in this life.

Actions

The first command is knowledge, the second is action that pertains to the practice of the pillars of Islam that are followed by one who submits to the will of God and seeks divine assistance in establishing the relationship between the self and God. Knowledge alone is not sufficient for the self who accepted the trusteeship of nature and was endowed with the divine spirit which includes its abilities to choose, to discern, and to gain consciousness of self. It is through actions based on knowledge that the centered self-benefits another as proof of being centered. The major pillars include ritual purity (*tahārah*), ritual prayer (*ṣâlāh*), ritual fasting (*ṣâum*), the paying of the alms tax (*zakāh*), the pilgrimage (*hajj*), counseling to positive dispositions and preventing the development of negative ones (*amr bi al ma' rūf wa nahy ᶜan al-munkar*), and *jihād* or struggle in the Way of God—the greater struggle of which is the inward struggle of the self (*jihād al-akbar*).[10] The last two are the major concern of psychoethics.

As a result of the performance of these acts of worship, if accompanied by divine assistance, the one who submits to the will of God will be receptive to the adoption of positive dispositions like temperance, courage, wisdom, and justice, and be able to avoid negative dispositions like anger, fear of other than God, cowardice, lust, envy, apathy unconsciousness (not knowing that you do not know) and over-consciousness (knowing but deceiving the self about it), but only on the condition that others benefit from the positive dispositions one has attained. This, then, makes it incumbent on the one who has submitted to the will of God to come to know and act upon the commands that underlie the relationship of self to others.

ESTABLISHING THE RELATIONSHIP BETWEEN THE SELF AND OTHERS

These commands give a framework for the establishment of the relationship between self and others including all social, political, and economic affairs undertaken among human beings. The model for all of this is the sunnah of Muhammad (sas) who said, "I was sent to complete the noble qualities of dispositions", explaining that God loves the positive dispositions and not the negative ones.[11] Al-Ghazālī also quotes another traditional saying in this regard, "By Him in whose hand is my life, no one shall enter paradise except the one who has positive dispositions."[12] Al-Ghazālī says,

> God taught [Muhammad (sas)] all the fine qualities of disposition, praiseworthy paths, reports about the first and last affairs, and matters through which one achieves salvation and reward in future life and happiness and reward in the world to come.[13]

Among the qualities listed are thirty obligations that one who submits has towards another.[14]

This process of the sunnah, whereby the positive dispositions of wisdom, temperance, and courage are kept in moderation resulting in the development of the positive trait of justice, is the traditional method of centering the self, and it begins by becoming conscious of the self; that is, by knowing the self.

<u>Know the Self</u>

The establishment of any of the relationships, according to al-Ghazālī, begins with gaining knowledge of one's self.

> *Know that the key to knowledge of God is knowledge of one's self. That is why it has been said, One who knows one's own self, knows one's Lord. That is also why God said, "We shall show them Our Signs upon the Horizons and within themselves until it is clear to them that He is the Real." (41:53)*

In short, nothing is closer to you than you. If you do not know your self, how will you know others? Moreover, you may think that you know your self and be mistaken, for this kind of knowing is not the key to the knowledge of the Real. The beasts know this much of themselves since of your self you know no more than the outward head, face, hands, feet, flesh, and skin. Of the inward dimension you know that when you are hungry, you eat bread, and when you are angry, you fall on the other person, and when "attraction to pleasure" dominates, you make for the marriage act. All the beasts know that much. Hence you must seek your own reality. What thing are you? From whence have you come? Where will you go? For what work have you come to this dwelling place? Why were you created? What and where is your felicity? What and from where lies your misery?

If you want to know your self, you should know that when you were created, two things were created: one is this outward frame, which is called the body. It can be seen with the outward eye. The second is the inward meaning which is called the self (or the soul), the spirit, and the heart. It can be recognized through inward insight but cannot be seen with the outward eye. Your reality is that inward meaning. Everything else follows upon it.[15]

Beginning with the self and moving towards centering it by completing the perfection of nature in its mode of operation is to submit to God's Will (*Islām*), thereby attaining happiness and well-being (*saʿādat*). It is an arduous task in which many who have attempted have not succeeded.

GOD'S WILL BE DONE: THE PRIMORDIAL GOAL OF THE SELF

The human being, then, is the trustee of creation, the human spirit at the time of its first creation having agreed to the terms of the trusteeship. Following the commands of God's signs in nature and within themselves, the human being is responsible for carrying out God's will so that all of nature may be allowed to center itself by completing the perfection of nature in its mode of operation. As an *ayah* says, "He gave unto everything its nature, and further, gave it guidance." (20:50). Everything in nature but the human self-perfects its own nature to the extent that life allows, by unconsciously submitting to the will of God, and the study of this is the concern of the Natural Sciences.

The area with which psychoethics is concerned is the completion of the perfection of nature in its mode of operation through centering in positive dispositions. Having ethically formed the covenant and accepted the trust, God breathed His spirit into human forms so that they gained the powers of consciousness of self which includes freely choosing positive dispositions from negative ones by consciously following one's conscience. The completion of the perfection of nature in its mode of operation, as God so willed, as opposed to all other natural forms, then, becomes a question of choice to do or not to do.

Psychoethics plays a central role in this process. Narāqī, (d. 1893) explains how all the other sciences were dependent upon this pivotal one:

> In fact, in the past, philosophers did not consider any of the other fields of learning to be truly independent sciences. They believed that without the science of psychoethics, mastery over any other science is not only devoid of any value, but it would, in fact, lead to the obstruction of insight and ultimate destruction of those who pursue it. That is why it has been said that knowledge is the thickest of veils which prevents the human being from seeing the real nature of things.[16]

CONCLUSION

Psychoethics arises out of the science of ethics, a branch of practical philosophy which is concerned with free-will actions of the self. The self is considered to be the highest evolutionary form of nature in its mode of operation because it has received the special divine gift of consciousness, a gift arising out of the divine spirit infused within the children of Adam. It was given when the human being made the covenant with God and accepted the trust of nature. As trustee of the Creator, the human being alone is responsible for the trusteeship which includes completing the perfection of nature in its mode of operation. Laws governing nature in its mode of operation are expressed through signs that appear on the horizon and within the self. The self has access to the language of the Signs through two kinds of guidance: *takwīnī*—universal to all of nature, and *tashrīʿī*—special guidance for human consciousness alone. Learning to read the signs on the horizon and within the self is a task undertaken by only the one who consciously submits to the will of God. Committed to the completion of the perfection of nature in its mode of operation, the self seeks Divine Assistance. In order for the trustee to perform the trust and complete the perfection of nature in its mode of operation, it should begin with knowing self, awakening to the self as it really is, becoming conscious of the self, including the development of the *tashrīʿī* guided conscience and free-will. In order to further this goal, psychoethics formulates the geography or topography of the self, its structure or morphology, and its dynamics.

NOTES

1. See al-Ghazālī, *Ihyā ʾʿulūm al-Dīn,* III, 22, 18 where the story originated. Also see the Mathnawi of Jalal al-Din Rumi, I. 3467 where the roles are reversed because his audience was in Asia Minor.
2. Al-Ghazālī, *al-Mīzān,* p. 115.
3. Al-Ghazālī, *Ihyā ʾʿulūm al-Dīn,* IV, 2.2255.
4. See also 3:73, 57:29, 3:171, 3:174, 49:8.
5. This is traditionally referred to as the soul.
6. Although all of the Prophets of the Old Testament and Prophet Jesus (as) are considered to have been human beings who in the most excellent way submitted to God's Will and completed the perfection of their divinely bestowed human nature, it is His Last Prophet in time, Muhammad (sws), known as the Seal of the Prophets, who is the main model of one who submits to His Will. This is because his every word and deed were recorded during his actual lifetime and therefore his example has greater reality as a model.
7. Al-Ghazālī also identifies a further stage of guidance as the light which illuminates, but this is a form beyond reason and rationality and therefore is discussed in *Jihad* Phase II. He refers to two verses in reference to it, namely, "Say: God's guidance is the guidance," (6:71) and "Whenever God wills to guide a human being, He enlarges his breast for surrender [to Him] (Islam)." (6:125)
8. Nasīr al-Dīn Tūsī, p. 115.
9. Al-Ghazālī, *Maqâsid,* p. 97
10. As opposed to that of armed conflict.
11. Ibid., Vol. 2, p. 10.
12. Ibid., Vol. 2, p. 10.
13. Ibid., Vol. 2, p. 10.
14. The theory, process, and mechanics of this are developed in *Jihad* Phase I: Centering the Self.
15. This implies that all of nature is sacred and that it is the human being who creates profanities.
16. Narāqī, p. 45.

Part III

Human Motivation
and Personality Types
in the Qur'ān

Human Motivation: An Islamic Perspective

SHAFIQ FALAH ALAWNEH

This paper is a modest attempt at describing the concept of human motivation from an Islamic perspective. Few studies have been directed toward this important topic, although great concern is given to motivation in general. Research in this domain usually includes topics like motivation theories, types of motivation, ways to motivate people, sources of motivation, and the role of motivation in high achievement and performance. Almost every source of information in psychology includes one or more chapters about motivation; sometimes whole books and journals are dedicated to this field.

The topic of motivating human behavior has occupied philosophers and thinkers since ancient times. The prophets were sent to ask people to believe in and obey the rules and the system chosen for them by Allah. The divine messages brought good news to those who believe in the messages and a warning to those who reject them. The miraculous acts of the prophets constituted one method of convincing people that what they brought was the truth. Many verses in the Holy Qur'ān describe the people and the way they received the teachings of their prophets. Such verses include (89:6-13), (79:15-25), (69:4-6), (71:1-4, 10-12), (11:58,66,94), and (7:72, 76-78). The following is an example of these verses:

> *Seest thou not how thy Lord dealt with the ᶜAd people of the city of Iram with Lofty pillars, the like of which were not produced in all the land. And with the Thamūd (people) who cut out huge rocks in the valley? And with Pharaoh, Lord of the Stakes. All these transgressed beyond bounds in the lands and heaped therein mischief. There f o re did thy Lord pour on them a scourge of diverse chastisements. (89: 6-13)*

It is clear from the preceding verses that motives are an essential component of human personality as created by Allah. Thus, the invitation of man to follow the system chosen for him by his Creator was almost always accompanied by some sort of motivation that stimulates him to do good deeds leading to Allah's acceptance and satisfaction. In the same vein, motivation may inhibit evil deeds that lead to Allah's anger and chastisement.

When Allah mentions ancient people in the Qur'ān like ᶜĀd and their prophet Hūd, Thamūd, and their prophet Salih, the people of Madyan and their prophet Shuᶜaib, and the Sons of Israel and their prophet Mūsā, He always asked his prophets to beautify good deeds in the eyes of the believers and make the picture of evil deeds ugly and hateful. In Islam, we find this matter even more obvious, for Allah describes Paradise in detail as if the believer is looking directly at it in his mind's eye. The same is true in describing Hell and its burning flames.

Allah, then, created man and endowed him with several instincts, incentives and motives that are significant for his well-being. It is true that instincts and incentives affect man's life and behavior, but their importance stems from their motivating force and influence. It seems necessary, however, to distinguish among several closely related concepts in this field such as instincts, incentives, drives, needs, and motives.

Instinct, for example, can be defined as a complex behavior that must have a fixed pattern throughout a species and that must be unlearned.[1] Most physiologists, though, view human behavior as directed by physiological needs and physiological wants in addition to simple innate instincts. This concept of instinct was put forward early in this century as a direct consequence of Charles Darwin's theory of evolution. After reviewing some 500 books on psychology and sociology, one sociologist compiled a list of 5,759 supposed human instincts.[2]

Incentives, on the other hand, are viewed as extrinsic forms of motivation. Teachers and educators always need these incentives. Since they cannot assume that students are enthusiastic about doing certain tasks like multiplying, dividing, and spelling because these activities are not fascinating in their own right, it is necessary for teachers and parents to look for incentives that magnify their impact.[3]

Unfortunately, instinct theory failed to explain all human motivation, a matter that resulted in proposing the concept of drive and the process of drive reduction as a mechanism of motivation. The idea behind drives is that a physiological need creates an aroused psychological state that drives the individual to reduce this need by satisfying it in some alternative way like eating or drinking. The aim of a drive is basically to lead the individual to homeostasis, i.e., the maintenance of a steady internal state.

The "drive" has been used sometimes to establish the concept and process of motivation. Woodsworth is credited with introducing "drive" into psychology in 1918, and drive is usually defined as the condition that imparts movement; it is also claimed that it can be understood through observable events. Some psychologists, however, prefer to use the terms "drive" and "motive" synonymously.[4]

A "need" comprises a major component in the content model of motivation. In this model, the major contributors like McClelland, Atkinson, and Maslow suggest that people act or behave to fulfil their needs and satisfy their desires. "Need" in this sense is a condition that exists within the individual. Some needs are basic and essential for the survival of the individual and thus rightly are called "primary needs." But many needs are not related to basic survival—they must be led for the development and the well-being of man. Needs usually give rise to "drives," which in turn compel the organism to act or behave.

Drives and incentives, however, are strongly interrelated, so that not only are we pushed by our need to reduce the drives and achieve optimum arousal, but we also are pulled by incentives. In this respect, incentives are viewed as positive or negative stimuli that lure or repel the individual. Our internal needs energize and direct our behavior, but so do the external incentives for a certain behavior for which we feel driven.

In the Qur'ān, this interrelation between internal needs and external incentives underlies the concept of reward and punishment. If one reads the Qur'ān, for instance, he or she will come across a myriad of these internal needs and external incentives that are used as the basis of what the Qur'ān and Muslim scholars describe as yearning (*targīb*) and awe (*tarhīb*). Instincts, internal needs, and external incentives are all used as components of the main principles of motivation, i.e., reward and punishment. Examples of these include eating, drinking, getting married to beautiful women, dwelling in lofty palaces and mansions, protection from fear and hellfire, success in this life and the Hereafter, high achievement, self-respect, and self-actualization, as well as being fed rotten food and boiling liquids, chastisement, being deprived of security and respect, being neglected and ignored, and dwelling forever in hellfire.

Motivation, the basic concept, runs through virtually all aspects of human life and behavior, especially those aspects related to learning and teaching. Forms of motivation, as will become evident throughout this article, are diverse and include among other things rewards and feedback, feelings of success and achievement, concern for others, and the development of one's capabilities. It goes without saying that motivation is the most important concept of education. It is important both as a concept that enhances educational behavior and as a goal of education. It is also important because other procedures, such as managing classrooms efficiently, maintaining discipline, preparing clear and attainable objectives, and teaching the gifted and talented, are all directed toward enhancing students' motivation to learn and teachers' motivation to teach.[5] To psychologists, a motivation is a need or desire that serves to energize behavior and to direct it toward a good.[6]

MOTIVATION IN MAJOR PSYCHOLOGICAL APPROACHES

Almost all psychologists agree that motivation is the basis for initiation, continuation or termination, and maintenance of human behavior. Motivation also directs human behavior toward the desired goals. Psychologists, however, differ in their interpretation of motivation according to the theoretical school to which they belong.

Psychoanalysts, for instance, view motivation as an unconscious impulse. Our behavior, according to this view, is totally determined by the multidimensional conflicts of the id, ego, and superego: the three major components of the human personality. The id is the actual personality at birth, the sole function of which is to fulfil the instincts and seek objects that satisfy them. In this sense, the id is usually guided and urged by lusts, pleasures, and instincts. An example of this are the baby's cries and agitated limb movements when it is hungry, which are believed, according to Freudian psychology, to be energized by the hunger instinct. The main principle that activates the id is the pleasure principle that seeks immediate gratification for the instinctual needs.[7]

According to Freud, the ego emerges when psychic energy is diverted from the id to energize the important cognitive processes such as perception, learning, and logical reasoning. It is the rational part of the human personality, and it serves the reality principle, i.e., finding realistic ways to gratify the instincts. The ego, moreover, must invest some of its energy to block the id's irrational impulses.[8]

The superego, which is the third component of the human personality, is the person's internalized moral standards. It develops from the striving of the ego for perfection rather than for pleasure or reality. It is normally developed between the ages of 3 and 5 as the child internalizes the moral values and standards of its parents. Thus, the superego is directed by culture and a social value system.

According to behaviorists, motivation constitutes the why of our behavior. When behavior is obstructed by some barrier and we feel imbalanced and tense, any release of this tension becomes a motivating force. Although there are various schools within behaviorism, such as radical behaviorism, neo behaviorism, and the school that embraces social learning theory, they all agree that the intensity and the continuity of our behavior are determined by contingencies of reinforcement and situational variables.[9] According to the behaviorist tradition, the major mechanism of human motivation is reinforcement and punishment, or what Thorndike described as the law of effect. Reinforcement or reward raises motivation by increasing the probability of certain behavior occurring in similar conditions, while punishment lowers motivation by decreasing the likelihood of some other behavior. These two (i.e., punishment and reinforcements) are the major, if not the only, consequences of human behavior. As Skinner has put it, behavior is totally governed by its consequences. If these consequences are pleasant, the individual will be motivated to continue with his present behavior. If otherwise, he will be motivated to stop and abstain from his present behavior.[10]

The cognitive approach emphasizes that motivation is a function of the individual's perception of the value and importance of his behavior on himself and his society, the individual's expectancy, and anticipation of the outcome of his behavior, and the performance level, i.e., the competence of behavior. When high personal competence is connected to skill, it is said that the individual has high self-efficacy.

As noted earlier in the discussion of the behaviorist tradition, motivation is mostly external. It is reflected in the form of reward or punishment. On the other hand, the cognitive approach emphasizes internal motivation, which springs from inside the individual. Accordingly, this approach speaks about achievement motivation, competence motivation, cognitive drive (knowledge motivation), curiosity and discovery motivation, arousal motivation and sensation seeking, and attribution motivation. The common factor among all these types of motivation is that they all stem from inside and thus become a distinguishing mark of the human personality, although, of course, they might be greatly affected by outside conditions and external factors as well.[11]

Humanists look at motivation from a content point of view and believe that motivation is strongly influenced by the needs of the individual. When a need is not satisfied, the individual becomes tense and anxious, and any behavior that reduces this tension is termed motivation. Moreover, humanists distinguish between basic needs (deficiency needs) such as food, drink, and safety, and meta needs (or growth needs) like the need for knowledge, beauty, and self-actualization.[12] Maslow even suggested that these needs are arranged hierarchically, so that the higher the need is, the less physical it becomes, and the less associated with survival it is. Growth needs are crucial in promoting the well-being of an individual, while deprivation needs form the physiological bases of human motivation.[13]

Motivation can be viewed as both physiological and psychological in origin, as is the case with arousal and sensation seeking. In this type of motivation, the stimulation of certain parts of the nervous system (mainly in the cortex) pushes the individual for more work and activity. But this is only one half of the process. Psychological states that characterize an individual are usually accompanied by physiological activities, mainly the active functioning of the sympathetic nervous system. Psychological states include the feelings of pleasure, satisfaction, and relaxation.

THEORETICAL EXPLANATIONS OF MOTIVATION

The psychoanalytic approach views motivation in terms of basic instincts, mainly the sexual instinct and the aggression instinct, each of which is demonstrated by several motives. This approach is attacked, however, because it proposes a group of obscure psychological constructs by which it tries to explain a complex human behavior. The suggestion that instincts motivate behavior does not satisfy the behaviorists, who consider those instincts vague and misleading.

Moreover, this approach is severely criticized by social psychologists who blame the instinct-oriented scientists for not agreeing upon a specified number of those instincts. Some claim there are hundreds of them, while others say there are two. Social psychologists also note that even if we assume the accuracy of the approach, we will notice wide differences between people and tribes for the same basic instinct.[14]

Unfortunately, the attack of behaviorists on the instinct theory is not complete. They argue that our behavior is completely governed from outside, and as Skinner put it, behavior is governed by its consequences. In his book A Matter of Consequences, he begins the chapter on education called "Science and Human Behavior" with the following lines:

> In an American school if you ask for the salt in good French, you get an A. In France you get the salt. And the A was probably reinforcing only as an escape from a threat of punishment. Students studied to avoid the consequences of not studying.[15]

In this case, they denied the role of the individual and his will in shaping his own behavior. According to behaviorists, our behavior is totally controlled by how others respond to it. If we receive any kind of reinforcement, we tend to repeat the behavior in similar conditions in the future. Otherwise, if we receive some sort of punishment, the behavior will stop and fade.

In modern psychology, motives can be divided into many types, depending on the basis /bases used for their classification. For instance, according to their origin, they can be classified into primary and secondary (acquired) motives; according to their consequences, either rewards or punishments; according to the level of being aware of them, either consciously or unconsciously; and according to the importance of their satisfaction, hierarchically, from biological needs at the bottom to safety needs, belonging needs, self-esteem needs, cognitive and knowledge needs, aesthetic needs, and finally self-actualization needs at the top.[16]

AN ISLAMIC PARADIGM OF MOTIVATION

In Islam, it is difficult to talk about motivation without reflecting first on man's origin, his aim, and his relationship with people and his Creator. This includes his place on this earth and how he should relate to the rest of creation, living or inanimate.

Man was created with the purpose of becoming God's representative on earth. We read in the Qur'ān the following verse:

Behold, thy Lord said to the angels: I will create a vicegerent on earth. They said: Wilt Thou place therein one who will make mischief and shed blood? Whilst we do celebrate Thy praises and glorify Thy holy name? He said: I know what ye know not. (2:30)

For the purpose of this representation and administration of earth and the investment of its resources, God endowed man with the ability to think and use his mind. This ability is essential for the concept of accountability. Since man can think and distinguish between good and evil, he must be responsible for his behavior and must be held accountable for his decisions.

The mental ability God endowed man with rests upon two important dimensions: knowledge and will (see Figure 1).

Figure 1. An Islamic Deconstruction of the purpose for creating man.

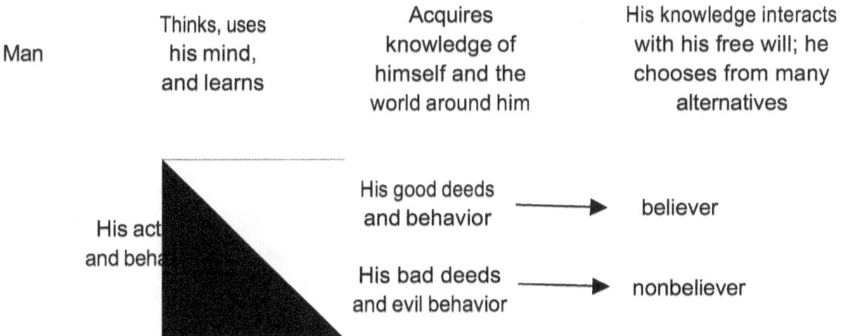

Without the necessary knowledge, it is difficult for man to behave in an enlightened manner, for knowledge enhances man's behavior. Recently, some psychologists have come to believe that knowledge comprises one important motive in human beings, and they termed it the "cognitive drive" or "cognitive motivation."[17] The more one knows about the world around one (and about him- or herself), the more one becomes motivated to obtain knowledge. The knowledge of import here, of course, is that which enables one to distinguish between right and wrong, between good and evil, and between lawful (ḥalāl) and unlawful (ḥarām).

Another motivation related to knowledge is achievement.

Psychologists like Atkinson and McClelland describe some people who are high in achievement motivation, based on their scores in some projective tests like that of the SAT. According to these psychologists, people who are high in achievement motivation are characterized by the full functioning of all their capacities, confidence in the face of the external world, a sense of responsibility for their own behavior, and high creativity.[18]

Once man acquires knowledge, he has to use another motive to direct and guide his behavior, namely, the motive of freewill. Whether man has free will or not is a philosophical question for which Islam has a moderate and rational answer. Having been endowed with the tools of knowledge and the devices of distinguishing between good and evil (ḥalāl and ḥarām), man can freely choose which route to follow. God says in the Qur'ān:

[Have We not] shown him the two highways. (90:10)

God showed man the two ways and left the choice up to him:

We showed him the way: whether he be grateful or ungrateful. (76:3)

Contingent on this free choice, which is an honor that God granted man, is the fact that man is fully responsible for his choice. This responsibility works as another motive for man's behavior, i.e., his behavior should be determined by his wisdom in choosing the right and avoiding the wrong deeds. There waits for man various rewards if he chooses the right path and various severe punishments if he decides to choose the wrong path. The delayed consequences of this choice must be kept in mind before man decides to choose.

The basic motive in Islam remains *Īmān* (faith). The evidence for it is the fact that *Īmān* is mentioned more than seven hundred times in the Qur'ān, whether directly or derivatively. This, then, is the basis and the energizing force for all motivation. Its functions include activating behavior, maintaining behavior, in addition to screening behavior and purifying it from all impurities.[19] *Īmān* comprises the strong Islamic base for directing, re-educating, and influencing man in this life. Abu Sulayman invites scholars and researchers to study this concept and states that it is a simple, clear, and very comprehensible concept. The essential components of this motive are the strong unshakable belief in Allah (the Eternal, the Absolute, and the Creator of the universe) and the strong unshakable belief in the fact that man must be held accountable for his deeds in this life.[20] *Īmān*, as the basic motive, is related to other types of motivation and to man's psychological state. This relationship is demonstrated below (see Figure 2).

Figure 2. The Relationship between *Iman* and Other Motives and Consequences of Human Behavior

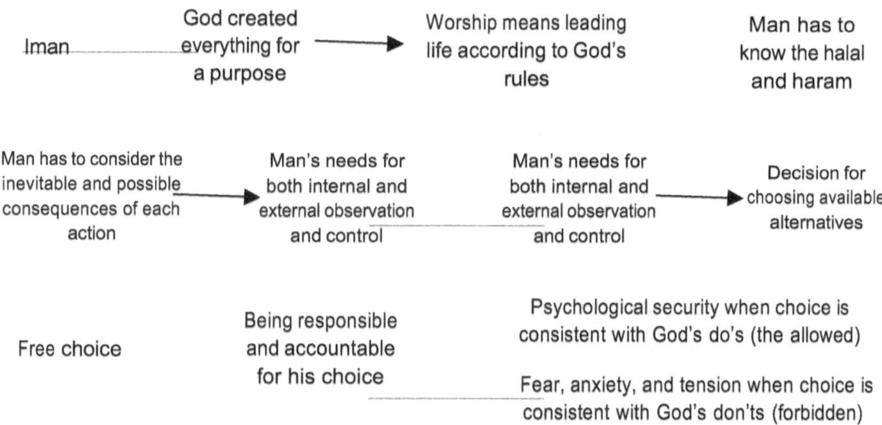

Clearly, once the motive of *Īmān* is connected with the motive of knowledge and controlled by external factors, they become the essential incentive for man's behavior. These two motives, however, are strongly related, since they both include the meaning of knowledge. Essentially, *Īmān* can be viewed as the highest level of knowledge, where one has no doubt whatsoever about the things he knows. While knowledge provides the individual with the necessary information about what is right and what is wrong, it is *Īmān* that causes man to do good and avoid evil.

In this sense, *Īmān* becomes a great force that is consistent with human nature. The relationship between the behavior of a Muslim and his *Īmān* is that of means and ends. This is the motive that shapes the spirit of Islamic ethics, Islamic brotherhood, the sense of responsibility toward this life and the Hereafter, the awareness in the unity of the Muslim society, the spirit of equality and belonging, and the protection of the idea of Islam and transferring it to other societies.

As a motive of human behavior, *Īmān* is not a simple declaration of belief on the tongue, the mere practice of certain Islamic rituals, or the cognitive knowledge of the cornerstones of Islam. God condemns hypocrites, those who say something that is not in their hearts. He says in this respect:

And the hypocrites also. These were told: Come fight in the way of Allah, or (at least) drive (the foe from your city). They said: Had we known there would be a fight, we should certainly have followed you. They were that day nearer to unbelief than to Faith, saying with their lips what was not

in their hearts. But Allah hath full knowledge of all they conceal. (3:167)

Īmān is, rather, a profound psychological belief that goes beyond doubt and that permeates the self overtly as well as covertly. Al-Qaradāwi says in this respect:

> *Īmān*, in its essence, is not only work done by the tongue, body or mind. Rather, it is a psychological function that reaches the depths of the self and touches all its dimensions whether they be cognitive, affective, or free will.[21]

According to this Islamic view, *Īmān* serves as a monitor for even the most basic psychological needs like food, drink, and sex. When the individual Muslim feels hungry and the desire for food urges him to act, it is *Īmān* that controls and monitors the whole process, allowing him to pick the right food, maintain the correct habits during eating, and consume the appropriate amount of food. In this respect, he will choose certain foods and avoid the others; he will use his right hand and will start the process with the name of Allah; he will not fill his stomach with food; he will end his eating by giving thanks to his Creator. The same is valid for drinking and even having sexual activities. When his heart is filled with *Īmān*, the Muslim goes on to choose freely but wisely from the alternatives available to him in any given situation.

Thus, *Īmān* leads to wisdom, which is mainly the choice of the correct thing from several alternatives. Allah says in the Qur'ān, addressing this issue of wisdom and true knowledge:

> *Say: Not equal are the things that are bad and the things that are good, even though the abundance of the bad may dazzle thee. So fear Allah, O ye that understand, (so) that ye may prosper. (5:100)*

Once this *Īmān* is established in the human personality, it must be coupled with free choice, so that man becomes fully responsible for his own behavior. In the Qur'ān, it is clearly stated that this religion is not compulsory since both ways are made clear to men:

> *Let there be no compulsion in religion (dīn). Truth stands out clearly from error. Whoever rejects tāghūt (anything worshipped beside Allah) and believes in Allah hath grasped the most trustworthy handhold, that never breaks. And Allah heareth and knoweth all things. (2:256)*

It has been decided this way because after knowledge of the *ḥalāl* and *ḥarām*, and strong belief (*Īmān*), there remains no excuse for the individual not to choose goodness and avoid evil.

Other internal and external motives accompany the *Īmān* motivation to maximize its effectiveness. Some of these are what I call the three "t's: *taqwā* (fear of Allah), *tahrid* (arousal), and *tawbah* (repentance). There are verses in the Qur'ān to support the existence of each of these motives. An example of the *taqwā* motivation is the following verse:

Enjoin prayer on thy people and be constant therein. We ask thee not to provide sustenance: We provide it for thee. But the Hereafter is for righteousness. (20:132)

The word *taqwā* and its derivatives are mentioned more than 258 times in the Qur'ān. As for *tahrid*, it is mentioned explicitly only once, while it is mentioned many times implicitly. Allah says:

O Prophet! Rouse the believers to the fight. If there are twenty amongst you, patient, and persevering, they will vanquish two hundred; if a hundred, they will vanquish a thousand of the unbelievers, for those are a people without understanding. (8:65).

And finally, there is a complete *sūrah* (chapter) in the Qur'ān named "Repentance" (*Tawbah*). Moreover, this word and its derivatives are mentioned 93 times. One example is the following:

Except for those who repent, mend (their life), hold fast to Allah, and make their religious devotion sincere to Allah; if so, they will be (numbered) with the believers. And soon will Allah grant to the believers a reward of immense value. (4:146)

The motivation of fear is the human emotion that enables man to either avoid danger and problematic situations, or face and solve them. This motivation is usually connected with types of anxiety and tension due to the threatening nature of the situation.[22] The Holy Qur'ān, however, looks differently at this motivation and views it in the context of *Īmān* mentioned earlier. In this context, fear is called *taqwā* and refers to the fear of God represented by adhering to His orders and commands and avoiding His disobedience. When someone says we have to fear God, he means that we have to be afraid of His punishment and thus avoid whatever He does not like. The concept of *taqwā* as a distinguished religious motivation, includes the following, according to al-Isāwb.

Abstaining from all that God asks us to avoid, such as disobedience, sins, and evil deeds. Thus, it is a kind of prevention from falling into these wrong deeds, protecting us from their unpleasant consequences. It is a kind of avoidance behavior.

Committing to all that God ordered people to do, including good work and good deeds, because in doing so man can protect himself from God's anger and punishment that He prepared (kept) for the disobedient.

Controlling man's instincts and biological drives in such a way that corresponds with God's orders, by seeking lawful means of satisfying these instincts, needs, and drives. By doing so, man learns obedience to God and His Prophet and respect for law, and he achieves the development of values, *taqwā* and *Īmān*.[23]

Taqwā in its sense, becomes a motivating force for human behavior that directs man towards the best and gears him towards more self-growth and control over his instincts and desires, leading consequently to personality growth and integration.[24] *Taqwā*, (the fear of Allah) soon becomes, by His help, "an internal feeling that is responsible for the execution of Islamic regulations. It becomes that latent guarantee that dominates all other guarantees, since it is superior to those man-made regulations that have only external control. It is so easy to cheat the external control when there is no internal conscience to guard human behavior."[25]

Figure 3. Model of Taqwā Motivation

External or Internal Stimuli	Fear of Allah and avoiding the forbidden (taqwa)	Behavior that removes or ends the previous state	Pleasant feeling for the end of the state of fear

As for the tahrid motivation, or the arousal of man's abilities and potentials, it is evident from the verse mentioned earlier (8:65) that once it is maximized, the ability of a believer becomes ten times that of an ordinary man. Rousing the believers, whether in war or in peace, requires, of course, the investment of all possible forms of reward and punishment. It is the desire of the believer to get the highest levels of these rewards that drive him to behave according to his Lord's regulations and laws.

The concept of *tawbah* (repentance) comprises another very important type of motivation, for without repentance the Muslim will stay on the wrong path without directing his efforts toward good deeds. Repentance urges the individual to do more good work to compensate for the wrong he has done, in addition to providing him with the assistance he needs to abstain from wrong deeds. Allah says in the Qur'ān:

When those come to thee who believe in our signs, say: Peace be on you. Your Lord hath inscribed upon Himself (the rule of) mercy. Verily, if any of you did evil in ignorance and thereafter repented and amended (his conduct), lo! He is oft-Forgiving, Most Merciful. (6:54)

Repentance is intertwined with the motivation of reward and punishment. Those who miss their prayers and follow their lusts will face destruction, except those who repent and follow their repentance with righteous work. Actually, being forgiven and accepted by the Lord is in and of itself a great reward sought by every Muslim. Not only will they not be wronged, but they will be admitted to the gardens of Heaven (19:59-60), and even their evil deeds will be changed into good ones, as is clearly stated in the Qur'ān:

Unless he repents, believes, and works righteous deeds, for Allah will change the evil of such persons into good, and Allah is oft-Forgiving, Most Merciful. (25:70)

The consequences of repentance, however, are not restricted to changing bad deeds into good, but go beyond that to include many other rewards. For instance, repentance is made a prerequisite for success in this life as well as in the Hereafter:

But any that (in this life) had repented, believed, and worked righteousness, happily he shall be one of the successful. (28:67)

It is also a necessary condition so that the believers open the way for the pagans and treat them as brothers. Allah says in the Qur'ān:

But when the forbidden months are past, then fight and slay the pagans wherever ye find them, and seize them, beleaguer them, and lie in wait for them in every stratagem (of war). But if they repent and establish regular prayers and pay zakāt, then open the way for them, for Allah is oft-Forgiving, Most Merciful. (9:5-6)

Allah even describes those who do not repent as being people who do wrong (*ẓālimūn*), and promises them with the hellfire:

Those who persecute the believers, men and women, and do not turn in repentance, will have the chastisement of the burning fire. (85:10)

Allah stresses the importance of repentance by the fact that he makes its rejection (i.e., He does not accept it from people) a kind of severe punishment by which He threatens the unbelievers:

But those who reject faith after they accepted it, and then go on adding to their defiance of faith — never will their repentance be accepted, for they are those who have gone astray. (3:90)

Finally, the consequences and rewards of repentance are not confined to those in the Hereafter but also are included in this life. Allah makes it a means for getting sustenance and improving the quality of life. Allah says:

And O my people, ask forgiveness of your Lord, and turn to Him (in repentance), He will soon send you the skies pouring abundant rain, and add strength to your strength. So turn ye not back in sin. (11:52)

However, it should be noted that the vehicle for all motivation is the great process of reward and punishment, or what the Qur'ān describes as yearning and awe (21:90). In the final analysis, it is to achieve a reward, or to avoid a punishment that people behave in the way they do. Here it must be mentioned that the reward and the punishment in the Holy Qur'ān are both qualitatively and quantitatively different from those mentioned elsewhere.

Reward and punishment in the Qur'ān are generally delayed rather than immediate. While contemporary psychology emphasizes the importance of immediate reinforcement (reward) following behavior, and that delay in presenting this reinforcement inversely affects behavior, the Qur'ān concentrates on the delayed rewards in the form of promises from Allah to be given to the believers, almost always, on the Day of Judgment. However, a Muslim is fully confident that those promises will be led, since they come from Allah who never breaks His promise.

The Qur'ān mentions all known or imagined rewards and punishments; for example, the basic biological and physiological rewards of food, drink, companionship, and clothing (76:17-18; 56:18-23; 78:23; 55:56-58; 47:15). A brief look at some verses of *Sūrat al-Naba'* will demonstrate what awaits the believers and those who reject the Truth.

Truly Hell is a place of ambush for the transgressors, a place of destination. They will dwell therein for ages. Nothing cool shall they taste therein, nor any drink, save boiling fluid. And a fluid, dark, murky, intensely cold (78:21-25). Verily for the righteous there will be achievement — gardens enclosed and grapevines, maidens of equal age, and a cup full to the brim. No vanity shall they hear therein nor untruth. Recompense from thy Lord, a gift, (amply) sufficient. (78:31-36)

No doubt, a wise person, endowed with true knowledge, full of fear of Allah and the desire not to make Him angry, roused effectively to behave, with the free will to choose, will try his best to be on the side of the believers and the righteous and will work hard to avoid being among the disobedient. Once man fully believes that the Hereafter is coming, and that people will be divided into two groups-those in misery and those in pleasure- he will be highly motivated to be among the second group.

Another look at the above verses (as well as others that describe reward and punishment) will show that the main types of reinforcement and punishment were addressed in the Qur'ān, long before they were specified by modern psychologists like Skinner. For instance, positive punishment is clearly represented by descriptions of, for example, staying in Hell for ages (78:21-32) and drinking boiling fluid if they ask for water (78:25).

Negative punishment on the other hand is demonstrated in many verses in the form of deprivation. Examples of negative punishment include being prevented from drinking any cool drink (78:24); being deprived of guidance and forgiveness (4:168); being prevented from speaking or even putting forth pleas (77:35-36); unrelenting punishment (43:75); sealing the mouths; and letting the hands and feet bear witness to what they did in this life (36:65). Indeed, there are hundreds of other examples of positive and negative punishments that encourage the individual to avoid punishment or end deprivation.

Positive and negative rewards are also stressed in the Qur'ān on many different occasions. Examples of positive reinforcement are numerous and include the following: raised couches upon which to recline with all kinds of meat and fruit to eat (36:56-57; 52:22); and meadows and gardens in which to play, with all that is wished for made ready (42:22).

Negative rewards mentioned by Allah include, for example, protection from fear and grief (46:13; 43:68, preservation from the chastisement of the blazing fire and from tasting death more than once (44:56).

The four types of punishment and reward are rarely referred to in the Qur'ān in isolation. Rather, they are often mentioned collaboratively. Sometimes punishment is associated with some sort of reward for the behavior; for example, the Qur'ān says that Allah is strict in punishment and oft-Forgiving (5:98), that He Forgives sins and accepts is severe in punishment (41:43; 40:3), and that He is swift in punishment and oft-Forgiving (6:165; 7:167)

Sometimes two types of reward (reinforcement) are mentioned side by side to emphasize a certain behavior, for example, the connection between the most generous sustenance (positive reinforcement) with the (negative reinforcement) in 34:4. Another example is from the hellfire (negative reinforcement) and admittance into the gardens of Heaven (positive reinforcement) mentioned in 3:185. At other times, positive and negative reinforcement are coupled together to emphasize the danger underlying a behavior. One example of this is joining severe chastisement and deprivation from purification and listening to Allah (negative reinforcement) as mentioned in 2:174.

Finally, it should be noted that all human motivation stems from and rotates around *Īmān*. Allah states clearly in the Qur'ān that people of faith are not like those who disobey. Allah says:

Shall we treat the people of faith like the people of sin? What is the matter with you? How judge ye? (68:35-36)

Evidently from the above verses, once man chooses to be among the people of faith, he will be treated as such by Allah, deserving distinguished treatment. The interrelatedness of this whole process is shown below in Figure 4.

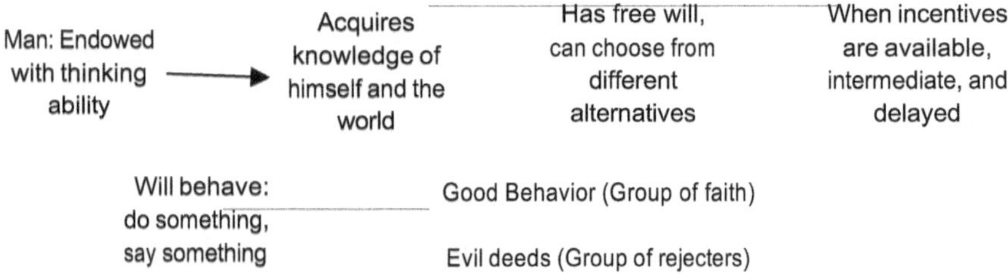

The figure shows that man, once endowed with the ability to think, will soon acquire the knowledge necessary to choose the correct path from several alternatives. Internal (free will) and external (incentives and rewards) motives activate human behavior and provide man with the energy and desire for correct behavior. Depending on his knowledge, free will, and wisdom, man will choose to be among one of two groups: the believers or the rejecters.

BASIC CHARACTERISTICS OF ISLAMIC MOTIVATION

The Islamic educational legacy pays great attention to the issue of motivation and discusses it under various headings, such as heart conditions; student and teacher morals; problems of knowledge, hope, and fear; imitation; control of consequences; and piety.

According to early Muslim scholars, motives are divided into two main types: those related to the teacher (inspiration, zeal, and having mercy on students), and those related to the student (curiosity, imitation, and self-respect). From these two types comes a third type that includes the common motives between the teacher and the student (love, respect, and desire for knowledge).[26] Early Muslim scholars specify the basic traits of Islamic motivation. One of these traits is the vertical interdependency of motives, or what can be called the hierarchical nature of motives. Al-Mawardi, for instance, discussed the hierarchical feature of human needs long before Maslow talked about them. Al-Mawardi's views in this regard can be considered the antecedent of Maslow's ideas about human motivation.[27]

Another characteristic of human motivation from an Islamic point of view is the clarity of aims and objectives. The aim of a Muslim, who is in the state of choosing to behave, is obvious: He seeks the acceptance of Allah. This clarity of aim leads the Muslim to choose the honest means for achieving objectives, and thus he knows beforehand how to reach his goal and achieve his objectives. Allah states this clarity of objectives in the Qur'ān:

> *Verily, (the ends) ye strive for are diverse. So, he who gives (in charity) and fears (Allah), and in all sincerity testifies to the best, We will indeed make smooth for him the path to ease. But he who is a greedy miser and thinks himself self-sufficient, and gives the lie to the best, We will indeed make smooth for him the path to misery. (92:4-10)*

Thus, the road is very clear in front of the individual, and he has to choose where to go. A third distinguishing feature of human motivation from the Islamic viewpoint is the vitality and high importance of goals and aims. The goal of motivation is highly significant for the well-being of the individual, both in this life and in the Hereafter.

When the goal is vital and important, the individual will double his efforts to achieve it.[28]

The fourth characteristic of human motivation from an Islamic perspective is realism. Motivation deals realistically with human beings in a very natural manner that corresponds to his pure nature. In this sense, man is considered a moderate being; he is not a devil, and he is not an angel. Since he is a human being, he is susceptible to falling into sin and error. But here comes the motive of *tawbah* (repentance), mentioned earlier, to make up for those errors and wipe out those sins, and even change them in his record into good deeds. Allah, who created man and knows him completely, offers him both positive and negative incentives to urge him to work properly. This combination of positive and negative incentives comprises the core of realism as a characteristic of human motivation from an Islamic perspective.

The final distinguishing characteristic of motivation as portrayed in the Qur'ān is comprehensibility. Human motivation encompasses all possible kinds of behavior, regardless of how simple and unimportant it might seem to be. Even the simplest good action, like smiling in the face of another Muslim, removing a thorn or a bone from the road, or even being familiar with one's spouse will deserve reward from Allah. The reward of a good deed depends on an individual's sincerity and the effect of the deed on others; this reward may be multiplied ten times or more, according to the will of Allāh. This comprehensibility of human behavior ensures the comprehensibility of the incentives used to reward man for his good work. These incentives, as was mentioned earlier, include every possible kind of positive or negative reward or punishment. They include all possible means of yearning and awe as the Qur'ān describes them.

NOTES

1. N. Tingbergen, *The Study of Instincts* (Oxford: Clarendon, 1951), p. 398.
2. D. Myers, *Psychology*, 4th ed. (New York: Worth Publishers, 1995), p. 397.
3. R. Biehler, *Psychology Applied to Teaching*, 3rd ed. (Boston: Houghton Mifflin, 1978), pp. 546-547.
4. B. Mukhopadyay, *Motivation in Education Management: Issues and Strategies* (New Delhi: Sterling Publishers, 1994), p. 11.
5. G. Davis, *Educational Psychology: Theory and Practice* (Reading, Mass: Addison-Wesley, 1983), pp. 244-245.
6. D. Myers, *Psychology*.
7. D. Shaffer. *Developmental Psychology: Childhood and Adolescence* (Pacific Grove, Ca.: Brooks/Cole, 1993), 47.
8. S. Freud, *The Ego and the Id* (London: Hogarth Press, 1974); original work published in 1923.
9. B. Mukhopadyay, *Motivation in Education Management: Issues and Strategies.*
10. W. Goodwin and H. Klausmeier, *Facilitating Student Learning: Introduction to Educational Psychology* (New York: Harper and Row, 1975).
11. R. Slavin, *Educational Psychology: Theory into Practice* (Englewood Cliffs, N.J.: Prentice Hall, 1991).
12. A.H. Maslow, *Motivation and Personality*, 2nd ed. (New York: Harper and Row, 1970), pp. 400-480.
13. Lefrancois, *Psychology for Teaching* (Belmont, Ca.: Wadsworth Publishing, 1994).
14. D. Stone and E. Nielson, *Educational Psychology: The Development of Teaching Skills* (New York: Harper and Row, 1982).
15. B.F. Skinner, *A Matter of Consequences* (New York: Alfred A. Knopf, 1983), p. 64.
16. Slavin, *Educational Psychology: Theory into Practice.*
17. Ibid.
18. Davis, *Educational Psychology: Theory and Practice*, p. 252.
19. A. Abu Sulayman, "Guiding Light: Selections from the Holy Qur'ān," *The American Journal of Islamic Social Sciences*, vol. 4, no. 2 (1987): viii.
20. Ibid.
21. Y. *Al-Qaradāwi, 'mān and Life* (Beirut: Ar-Risālah, 1984), 30 (in Arabic). p. 22.

22. Davis, *Educational Psychology: Theory and Practice*, p. 558.
23. A al-Isawi, *Components of Islamic and Arabic Personality and Methods of Their Development* (Cairo: Dar al-Fikr al-Jami', 1986) (in Arabic).
24. M. Najāti, *Qur'ān and Psychology* (Beirut: Dār al-Shurūq, 1982), p. 254 (in Arabic)
25. S. Quṭb, *Fi Zilāl al-Qur'ān*, vol. 1 (Beirut: Dār al-Shurūq, 1981), p. 205 (in Arabic).
26. M. Mansi, Readings in Psychology (Alexandria: Dār al-Maʻrifah, al-Jāmiʻiyyah, 1982) (in Arabic).
27. J. Al-Alousi, Psychological Foundations of Al-Mawardi's Educational Views (Baghdād: Matbaʻat Baghdad, 1988), pp. 30-31 (in Arabic).
28. Mansi, Readings in Psychology.

12

The Drives of Human Behaviour in the Qur'ān

MUHAMMAD UTHMAN NAJATI
Translated, with introduction,
By Yasien Mohamed[1]

INTRODUCTION[2]

The discussion of drives is pertinent to personality in so far as "personality is the relatively stable organization of a person's motivational dispositions, arising from the interaction between biological drives and the social and physical environment".[3] The study of personality has until recently been ignored by psychologists partly because the focus in the past has been on the investigation of processes that are common to all organisms, and which could be investigated in the laboratory, rather than on the wholistic man and his motivation. An investigation into human drives is an important part of the study of personality in so far as it explains the motivations that drive human personalities to behave and think in a distinctive way.[4]

The closest English equivalent that I could find for the Arabic word *dawāfiᶜ* is "drives", and this seems to be exactly what Najātī means, judging from the context in which he uses the term and the sources that he cites. However, this term is outmoded, though not out of use in modern psychology, as it was originally used by Woodworth in 915 to refer to "force of energy", which applies to instinctive behaviour in lower animals.[5] Later, the term became applicable to human social behaviour, and it is in this sense that Najātī uses the term. For the sake of accuracy of translation, I retain the term, but it is not necessarily the one that I would prefer to describe the drives of human motivation and personality.[6]

Freud employed the mechanistic philosophy of the drive concept and was the first to hold that sexual drives are the sole sources of motivation for human behaviour. Most psychologists today, however, have abandoned the hope of explaining social motives in terms of drives. Hull introduced the term "incentive", which is more appropriate for explaining human social behaviour. Whereas a "drive" is unlearned and has a presumed physiological basis, an "incentive" depends on prior learning, occurs in particular situations, and lacks any discernable physiological basis.[7] In contrast to Freud, Adler stressed the positive striving of the future rather than the determination of personality from the past. Allport argued that new interests and motives can be acquired at any time of life, becoming "functionally autonomous". This notion of the individual creating his own personality fits in with Roger's and Maslow's theories of self-actualization as the fundamental principle in personality growth and development.[8] Attempts to explain learned behaviour and acquired personality in terms of "drives" are therefore not compelling, and we are sure to enter an era where this term will no longer be used for human behaviour.

> The term "drive" should be distinguished from the term "instinct"; the former applies to both animals and humans, and the latter applies primarily to animals. Najātī therefore uses the term "drives" to encompass both the physiological and psychological dimensions of the human personality. Thus, the "religious" drives, for example, is a sub-category of the "psychological" drives. Emotions such as love, and fear are also included as part of the psychological drives. These are subjective states which are recognized by existentialist psychologists but rejected outright by the behaviorists who are only concerned with outwardly observable behaviour. As a Muslim psychologist, Najātī employs the Qur'ān as his guideline, and finds verses in the Qur'ān to support the human drives in modern psychology.

Najātī cites Maslow and supports his distinction between the primary or physiological drives such as hunger and thirst, and the secondary or spiritual drives such as the need for the values of justice and beauty etc. The fulfillment of both these levels of drives leads to the development of the complete personality who has both biological and spiritual needs. Maslow makes it clear that in recent years more and more psychologists are moving away from the "drive" theory of human behaviour, which is more focused on the notions of equilibrium, homeostasis, and tension reduction. Rather, there is a tendency to supplement these concepts with the notions of personality growth and self-perfection. Maslow himself supports the notion of self-actualization or self-realization but he states that it is not a sharply defined concept, but its meaning is more easily "indicated" than defined. Growth to him is not a static concept but something continuous throughout one's life. Growth needs are to be distinguished from "basic", physiological needs such as sex, elimination, sleep, and rest. These are tension-reduction needs when they are satisfied, but when thwarted they lead to frustration and unhappiness. Failure to satisfy basic needs or primary drives could lead to a miserable and psychologically disturbed personality.[9] Freud demonstrated the problem of sexual repression with his Viennese patients who conceived of sexuality as something innately sinful and dirty. He rightfully proved that Stoic or Christian concepts of the evil nature of instincts can produce a mentally unhealthy or neurotic personality, but he wrongfully generalized the problem to all religions. Islam has a positive view of sexuality, indeed, of all drives, if it is directed in a religiously lawful manner. It is in this positive spirit that Najātī projects the Islamic attitude to sexuality and other drives of human behaviour.

The original concept of drives perpetuates a negative attitude to the human personality, concerned only with the gratification of primary drives or needs. Practically all theories of motivation unite in sharing the view that drives are annoying and irritating, and have to be rid of, and all motivated behaviour is directed at getting rid of such discomforts. Pushed to the extreme we wind up with Freud's death instinct.[10] Hence the notions of tension-reduction and needs reduction. Maslow states:

> "Almost always associated with the negative attitude toward the need is the conception that the primary aim of the organism is to get rid of the annoying need and therefore achieve a cessation of tension, an equilibrium, a homeostasis, a state of rest, a lack of pain".[11]

This approach is understandable in animal psychology and behaviorism, which is heavily based on the work of animals, but it is problematic for many psychologists such as Allport and Maslow who criticized it for not being able to account for the human tendency for growth, self-realization, and individuation. Maslow states: "If the motivational life consists essentially of a defensive removal of irritating tensions, and if the only product of tension-reduction is a state of passive waiting for more unwelcome irritations to arise and in their turn, to be dispelled, then how does change, or development or movement or direction come about? Why do people improve? Get wiser? What does zest in living mean?"[12]

The mechanistic concept of a "drive" originated in modern psychology, and Najātī, in his attempt to Islamise the concept, identifies firstly the broader understanding and application of the concept to humans, and secondly, cites the verses from the Qur'ān that support the various drives, both those which we share with animals and those which are unique to us as humans. Najātī also reminds the reader that these drives are not to be obliterated, but to be controlled and directed in a lawful manner, in accordance with Islamic law. The gratification of these drives, even the basic, biological ones, ought to direct man towards God, in submission and gratitude to Him. The appropriate satisfaction of man's basic and higher needs will lead to acceptable, lawful behaviour and to a healthy personality. The inappropriate gratification of drives will cause man to deviate from his *fiṭrah*, from his innate human nature, which is inclined towards devotion to God, and consequently to an unhealthy personality.

TRANSLATION

Drives motivate living organisms to achieve specific goals like satisfying basic biological needs. Modern psychologists distinguish between physiological drives (or primary drives) and psychological drives (or secondary drives). Physiological drives satisfy physical needs, that is, if there is loss or imbalance in the body, they direct human behaviour to compensate for the bodily loss or to restore it to its former state of balance. Psychological drives, however, are mostly acquired through education and socialization.

<u>Physiological Drives</u>

Divine wisdom necessitates that God lodges within every created being certain special qualities that enable it to perform its functions: *"Our Lord is He who gave everything its nature, then guided it"* (20:50). God has placed within both man and animals two types of physiological drives: one is essential for the preservation of the individual, and the other is essential for the perpetuation of the species.

Physiological drives have certain important physiological functions, which attend to the needs of the body when an organic or chemical loss occurs. Their aim is to preserve the life of the body by restoring it to its original state of balance. If there is a loss of homeostatic balance in the body due to lack of nourishment, heat or cold and tiredness, the drives do what they have to do to bring the body to its normal state of balance, i.e., to a state of homeostasis.[13] Thus, the individual will eat, change his clothes or rest, depending on his need or the cause of the homeostatic imbalance. These activities are physiologically based and are not controlled by man's will. Sweat is due to bodily heat and eating is due to hunger. Modern psychologists only discovered this principle of homeostatic balance recently[14], but the Qur'ān referred to it fourteen hundred years ago:

> As for the earth, We have spread it out, laid down upon it firm mountains and caused to grow therein all sorts of fare [plants] (15:19);

> To whom belong the heavens and the earth and He has not taken to Himself a child, and has no associate in this dominion, and He created everything, preordaining it fully[15] (25:2);

...and everything with Him is by measure (13:8).

The Drive of Self-Preservation

The Qur'ān mentions the drive of self-preservation in verses connected with hunger, thirst, tiredness, heat, cold, pain and breathing. God reminds Adam of the paradise, where he was free of the pains of hunger or thirst. God warns him of Satan, who wants to expel him from paradise and bring him to earth to struggle and to toil.

Man hunts and farms to satisfy his hunger and thirst; makes clothes to cover his nakedness in cold weather; and builds houses to protect him from heat and cold:

> *So, we said: "O Adam, this is surely an enemy of you and your wife; so do not let him drive you out of Paradise; for then, you will be miserable. You will certainly not be hungry therein, nor be naked, and you will not thirst therein, nor be exposed to the heat of the sun." But the Devil whispered to him, saying: "O Adam, shall I show you the Tree of Immortality and a kingdom which shall never perish?" (20:117- 120).*

This verse refers to the drives of thirst, hunger, and avoidance of extreme heat and cold. It also refers to the drive for self-perpetuation and the drive for acquisition (*tamalluk*). The drives of self-preservation serve the drive of self-perpetuation; but the drive for acquisition is a psychological drive.

Satan is aware of these drives in his attempt to drive man to seek immortality and permanent ownership. We note above that Adam forgot the divine warning, and disobeyed God by eating from the forbidden fruit.

The following verses refer to the drives of self-preservation such as avoiding heat and cold, and coping with tiredness and pain:

> *Allah has made of your homes places for you to dwell in and has made for you from the hides of cattle light houses to carry on the day of moving and on the day of settling down. And from their wools and their furs and their hair He [has made for you] furnishings and means of enjoyment for a while. Allah has made for you from what He created, sunshades, and from the mountains, places of retreat, and has given you garments to protect you from the heat and coats of mail to protect you while fighting. Thus, He perfects His blessing to you so that you may submit (16:80-81).*

Man turns to the mountains, caves, tents, and houses to protect himself from wild animals and his enemies. Man also protects himself from extreme weather conditions by sitting under the shade of the tree and by making suitable clothes; by making weapons, he protects himself in war from his enemies and from being wounded. Thirst, hunger, and fatigue cannot be unsatisfied for a long period of time, but God promises a reward to those believers who are patient with these unsatisfied drives for His sake:

It is not given to the people of Medina and the desert Arabs around them to stay behind the Apostle of Allah, nor to prefer their own lives to his life for they are afflicted neither by thirst nor fatigue nor hunger in Allah's way, nor do they take a step that upsets the unbelievers, nor inflict a blow on the enemy but a good deed is recorded for them on account of it. Allah does not allow the beneficent to lose their reward (9:120).

Fear and hunger contribute to a miserable personality. The fear of death, the fear of the unknown future and the fear of the enemy contribute to the individual's unhappiness:

We will certainly test you with some fear and hunger and with some loss of property, lives, and crops. Announce the good news to those who endure patiently (2:155).

Allah has given as a parable a town which was safe and secure, and its provision came in abundance from every side; then it denied Allah's blessing, and so Allah made it taste the engulfing hunger and fear on account of what they used to do (16:112).

Let them worship the Lord of this House, "Who has fed them when they were hungry and secured them against fear" (106:3-4).

Man needs rest, and the Qur'ān refers to man's need for work during the day and rest at night. Man wakes up in the morning alert and active, ready to perform the activities of the day with enthusiasm but comes home tired. He sleeps to relieve himself of bodily tensions and psychological fears. These are the favours of God, providing man with relief after a hard day's work:

It is He who created the night for you to rest therein and the day to see. Surely, in this are signs for a people who listen (10:67).

It is He who made the night raiment for you, and sleep a period of rest, and made the day a rising up (25:47).

And it is He who makes you die at night and knows what you do by day. He raises you up in it, until a fixed term is fulfilled; then unto Him is your ultimate return. He will declare to you what you used to do (6:60).

The Drive for the Perpetuation of the Human Species
We have already discussed the instinct for self-preservation, and we turn

now to a brief discussion of the sexual drive and the drive of motherhood.

The Sexual Drive:
The sexual drive plays a vital role in the perpetuation of the human species. It is through this drive that a family is formed, and it is through families that societies and nations are formed. It is through society that the earth is cultivated, that people come to know one another, and that civilization is built through progress in knowledge, industry and culture. God states, *"O mankind, We have created you male and female[16] and made you nations and tribes, so that you may come to know one another. Surely, the noblest of you in Allah's sight is the most pious?"* (49:13). Through a family, the husband lives with his wife in safety and tranquility. The feelings of love and mercy that are nurtured through this relationship lead them to a marital life of harmony and cooperation, creating a sound atmosphere for the care and upbringing of children. Thus, God states:

> *And of His signs is that He created for you, from yourselves, spouses to settle down with and He established friendship and mercy between you (30:21);*

> *O people, fear your Lord who created you from a single soul, and from it He created its mate, and from both. He scattered abroad many men and women; and fear Allah in whose name you appeal to one another and invoke family relationships. Surely Allah is a watcher over you (4:1).*

The Drive of Motherhood:
God, in His wisdom, determined that there be a natural drive in a woman for the perpetuation of the species. She is naturally disposed to bear the burden of pregnancy and birth; she is able to suckle the child, and care for him until he is able to care for himself. She carries this responsibility naturally, without complaint or hesitation. The Qur'ān refers to the mother bearing the pains of pregnancy and birth:

> *We have admonished man regarding his parents; as his mother bore him in weakness upon weakness, weaning him in two years: "Give thanks to Me and to your parents. Unto Me is the ultimate return" (31:14).*

In the narration of the story of Moses (Mūsā), the Qur'ān describes the love and affection of the mother towards her children. She is worried about them, and she is sad when they are not with her. Moses' mother was distressed on account of her son's departure, but her faith in God's providence was strong, and she was able to sustain her inner tranquility:

> *The heart of Moses' mother became vacant; she almost exposed him, but*

for Our fortifying her heart, so that she might be one of the believers (28:10).

When her son returned to her, her sadness disappeared, and she was happy once again:

Then We returned him to his mother, so that she might be comforted and not grieve, and that she might know that Allah's promise is true; but most of them do not know (28:13).

Psychological Drives

Man's personality is unique, and unlike the animal whose behaviour is driven by his instincts alone, man's behaviour is determined by his basic, primary as well as secondary, psychological drives. These psychological drives (*al-dawāfiᶜ al-nafsiyyah*), such as the acquisitive and religious drives, do not have a discernable physiological basis. Whereas most modern psychologists hold that psychological drives are acquired from the social environment, others such as Erich Fromm consider psychological needs such as prestige, belonging, identity and a frame of orientation as intrinsic to humans.[17] Abraham Maslow, who introduced the distinction between primary drives (e.g., hunger, thirst and sex) and secondary (or spiritual) drives (e.g. values of justice, goodness, beauty), regarded the latter type innate in human nature. For both Fromm and Maslow, the fulfillment of the secondary drives is essential for the growth and development of the human personality. We shall place these secondary drives below under the category of psychological drives. We agree with Fromm and Maslow who state that many of these psychological drives are not acquired but innate to human nature. Western psychologists tend to focus on man's physiological dimension and ignore his spiritual aspect, which is the more important aspect from an Islamic point of view. Fromm and Maslow are particularly critical of the behaviorists who tend to focus only on the outward, observable aspect of man. Fromm, for example, identifies the religious drive as something innate in man, and states,

The thesis that the need for a frame of orientation and an object of devotion is rooted in the condition of man's existence seems to be amply verified by the fact of the universal occurrence of religion in history. …the psychoanalyst whose laboratory is the patient and who is a participant observer of another person's thoughts and feelings can add another proof to the fact that the need for some frame of orientation and object of devotion is inherent in man.[18]

The Acquisitive Drive

Man acquires the acquisitive drive from his social and cultural environment. Human experience testifies to man's love for wealth and material possessions, which make him feel safe and secure, and protect him from poverty and powerlessness. The Qur'ān mentions this drive in many places:

> *Attractive to mankind is made the love of the pleasures of women, children, heaps upon heaps of gold and silver, thoroughbred horses, cattle, and cultivable land. Such is the pleasure of this worldly life, but unto Allah is the fairest return (3:14).*

> *And you love wealth ardently (57:20).*

Satan tempted Adam to disobey God by appealing to his acquisitive needs: "But the Devil whispered to him, saying: *"O Adam, shall I show you the Tree of Immortality and a kingdom which will never perish?" (20:120).* Do not misinterpret the expression "a kingdom which will never perish" to mean that the acquisitive drive is instinctive in man. Satan was instrumental in fashioning the presence of a drive which was not previously there. It is therefore acquired, and not instinctive as considered by McDougall[19], whose view is also not supported by modern anthropological and psychological studies.

The Aggressive Drive

The aggressive drive manifests itself in the human personality through aggressive behaviour, physical or verbal. The Qur'ān states:

> *But Satan caused them to fall down from it and be turned out of the bliss they had been in. And We said: "Go down, being enemies one to the other. And you will have in the earth an abode and sustenance for a while" (2:35).*

This verse points to the reality of conflict, hostility and oppression that occurs in a competitive situation with individuals who seek to assert their own desires. When God told the angels about man as the vicegerent on earth, they reacted in an aggressive manner. "Will you place one who will make mischief in it and shed blood?" (2:30). In commenting on this verse, Imam Fakhr-al-Dīn Rāzī states: "It means that the combination of anger, desire and the intellect in the human constitution enables the execution of desire and anger, through which corruption occurs."[20] For example, the first aggression that occurred in the life of mankind is Cain's (Qābil) killing of his brother Abel (Hābil) out of envy.

> *And recite to them in all truth the tale of Adam's two sons, when they*

offered a sacrifice, which was accepted from one, but not accepted from the other. The latter said: "I will surely kill you", the other replied: "Allah accepts only from the God-fearing". "Should you stretch your hand out to kill me, I will not stretch my hand out to kill you; for I fear Allah, Lord of the Worlds." "I only wish that you be charged with my sin and yours and thus be one of the companions of the Fire; and that is the reward of the evildoers". Then, his soul prompted him to kill his brother; and so he killed him and became one of the losers (5:27-30).

Also, with reference to verbal aggression, the Qur'ān states:

O believers, do not take as close friends other than your own people; they will spare no effort to corrupt you and wish to see you suffer. Hatred has already been manifested in what they utter, but what their hearts conceal is greater still. We have made clear Our signs to you if only you understand (3:118).

Is the aggressive drive something instinctive or acquired? Lorenz and Freud hold that it is instinctive, but other psychologists reject this pessimistic view, and argue that it is acquired. Erich Fromm and Abraham Maslow hold that man is innately good and that the aggressive drive is acquired. Modern experimental studies have demonstrated aggressive behaviour in children as the result of the restriction or thwarting of their physical movements. When they are older, they display aggressive behaviour in numerous other situations when faced with obstacles of a social, legal or financial nature. Other studies have contradicted this view and have shown that the child whose physical movements have been thwarted does not necessarily behave in an aggressive manner. Some children seek help in a non-aggressive manner, others adopt a withdrawal strategy or resort to drugs or alcohol. Much has to do with the child's education, his relationship with his parents and whether he had learned to respond to obstacles with aggression or not. Many modern psychologists hold the view that aggression is partly acquired[21], and this conforms to the Qur'ānic view that within human nature there is the readiness for both good and evil: "And guided him onto the two highways" (90:10). The duality of human nature suggests that man is disposed to the two highways, one which is the steep and difficult path of virtue, the other is the easy path of vice. Man chooses between the paths of good or evil, of kindness or aggression to others. At the end of the day, man's response to the obstacles with aggression or withdrawal, or in some other way, depends largely on his upbringing and social-cultural environment.

The Competitive Drive
The competitive drive is acquired through education, which approves of

certain types of competition, be it economic, political or intellectual, i.e., they correspond to what society considers to be valuable. The Qur'ān encourages man to compete in piety (*taqwā*) and good deeds. He is urged to adhere to profound human values and to follow the Divinely designed way of life, whether in his relationship with God, his family, or his society. Competition is directed at forgiveness and pleasure of God, and final entry into paradise. God refers to the competitive drive in the following verses:

Witnessed by those well-favoured. The pious are indeed in bliss; Upon couches gazing round. You will recognize in their faces the glow of bliss; They are given to drink a seal of wine; Whose seal is musk. Over that, let the competitors compete (83:22-26).

To everyone there is a direction towards which he turns. So, hasten to do the good works. Wherever you are, Allah will bring you all together. Surely Allah has power over all things (2:148).

Vie with one another unto forgiveness from your Lord and a garden the breadth whereof is like the breadth of the heavens and earth; it has been prepared for those who believe in Allah and His messengers. That is Allah's bounty, which He confers upon whoever He pleases. And Allah's is the great bounty (57:22).

The Religious Drive

The religious drive is instinctive; deep within man's soul is something that impels him to reflect on God and His creation, and to worship Him and seek his help in difficult times. A sense of God's protection and care make man feel secure and tranquil. This is clearly demonstrated in human nature throughout history. Although different societies have different conceptions of God and modes of worship, they have a common concern for religion and worship of God, which testify to the religious drive in all men. It is a drive that lies deep within the human soul. The following verses of the Qur'ān refer to the innate religious drive in man:

So, set your face towards religion uprightly. It is the original nature according to which Allah fashioned mankind. There is no altering of Allah's creation. That is the true religion; but most men do not know (30:30).

And [remember] when your Lord brought forth from the loins of the Children of Adam their posterity and made them testify against themselves. [He said]: "Am I not your Lord?" They said: "Yes, we testify," [This] lest you should say on the Day of Resurrection: "We were in fact unaware of this" (7:172).

The second verse makes clear that man, before his creation on earth, testified about himself in acknowledging God as his Creator. Thus, on the Day of Judgement, he cannot say that he was unaware of this. It shows that in human nature there lies an instinctive preparedness to know God and His Oneness. Therefore, knowledge and recognition of God is connected with fiṭrah (original innate nature). This recognition was present from the very beginning in the deepest recesses of man's spirit (*rūḥ*). However, since man's spirit has been encapsulated by his body, he has forgotten God and his original recognition of God. Man needs to awaken this unconscious recognition of God to come to know God. He can attain this knowledge of God by coming to know his true self. One of the ways of coming to know his true self is when man is faced with life-threatening situations.[22] Thus, God states:

It is He who makes your journey on land and on sea; so that when you are in the ships and they sail with them driven by a fair wind, and they rejoice in it, a stormy wind comes upon them and waves surge over them from every side, and they think that they are being overwhelmed. Then they call upon Allah, professing submission to Him sincerely: "If You save us from this, we shall be truly thankful" (10:22).

The Unconscious Drives and the Conflict Between Drives

Drives that are socially unacceptable are suppressed within the unconscious and they can be expressed in the form of slips of the tongue and speech errors. The Qur'ān refers to such unconscious drives and man's attempt to conceal them in the following verse:

Or do those whose hearts is a sickness think that Allah will not bring their rancours to light? Had We wished, We would have shown them to you, so that you might know them by their mark. And you shall surely know them by their distorted speech. Allah knows your works (47:29-30).

This verse indicates that the Qur'ān revealed the power of the unconscious long before Freud, who established his school of psychoanalysis as recent as a hundred years ago. The conflict of drives occurs when an individual finds himself hesitant, helpless, or confused in the face of two opposing drives. The Qur'ān makes mention of these individuals who face such psychological conflict in the context of faith. They are uncertain and stand mid-way between belief and unbelief. God states:

Say: "Shall we call, besides Allah, on what neither profits nor harms us, and turn on our heels after Allah has guided us?" [We shall then be] like one who, being tempted by the devils in the land, is bewildered though he has friends who call him to guidance [saying]: "Come to us." Say: "Guidance from Allah is the true guidance. And we are commanded to submit to the Lord of the Worlds". (6:71)

This verse refers to a psychological conflict in the individual who is torn between the demands of Satan and the demands of believers. Note the following verse pertaining to the psychological effect of doubt.

Those who believe in Allah and the Last Day do not ask you for [exemption from] fighting in the way of Allah with their wealth and lives. Allah knows well the righteous (9:44);

Vacillating between the two, inclining neither to these nor to those; and whomever Allah leads astray, you will not find him a way out (4:143).

Control of Drives

The satisfaction of basic drives is essential for human survival; it is natural and therefore does not violate human nature, if it remains within the limits prescribed of Islamic Law (*Sharīʿah*). Islam therefore does not support the repression of man's natural drives but encourages their control and canalization[23] within prescribed limits to benefit the individual and the society.

A distinction should be made between desisting from desire and repressing desire. Desisting from desire is a conscious refusal to satisfy desires in unacceptable situations. It does not involve a denial of these desires, considering them impure, which implies repression of desire. It also involves an attempt to remove it entirely from one's consciousness, which could create feelings of guilt and anxiety.

Eventually, repression of desire affects the unconscious level. It [i.e., the desire] is removed from consciousness, and becomes stored in the unconscious, manifesting itself in many forms of disturbed behaviour.

The Qur'ān calls for the control and canalization of desires within prescribed limits. The individual should control his instincts, not the instincts to control him. The Qur'ān encourages the satisfaction of physiological drives in a lawful manner:

O people, eat from the earth lawful and pleasant produce, and do not follow in Satan's footsteps; for he is a manifest enemy of yours (2:68).

O believers, wine, gambling, idols and divining arrows are an abomination of the Devil's doing; so avoid them that perchance you may prosper! The Devil only wishes to stir up enmity and hatred among you, through wine and gambling, and keep you away from remembering Allah and from prayer. Will you not desist, then? (50:90-91).

If you fear that you cannot deal justly with the orphans, then marry such of the women as appeal to you, two, three or four; but if you fear that you cannot be equitable, then only one, or what your right hands own. That is more likely to enable you to avoid unfairness (4:2).

Your women are a tillage to you. So, get to your tillage whenever you like (2:23).

The above verses do not call for the negation or repression of the sexual drive, nor for their unlimited satisfaction, but advocates their satisfaction in a properly regulated and lawful manner.[24] The regulation of drives has two aspects to it: the one is to satisfy drives within the context of Islamic law; the other is not to go to extremes in the satisfaction of these drives. Concerning the first aspect, for example, Islam prohibits the satisfaction of hunger and thirst with unlawful food and drink. It also prohibits the consumption of foods that are harmful to the body, such as wine and swine. Islam also makes unlawful the satisfaction of the sexual instinct outside marriage. God has created male and female to satisfy the sexual drive within marriage, to start a family and to find stability and tranquility within marriage, as God states:

And of His signs is that He created for you, from yourselves, spouses to settle down with and He established friendship and mercy between you. (30:21)

However, if circumstances do not permit a person to marry, then he is required to be chaste and to control his sexual urges until his conditions have improved: "Let those who do not find the means to marry be abstinent, till Allah enriches them from His bounty" (24:33). The Qur'ān urges man to live in a society that will help him control his sexual instincts, and not stir them. Men and women are therefore required to lower their gaze and to dress modestly. Fasting and physical exercises will also help in the curbing of the sexual appetite (see 24:30- 31). The free intermingling of mature males and females are prohibited in Islam. The law helps the individual to control his sexual passions (see 24:58-59).

The second point is to be moderate in the satisfaction of drives. Medical research has proven that that extremity in eating, drinking and rest can be harmful to human health. God prohibits greed in the following verse:

O Children of Adam, put on your finery at every place of prayer. Eat and drink but do not be prodigal, He does not like the prodigal (7:31)

This verse does not refer only to moderation in eating and drinking, but to all physiological drives. Perhaps the mention of only these two drives brings us back to the point about the importance of these drives for self-preservation and man's tendency to be extravagant with respect to them.

The Qur'ān also refers to psychological drives such as the acquisitive and aggressive drives. Concerning the latter, it prohibits people from being aggressive, physically, or verbally: "Help one another in righteousness and piety, but not in sin and aggression" (5:2).[24] The Qur'ān also calls man to control his acquisitive drive. It prohibits interest, exploitation, and theft, and prescribes charity and *zakāh* (alms)[25] In general, the Qur'ān calls man to control his drives and his desires in a moderate manner and lawfully in accordance with Islamic law. Man should not be a slave of his desires (*nafs*), the source of his physiological and lower psychological drives, but should have full control over them. Thus, God states:

> *Then, as to him who has transgressed, and preferred the present life; Hell is indeed the refuge. But as to him who fears the station of his Lord, and forbid s his soul from passion; then Paradise is the refuge (79:37-41).*

The Qur'ān calls upon man to balance his life and satisfy both the demands of his body that seeks satisfaction in its daily life and the soul (*rūḥ*) that longs for its Creator and the happiness of the Hereafter. It is man's duty to satisfy both these physiological and spiritual drives to fulfill the divine mission that God has decreed for him in this world. By so doing, he will come to acknowledge God as his Creator and worship Him alone, and he will earn God's forgiveness and pleasure in the Hereafter. If man can meet the demands of this world as well as the demands of the Hereafter, then he will be liberated from psychological conflicts and live a life of security, tranquility, and happiness, as God states:

> *But seek, thanks to what Allah gave you, the Hereafter, and do not forget your portion of the here below (28:77).*

> *O believers, let not your possessions or children distract you from the remembrance of Allah. Whoever does that-those are the real losers (63:9).*

These verses make it clear that Islam does not stand for monasticism: it seeks to satisfy both man's physical and spiritual needs. The satisfaction of physical needs is not an end in itself; rather, it is a means to attain a higher, more lasting goal of eternal happiness in the Hereafter. Thus, in the verses below, the Qur'ān makes mention of the satisfaction of one's worldly, physical needs. This is followed by a reminder that the fear of

God is better than the mere preoccupation with the physiological and psychological drives that pertain to this world. It is only through being god-fearing (*taqwā*) that man will realize God's pleasure and the happiness in the Hereafter. This realization will help him control his drives and instincts, and direct their satisfaction in a lawful manner and in moderation:

> *Attractive to mankind is made the love of the pleasures of women, children, heaps upon heaps of gold and silver, thoroughbred horses, cattle, and cultivable land. Such is the pleasure of this worldly life, but unto Allah is the fairest return. Say: Shall I tell you about something better than all that? For those who are God-fearing, from their Lord are gardens beneath which rivers flow, and in which they abide forever [along with] purified spouses and Allah's good pleasure. Allah sees His servants well! (3:14-15).*

> *The earthly life is nothing but sport and amusement, and the world to come is surely better for those who are God-fearing. Do you not understand? (6:32).*

These verses confirm that man's preoccupation with the satisfaction of his lower drives and desires in preference to the life Hereafter will cause him to forget his Creator; but if man does not allow his worldly life to divert him from worshipping God and doing good deeds, he will be in full control of his drives and desires and will thereby gain God's pleasure and forgiveness.

The Deviation of Drives

The phrase "the deviation of drives" actually means "the deviation from the true purpose of the drives". In other words, when a person seeks the satisfaction of his drives for their own sake in an immoderate and unlawful manner, then he has deviated from his true purpose. But if he controls his lower drives he will not be deviating from his true purpose. The most obstinate of all drives is the sexual drive. The Qur'ān makes mention of how the sexual drive was corrupted in the people of Lot:

> *And [remember] Lot when he said to his people: "Do you commit indecencies which no one in the whole world committed before you? You approach men instead of women lustfully; you are rather a people given to excess. (7:80-81).*

Of the psychological drives, the most familiar one is the acquisitive drive, which stems from man's excessive love for wealth. Wealth is a trust from God, which man is required to spend in a lawful manner in the path of God and for His pleasure. It is also important for the cultivation of the land, the building of civilization and for human progress. For some people, the pursuit of wealth becomes an end in itself; they hoard it and do not help others with it in the way of God. The immoderate satisfaction of these drives and man's inability to control them diverts man from his true goal, which is self-preservation and welfare for the society. Immoderate and inappropriate anger, for example, makes a person oppressive and violent towards others. Extremity with respect to the competitive drive makes a person obsessed with power and domination. Excessive rest, inactivity and sloth make a person irresponsible, uncooperative, and unhelpful. All these extremities will lead to deviation, except for the middle path, which is the best way.

God states: "And those who, when they spend, do not squander or stint, but choose a middle course between that" (25:67); Also, "Do not keep your hand chained to your neck, nor spread it out fully. Lest you sit around condemned and reduced to poverty" (17:29).

NOTES

1. Besides holding positions mentioned in the "List of Contributors", he is also the translator of several works of Sigmund Freud into Arabic.
2. This article comes from a chapter in Najātī's book, *al- Qur'ān wa-'ilm al-nafs*. See 'Dawāfic al-Sulūk fi al-Qur'ān' in *al-Qur'ān wa-cilm al-nafs* (Cairo: Dār ul-Shurūq, 1989), pp. 23-65.
3. T. Takuma, 'Personality' in *Encyclopedia of Psychology*, H. J. Eysenck (ed.) et al, Vol 2, p. 779.
4. T. Takuma, 'Personality' in *Encyclopedia of Psychology*, H. J. Eysenck (ed.) et al, Vol 2, p. 779.
5. R.C. Bolless, 'Drives' in *Encyclopedia of Psychology*, H. J. Eysenck (ed.) et al, Vol 1, p. 290f.
6. The translator took the liberty of providing a free translation for the sake of brevity and readability. In places where the author cited several verses from the Qur'ān to substantiate a particular point, the translator has reduced the number of verses. For the translation of Qur'ānic verses, he used Majid Fakhry, The Qur'ān: *A Modern English Version* (London, 1997).
7. Ibid, p. 290f.
8. T. Takuma, 'Personality' in *Encyclopedia of Psychology*, H. J. Eysenck (ed.) et al, Vol 2, p. 780.
9. A. Maslow, *Toward a Psychology of Being* (Princeton: Princeton University Press, 1962), pp. 19-25.
10. Ibid, p. 27.
11. Ibid, p. 27.
12. Ibid, p. 27.

13. The term 'homeostasis' was used by the American physiologist Cannon (1932) to characterise the totality of effects responsible for maintaining a certain physiological constancy (e.g. Body temperature, blood sugar). Trans. note.

14. W.B. Cannon, *The Wisdom of the Body* (New York: Norton, 1932).

15. That is, 'He created everything according to the wisdom He intended'; see Al-Qurtub – ī, Abu Abdullah Muhammad ibn Ahmad al-Ansāri, *al-Jāmiʿu li al-Ahkām al-Qur'ān* (Cairo, 1967), vol., 13, p. 3.

16. The idea of the creation of pairs pertains not only to humans but to the whole of creation; compare the chapter 36, verse 36. Note Quṭb's commentary on this verse, see Muhammad Quṭb, *Dirāsāt fī al-nafs al-insāniyyah* (Beirut: Dar al-Shur'q, 1979), pp. 195-196.

17. G. Lindzey, C.S. Hall and R. F. Thompson, R. F., Psychology (New York: Worth, 1976), p. 360; cf. Erich Fromm, *al-Dīn wa-tahlīl al-nafsī*, trans. Fuad Kāmil, (Cairo: Maktaba G h ā r i b, 1977). [cf. Erich Fromm, Psychoanalysis and Religion, New Haven and London, 1950.

18. Erich Fromm, *Psychoanalysis and Religion* (New Haven and London, 1976), p. 27.

19. Fakhrudin Muhammad ibn ᶜUmar al-Rāzī *Kitāb al-Nafs wa al-rūh wa-sharhu qawāmuhā*, ed. Muhammad Husayn al-Macsūmī,(Cairo, n.d.), p. 4.

20. Charles G. Morris, *Psychology: An Introduction* (Englewood Cliffs, New Jersey, 1979), pp. 368-370.

21. Al-Bāhī al-Khoulī, *Adam al-Yūhī Salām, Falsafatu Taqwīm al-Insān wa Khilāfātuhu* (Cairo: Maktabah Wahba, 1974), p. 176.

22. Canalization refers to the consolidation of certain kinds of behaviour and specifically the definite means of drive satisfaction from among several initial possible choices.

23. Muhammad Quṭb, *al-Insān Bayna al-Mādiyyah wa al-Islām* (Cairo: ᶜIsā al-Bābi al-Halabī wa-shurakā'uhu,1960), pp. 84-91; cf M. Quṭb, *Manhaj al-Tarbiyyah al-Islāmiyyah* (Beirut: Dār al Shurūq, n.d.), pp. 128-129; p. 140.

24. Cf. Q. 33: 58; 58:9; 6: 151; 49: 9-11

25. Cf. Q. 9: 34 and 35, 3: 80, 64: 16; 63: 10; 57:7

13

The Concept of Personality In Islam

RASHID HAMID

The concept of personality is clearly the heartbeat of psychology and continues to present the contemporary psychologist with the challenge of self-discovery both in an individual and collective sense. As a construct, personality is used interchangeably with terms like the self, character, soul, and particular behaviors of an individual. When viewed singularly, these terms are insufficient in defining that aspect of our being we call personality. The common thread in numerous definitions of personality is a reference to the distinctive characteristics of an individual that make her or him unique from others. The "others" may be different species, socio-cultural groups, or another person. The Arabic word for psychology, *nafsanīyya*, indicates that the focus of the discipline is on the study of the self (*nafs*)—what the individual is, what he has been, and what he can become. The relative "causes" of personality are as numerous as the multi-faceted nature of human experience. The purpose of this presentation is to provide the reader with what I believe to be the fundamental and essential constructs included in the Islamic concept of personality. The word *shakhsiyyah* refers to the distinctive character, identity, and way of life of a person (*shakhs*). The related term *mushākhi* includes the influences or factors leading something to its distinctive characteristics. The *major* or *universal* factors contributing to unique characteristics of any person are shared by all humans. These factors are discussed below.

PERSONALITY: UNIVERSAL CHARACTERISTICS

As revealed in the Arabic lexical structure of the terms cited above, it would be inappropriate to speak of non-human species as having "personality". It is important to know which characteristics distinguish mankind from other species and to acknowledge that such characteristics cannot be understood or explained in biological/reductionist terms.

MAN: A SPECIAL CREATION

The most important characteristic of man is that he is a special creature—his nature being linked to the Divine and Eternal. Man is Allah's vicegerent on earth and his inner self can only be properly understood in this context.

> *And when thy Lord said to the angels: "Lo! I am about to place a vicegerent in the earth," they said: "Will thou place therein one who will do mischief and shed blood, while we hymn Thy Praise and Glorify Thee?" He said: "Surely, I know that which you know not". (2:30)*

> *And (remember) when thy Lord said into the angels: "Lo! I am creating a mortal out of potter's clay (mud). Lo, when I have made him and breathed into him of My Spirit, do you fall down prostrating yourselves to him". (5:28-29)*

The angels were commanded to prostrate to man in that he is to come into the knowledge of the natural laws and harness them in obeisance to God. Man's growth and activity in this world are not without purpose.

> *I have created the jinns and the humans for the sole purpose of worshipping Me. (51:56)*

On this foundation rest all subsequent approaches to the study of personality. To deny the origin and purpose of humanity is to deny the fundamental distinctive characteristics of mankind. On this point, I repeat that:

> Because of ignoring the infinite spiritual qualities within the human being and relegating inquiries about them to philosophers and theologians, psychology (as defined in the West), has presented a concept of human personality devoid of a soul, and absolved of spiritual faith and ambition and an integrated well-being.[1]

Most of the texts published in psychology and the sciences of man continue to state that mankind is a descendent of apes despite the certain truth as revealed in the authentic scriptures. The authors of one text on personality said:

> Australopithecus, the first step in human evolution, was a small, apelike creature, a vegetarian living in wooded areas and limited to near-tropical regions

…Australopithecines and the millions of humans who followed them migrated in response to environmental demands.[2]

In response to the Divine origin of mankind, the author of a new biology text tailored for social science students suggested that the concept of special creation is contrary to rational scientific inquiry.

> Such a concept of special creation by a supernatural force is outside the realm of science because it is simply not possible to test its validity by scientific methods…The scientist, on the other hand, must seek a rational explanation that will be consistent with what is known about natural forces and with established scientific principles.[3]

Representing the mainstream thought in Western philosophies of knowledge, this author's remarks clearly reflect an awareness of what constitutes science and a constricted knowledge of natural law (i.e., Divine law). His comments are consistent with the contrived segmentation of life into "sacred and secular realms" and reflect a "spiritual tone-deafness" prevalent in secularized materialistic cultures. Without belabouring the issue, I now proceed from this point with the diagnosis of this view in the Qur'ān:

> *This is because they believed then disbelieved, therefore their hearts are sealed so that they do not understand. (63:3)*

LIMITED FREE WILL

Man is created with a limited free will to use to his advantage or detriment. To the extent that his volitional acts are consistent with his true nature, man makes psycho-spiritual progress. When he intentionally deviates from Divine Law, man retards and stunts his own inner growth.

> *And, if thy Lord willed, all who are in the earth would have believed. Would you (O Muhammad) compel men until they are believers? It is not for any to believe except by the permission of Allah. He has sent uncleanness upon those who have no common sense. (10:99-100)*

Common sense, being essential for healthy personality development, refers to the fundamental inherent ability to discern what the correct course of action should be in a given situation, independent of conflicting majority behavior, expectations and standards.

Common sense is not necessarily what is commonly practice by society.

> *Were you to follow the common practices of those on earth, they will lead you away from the way of God. They follow nothing but conjecture [empty talk— author's note]: they do nothing but lie. (6:116)*

In verse 10:99-100, we are reminded that (1) no individual can force another to privately accept the truth and (2) man's free will is a test from Allah. The individual's "degrees of freedom" lies within a finite range of possibilities and potentials. Whatever one chooses to believe, to do or become should be grounded in the knowledge of the truth. Since man's knowledge is relative and finite, he should rely on the perfect guidance of God in regulating his affairs and promoting self-development. The critical importance of this Universal Criterion for human action is discussed in more detail later.

With the exception of involuntary reflex actions, most human behavior is *functionally autonomous*.[4] That is, the behavior is free of the initial precipitating conditions which led to its emergence. Humans retain conscious control over whether most of their behavior is repeated. Man can also modify the conditions in which certain behaviors take place. For example, an infant may initially drink water to satisfy the thirst drive, but the child soon begins to drink water for the sake of it or some other unrelated motive (i.e., imitation of parent's behavior). In every situation, the individual has a choice between alternative courses of action even if one of them involves no activity. Personality and behavior are not solely determined by forces and influences beyond the control of the individual.

A frequent practice among lawyers in Western societies dating back to the tenth century (C.E.) is to plead that an individual accused of a serious violent crime "behaved under duress", "was temporarily insane", "was a victim of a neurotic past" or "was in a fit of passion and rage". The underlying psychological assumption in each case is that the accused was not in control of him- or herself. However, often it is more accurate and truthful to infer that the accused did not intend to choose to control himself. Humans are held responsible for their willful actions.

> *Say (O Muhammad): "Shall I seek for my Cherisher other than Allah when He is the Cherisher of all things that exist? Every soul draws the consequences of its own acts on none but itself: no bearer of burdens can bear the burden of another. Your goal in the end is toward Allah. He will tell you the truth about the matters wherein you disputed." (6:164)*

The significance of a limited-free will in personality development is further emphasized in the following verse:

> *Surely Allah does not change the condition in which a people are in until*

they change that which is in themselves. (13:11)

The outer characteristic conditions, as reflected in the quality of life, mirror the inner characteristics of people. This same principle holds true for the individual who has been given the capacity to change himself. Instead of passively waiting for something to happen, the individual must take some initiative in changing his values and behaviors to foster improvement.

Sheikh Jaafar Idris (1977) has aptly summarized the relationship between the Will of Allah and human freedom.

> Man cannot do anything against the Will of God, but God has willed to give him the freedom to choose and the power to realize some of his intentions even if they go against the Guidance given by God. One of the important areas on which God gave man to act is his internal state. But since much of what happens to man depends upon what kind of internal state he has, man can be said to be largely responsible for his destiny.[5]

HIGHER FACULTIES AND MORAL CONSCIENCE

Man has been granted additional faculties which enable him to (1) gain knowledge of the natural laws of creation, (2) distinguish between right and wrong, and (3) exercise his free will.

> *Did we not assign unto him two eyes and a tongue and two lips and guide him to the parting of the mountain ways! But he has not attempted the Ascent. (90:8-11)*

> *By the soul, and the proportion and order given to it and to its enlightenment as to its wrongs and its rights. (91:7-8)*

> *Read! And thy Lord is Most Gracious, who taught by the pen, taught man that which he knew not. (96:3-5)*

Man's intelligence and his capacity for speech and language also enable him to share his thoughts, ideas and discoveries with contemporaries and future generations. By means of his imagination, man can transcend the physical dimension of time/space and peer into his past and probable future. He has been granted the faculty of insight into which he can become aware of his own psychological and spiritual characteristics. Man's insight and intelligence is coupled with a personal sense of self-surveillance or moral Conscience. The self-reproaching "spirit" (*al-nafs al-lawwāmmah*) is the inner counselor, which enjoins and leads to righteousness and warns against evil. Yet the individual has been given the power to even ignore his moral conscience. The person who is devoid of moral consciousness *and* behavior is not intelligent irrespective of his proficiency in abstract reasoning and logic, and the use of the empirical method.

Surely, these higher faculties and qualities in man point to a higher purpose and destiny for him, provided he chooses to aspire toward them. If he foolishly ignores the guidance of God, he regresses to the lowest of states and whatever remains of a healthy personality in him is from the mercy of God.

> *We have indeed created man in the best of molds, then do we abase him (to be) the lowest of the low, except those who believe and do good; and theirs is a reward unfailing (95:4-6)*

THE ORIGINAL HUMAN NATURE (FIṬRAH AL INSAN)

Human beings are born in a state of obedience and submission to divine law as revealed in the Qur'ān:

> *So set thy purpose (O Muhammad) for religion (a way of life) as a man who is by nature upright (hanīfah)—the nature of man into which Allah created (him). There is no altering (the law of) Allah's creation. That is the right religion, but most know me not. (30:30)*

The nature (*al-fiṭrah*) of uprightness put in man by Allah is characterized by an inclination to what is good and pure, the desire to keep the commandments of Allah and submission to His will. An example of this goodly nature is seen in the conduct of the Prophet Muhammad (SAS) during the Ascension (*Miᶜrāj*) as narrated on the authority of Abū Huraira. The Prophet Muhammad (SAS) was offered two drinking vessels, one containing milk and the other wine. The Prophet (SAS) chose the milk. The angel said to him: "You have been guided on *al-fiṭrah* or you have attained *al-fiṭrah*; Had you selected wine, your *Ummah* would have been misled." Although born in *al-fiṭrah,* man nevertheless, is weak in that he may choose to follow inclinations of the evil self (*al-nafs al-ammārah*) in opposition to his true nature. Again, we are reminded of the importance of free-will and personal responsibility in molding character and behavior. Depending on whether the moral conscience is heard, the individual may choose what is best for him or what is detrimental to him. One cannot separate the moral conscience from the nature of uprightness. Carl Jung, an imminent psychoanalyst who recognized the importance of religion and the moral conscience in personality development, said:

> Conscience, and particularly bad conscience, can be a gift from heaven; a genuine grace, if used as a superior self-criticism. Self-criticism, as an introspective discriminating activity, is indispensable to any attempt to understand one's own psychology.[6]

Consistent with man's true nature, Jung described man as "homo religios"[7] In sharp contrast to the Islamic concept of man's true nature, the Judeo-Christian perspective presumes that humans are "born in sin". They inherit the sins of their original forebear, Adam (AS). It is not uncommon to find people referring to someone as being "a born criminal" or "coming from a bad seed", yet the contrived concept of "original sin" is totally alien to Islam. Personality development in Islam does not proceed from a point of self-negation and rejection. It may be that the notion of "original sin" constitutes part of the psychological sediment underlying collective existential anxiety and inner turmoil in Judeo-Christian culture. Many people are not fully cognizant of the virtuous qualities of the true human nature. If they were, such serious problems as aggression, violence, and socio-ethnic conflict might be more readily solved.

PERSONALITY: PARTICULAR INDIVIDUAL CHARACTERISTICS

In addition to the universal characteristics shared by the whole of humanity, each person has certain qualities or attributes that clearly distinguish them from anyone else. It is because of their uniqueness to the individual that such characteristics can only be described in general terms. One sign of the uniqueness of individual is the fingerprint or fingertip as described in the Qur'ān.

Nay, We are able to put together in perfect order the very tips of his fingers. (75:4)

The configuration of the fingerprint of each human being is not shared with any other person, despite the immense number of people who are living and have lived on the earth. The fingerprint is the most accurate means of identifying a person in the absence of all other information. Even monozygotic twins fertilized from the same egg do not have the same fingerprint. Allah (SWT) tells us that He can reassemble our forms down to the most intricate, unique detail. The pattern of the fingerprint as a phenotype reflects a unique mixture or constellation of genotypic characteristics in each person. By analogy, we should see that, like the physical fingerprint, each individual is a unique personality in a universe of personalities. Expressing the same idea in different words, Seyyed Hossein Nasr notes:

The uniqueness of the temperament of each individual indicates that each microcosm is a world of its own, not identical with any other microcosm. Yet, the repetition of the same basic humors in each constitution bears out the fact that each microcosm presents a morphological resemblance to other microcosms.[8]

Inner growth is not entirely the same for everyone in as much as each person is a unique microcosm in his or her own right. Individuals also have particular goals in life that should all be subsumed under the universal goal of obeisance to Allah.

Surely your effort is dispersed (toward diverse ends). As for him who gives and is dutiful toward Allah and believes in (and practices) good deeds; surely, We will ease his way unto the state of ease. (92:4-7)

This means, in no uncertain terms, that individual development should take place in the light of the divinely ordained paradigm of life for mankind. In the absence of this paradigm, there is no real character development.

But as for him who is a miser and regards himself as independent (self-sufficient), and does not practice good deeds; surely, We will ease his way into adversity (difficulty). (92:8-10)

DEVELOPMENT OF PERSONALITY

The theme of personality development in Islam can be construed in the context of the term (*fasᶜala*) which means: "to separate, wean or evolved towards completion." Another term used in the Qur'ān (*aṭwārā*) points out that this evolution or development takes place in stages or phases.

What ails you that you place not your hope in Allah, when it is He that created you in diverse stages. (71:14)

The stages are compared to the growth of the plants and foliage as reflected in the term (*nabātā*).

And Allah has caused you to grow (anbātakum) from the earth like other growth (nabātā) (71:17)

The stages in the prenatal physical development of man identified in the Qur'ān are: (1) lodgment in the earth, (2) quintessence in male spermatozoa and female egg, (3) placement in the mother's womb, and (4) formation of the biological form.

Man, We did create from a quintessence of clay; then We placed him as a drop of sperm in a place of rest, firmly fixed; then We made the sperm into a clot of congealed blood; then of that clot We made a (fetus) lump;

*then We made out of that lump bones and clothed the bones with flesh;
then We developed out of it another creature. So blessed be Allah, the
best to create. (23:14)*

Following birth, each person physically matures, experiences death, and
will be raised from the dead on the Last Day.

*After that (birth), at length, you will die. Again, on the Day of Judgment
will you be raised up. (23:15-16)*

Again, we note that at a critical point (known only by Allah) in this prenatal
development man becomes "another creature"—a higher being into whom
Allah has breathed His Spirit and granted higher faculties.

*But He fashioned him in due proportion and breathed into him something
of His spirit. And He gave you the faculties of hearing and sight and
feeling (and understanding): Little thanks do you give! (32:9)*

The development of personality can be essentially regarded as the
development of man's higher nature as a psycho-spiritual being.
Analogues but not identical to physical development, psycho-spiritual
growth also takes place in stages.

That you shall journey from plane to plane. (ṭabaqan°an ṭabaq) (84:19)

Personality development is not equivalent to intellectual achievement in
the peripheral sense of the individual being regarded as a "smart person"
who excels in perceptual-cognitive tasks, academic pursuits, and the
retention of facts. Sheikh Muhammad Quṭb observes that the Islamic
concept of personality development also reflected in the word (*tazkiyyah*),

… means development of the good side of man and its promotion, to the
end of making it fulfill God's description of His creation in the best of
forms…

Islamic development, or growth is equally fulfilled by the disciplining of
the self (*nafs*) which is "capable of evil", by enabling it to master its
affections and passions.[9]

Self-discipline and weaning away from blame-worthy
characteristics constitute the "ascent" or "path that is steep" described in
Surah al-Balad (10-18). Related but not identical concepts have been
forwarded by some Western psychologists. For example, Carl Rogers
characterizes this as the growth of "becoming a person",[10] while Abraham
Maslow describes it as "self-actualization".[11] There is mutual agreement

among Islamic psychologists and self-theorists in the Western tradition that self-development involves freeing oneself from egocentric, defensive and counter-productive attitudes, and behavior. Yet, the Islamic concept of self-development, in contrast to most Western self-theories, emphasizes the importance of inculcating noble, spiritually dynamic qualities in the self to please Allah.

> *But those will prosper who purify (tazakkā) themselves and glorify the name of their Guardian-Lord and lift their hearts in prayer. (87:14-15)*

> *Truly he succeeds that purifies (zakkāhā) his (soul), and he fails that corrupts it (91:9)*

> *Those who spend their wealth for increase in self-purification (yatazakkā) and have in their minds no favor from anyone for which a reward is expected in return, but only the desire to seek for the Countenance of their Lord Most High. (92:18-20)*

The advance towards *tazkiyyah al-naf*s is not without effort and struggle. This constructive struggle involves confrontation with the weaknesses in human nature with an eye towards overcoming them. Yet often, the individual's struggle to achieve this noble objective is burdened by man's lack of knowledge of himself and creation, and he is often foolish to himself.

> *The prayer that man should make for good, he makes for evil; for man is given to hasty deeds. (17:11)*

> *God does wish to lighten your (difficulties): for man was created weak (in flesh). (4:28)*

> *Truly man was created very impatient; fretful when evil touches him; and niggard when good reaches him. (17:19-21)*

An additional dimension of personality development in Islam is reflected in the phrase "*Tajdīd-ul-nafs*", meaning renewal, restoration, rejuvenation, regeneration, and to refurbish. All these terms imply some type of return to a previous state or condition. Dawud Rosser-Owen points out that *tajdīd:*

> …is the process of renewal of the pristine form of Islam and *fiṭrah* within the individual and his close associates. The *mujaddid* (renewal) is the *imām* of the body namely the *qalb* (heart), acting under direction.[12]

When viewed from this perspective, the process of self-purification or personality development represent a conscious, determined, and sincere effort on the part of man to advance his "good side"– *al-fiṭrah*. This advance is a return to *Hanīfah* "the nature of man as Allah created him", in harmony with divine law. The self which is moving away from this advance or return is not identical to the self that is returning or advancing. The self which has returned may also be called *nafs mujaddad*—the restored and rejuvenated self. The guidelines underlying this whole process of *tajdīd-ul-nafs* are embodied in the Shariah of Islam.

Three stages of personality development are described in the Qur'ān. They are: (1) *al-nafs al-ammārah*—the self-prone to evil, impelling, headstrong, and passionate; (2) *al-nafs al-lawwāmmah*—the self-reproaching spirit which resists and warns against evil, and desires to please Allah; and (3) *al-nafs-al-mutma'innah*—the righteous soul in complete rest and satisfaction. The state of rest and satisfaction does not signal an end to personality development. In fact, it represents a soul at peace with itself because the person has inwardly submitted to God and loves to serve him. The inner growth continues throughout life.

> *Nor do I absolve myself (of blame); the human soul is certainly prone to evil, my Lord bestows His mercy; but surely my Lord is oft-forgiving, Most Merciful. (12:53)*

> *And I do call to witness the Self-Reproaching Spirit (which warns against evil). (75:2)*

> *(To the righteous soul it will be said:) "O soul in complete rest and satisfaction, come back to thy Lord, well pleased, and well pleasing unto Him." (89:27-28).*

The second stage, according to A. Yusuf Ali is regarded as a "faculty"[13] in Western psychology and is not considered critical in personality development. The moral conscience is more often described as a "superego" reflecting the prohibitions of one's culture. In formulating the concept of a "superego", Freud[14] wanted to de-emphasize the importance of God-consciousness in personality development. This desire to de-emphasize religion in his theory of personality was a reflection of Freud's own personal conflicts and the collective anxieties and contradictions experienced by many in Victorian Judeo-Christian society. Carl Jung, taking issue with Freud on this point, later said:

> The individual who is not anchored in God can offer no resistance of his own resources to the physical and moral blandishments of the world.[15]

While the ability to discriminate between good and evil is acknowledged as crucial to self-actualization, Western psychology does not offer its students explicit constructs or stages of development (like *al-nafs-al-mutma'innah*) related to actualization in submission to God (Allah). On this point, Fadiman and Frager observed that:

> These traditions (Eastern religions) also offer clearly defined techniques for psychological and spiritual development. Maslow found an essentially religious or spiritual dimension in the self-actualizing individuals he studied.[16]

However, let us keep in mind that the divine paradigm for self-development is neither "Eastern" or "Western". On this note, I now turn your attention specifically to Islam as the Divinely revealed way of life for personality development.

ISLAM—THE BASIS OF PERSONALITY DEVELOPMENT

Growth and development do not take place in a vacuum. As noted above, Allah (SWT) has compared the growth of human beings with that of plants and herbage (71:17). Again, in *Sūrah Wāqiᶜah*, Allah (SWT) says:

> *Do you then see? The (human seed) that you throw out? Is it you who create it or are We the Creator? (56:58-59)*

> *See you the seed that you sow in the ground? Is it you that cause it to grow or are We the Cause? (56:63-64)*

These verses recall the importance of culture in the growth of living things. On the meaning of culture, Mir Valiuddin pointed out that:

> Culture, as we know, is derived from the Latin word *cultura* and is primarily applicable to the cultivation of land and tillage… But it is the universal character of culture, be it of flowers, or of fruits, that what is important is the seed that is sown and the soil in which it is sown. Nor can the conditions which favor growth and development be neglected.[17]

The definition of culture, in the human context, encompasses the socio-psychological medium, including the values and the ideals, to which a person is exposed. Moreover, it includes the complete way of life that the individual adopts and his ultimate frame of reference which gives meaning to life. Allah (SWT) provides mankind with a divinely ordained culture or way of life to promote self-development in all its dimensions. This culture is Islam. In part of verse four in *Sūrah Mā'idah*, Allah says:

.... this day have those who reject faith given up all hope of your religion (way of life): yet fear them not but fear Me. On this day have I perfected your religion for you, completed My Favor upon you, and have chosen Islam as your Religion.

In *Sūrah Ali-Imrān*, we are told:

Surely, the Religion before Allah is submission to His will (Islam)... (3:19)

Seek they other than the religion of Allah when, to Him submits all there is in the heavens and earth, willingly or unwillingly, and unto Him they all will be returned. (3:83).

The laws of Islam are embodied in the Holy Qur'ān and the sunnah of the Prophet Muhammad (SAS). The word (*sunnah*) derives from (*sanna*) and means "a pattern or form". Allah created human beings and the ideal pattern for humanity to follow in harmony with divine law. To make sincere efforts to live in accordance with the teachings in the Holy Qur'ān and to follow the pattern of conduct of the Prophet Muhammad is to obey Allah.

All who obey Allah and the Apostle are in the company of those who are in the Grace of God — of the Prophets (who teach), the sincere (lovers of truth), the witness (who testify) and the righteous (who do good): Ah! What a beautiful fellowship! (4:69)

And thou (O Muhammad) are on an exalted standard of character. (68:4)

Allah (SWT) brings about a person's self-development.

Those who believe and work righteous deeds—from them shall we blot out all evil (that may be) in them, and we shall reward them accordingly to the best of their deeds. (29:7)

To the extent that the individual's inner state and outer environment cannot be described as Islamic, personality development may be constrained. This is one reason why it is so important to provide the proper Islamic culture or environment for the individual's psycho-spiritual growth. In this regard, the Prophet Muhammad (SAS) said:

"No baby is born but upon al-fiṭrah (human nature in submission to Allah). It is his parents who make him a Jew, a Christian or an idolater (Sahih Muslim)."[18]

Parents serve as role models for the children, and to a large extent, they try to inculcate their own values and beliefs in their children. The family is the basic social unit in all cultures, and it serves as a microcosm of the larger society. Outside of the family, one's associates, peers, and the general populace also exert some influence on personality development. This relationship between the individual's beliefs and behaviors and cultural influences has been repeatedly confirmed by the psychologists and anthropologists, such as Bandura, Hongiman, Thompson and Walters.[19] The impact of culture on personality is reflected in the common Western adage: "You can tell a man by the company he keeps." On this point, the Holy Prophet (SAS) said:

> The similitude of good company and that of bad company is that of the owner of musk and of the iron-smith blower; and the owner of musk would either offer you it free of charge, or you could buy it from him, or you could smell its pleasant odour. And, so far as one who blows is concerned, he might either burn your clothes or you shall have to smell its repugnant smell.[20]

In the Qur'ān, Allah (SWT) says:

> *O you who believe, take not for friends and protectors those who take your religion (way of life) for a mockery or sport—whether among those who received the Scripture before you or among those who reject faith; but fear Allah if you have (true) faith (5:57).*

This does not mean that one has to cut oneself off from most human associations in an effort to develop an Islamic personality. However, one has to exercise discretion based upon the guidance of Allah in choosing associates and guard oneself from negative influence of un-Islamic surroundings. The absence of God-consciousness in a society soon ushers in the moral deterioration of its members and retards their self-development.

Carl Jung (1963) has observed that,

> If dull people lose the idea of God, nothing happens—not immediately and personally at least. But socially the masses begin to breed mental epidemics, of which we have now a fair number.[21]

One does not have to look very far to see that materialistic, irreligious cultures in many parts of the world have given rise to all manner of psychological perversions and illness (i.e., the breakdown of the family, homosexuality, sexual promiscuity, alcoholism and drug addiction, and violence) As Horney notes, a "neurotic personality" shared by many in such cultures is the end result.[22] From an Islamic perspective, the reference to many cultures or nations in the West and elsewhere as "developed nations" surely ignores the critical dimension of psycho-spiritual growth.

Obviously, there are people living in non-Islamic societies who are morally upright and sincerely practice righteousness. Their behavior can be generally described as Islamic, even though such individuals may not be consciously Muslim. Why? Because Islam means submission to Allah as evidenced in righteous conduct, and, secondly, Islam is the all-encompassing divine way of life transcending any society and time. Thus, it would be incorrect to claim that Islam was created by Muslims. The culture of Islam is implemented by humans but is man-made. In contrast, Judeo-Christian culture is largely a manmade dictum in the sense that its scriptures have been altered and distorted with the inclusion of contrived dogmas and teachings of select groups. The "dīn" now underlying Judeo-Christian culture does not reflect the true guidance of divine law– *Sharīᶜah*. This is why a religious Christian is not a Muslim in the complete sense of surrender and submission to the One God and His Law. On this point, the Prophet Muhammad (SAS) said:

> By Him in whose hands is the life of Muhammad, he who is among the community of Jews and Christians hears about me but does not afford his belief in that with which I have been sent and dies in this state (of disbelief), he shall be one of the denizens of Hell. (Narrated by Abū Huraira).

The Prophet (SAS) also said that:

> One among the people of the book (i.e., Jews and Christians) who sincerely believed in his apostle (and practiced his religion) and later lived to see the time of Prophet Muhammad and affirmed his faith in him (Muhammad as God's last messenger) and followed him and attested his truth, for that person is a double reward.

These two *Āhadīth* clearly reveal that during the prophetic life of Muhammad (SAS) and in all times thereafter, the previous scriptures are abrogated in as much as it was Allah's will and plan to reveal the Holy Qur'ān as a universal Mercy and Guide to mankind. No individual or group can truthfully claim that it's way of life is superior to the finalized divine law and way of life revealed by Allah (SWT). In the context of self-development, Islam constitutes "the culture of personality" sine qua non— the richest soil in which to sow the psycho-spiritual seed." *Tatmīm al-nafs*, true self-realization and actualization, takes place in the state of Islam.

ADJUSTMENT AND PERSONALITY

With a basic introduction to the universal and particular characteristics of personality, the essential themes in personality development, and the influence of culture, we can now proceed to discuss the Islamic perspective of psychological adjustment. Every person, irrespective of his station, meets with good and bad situations which tests his spiritual mettle, age-linked emotional maturity, and faith in Allah. Life, death, freewill, and knowledge all constitute tests for mankind, collectively and individually.

> *Every soul shall have a taste of death; and We test you by evil and by good by way of trial. To Us you must return (21:35).*

The Islamic concept of trial or test, (*fitnah*) includes the dimensions of trials and tests, (good and bad), temptations, tumult, oppression, and situations warranting self-examination. *Fitnah* varies in nature and degree according to Allah's plan for every soul.

> *And surely, We shall test you with some fear and hunger, and loss of wealth and lives and crops; but give glad tidings to the steadfast—who say when misfortune strikes them: "surely, to Allah we belong and to Him is our returning." (2:155-156)*

As indicated in the above verse, tests in life are not restricted to any one portion of humanity. No individual is without some limitations and faults. *Fitnah* are necessary to allow each person the opportunity to recognize and overcome blameworthy characteristics in their character and behaviour. Yet, Allah (SWT) assures all that He places no burden on the person greater than he can bear.

> *On no soul does Allah place a burden greater than it can bear. It gets every good that it earns, and it suffers every ill that it earns… (2:286)*

This assurance is the bedrock of a balanced self-concept which allows the individual to meet life's situations in a psychologically sober and stable fashion. The individual cannot repeatedly claim that he or she is helpless and unable to improve one's life. A basic confidence that life situations are not insurmountable is characterized as inner strength.[23] The source of inner strength, in contrast to "ego strength", is sincere acceptance of *fitnah* as a potential stimulus for psycho-spiritual growth. Inner strength is realized and cultivated through submission to Allah.

Failure to adequately interpret and respond to life situations is usually due to: (1) external constraints beyond the individual's control, (2) rejection or distortion of the truth and (3) ignorance of the truth underlying one's experiences. If the person remains ignorant of the truth, personality development and healthy life adjustment are not fully realizable. Yet, Allah (SWT) has clearly made the truth known to every soul in as much as each person is obliged to seek solutions to life's difficulties and utilize his intelligence and moral conscience in the right way. Because of human weaknesses and limitations, some mistakes and wrong decisions in life are unavoidable.

> *But surely thy Lord—to those who do wrong in ignorance, but who thereafter repent and make amends—thy Lord, after all this, is oft-forgiving, Most Merciful (16: 119)*

> *Allah forgives souls who sincerely seek the truth ... (20:82)*

The intentional rejection or distortion of the Truth stunts inner growth and is a form of self-oppression. In this case, one has the characteristics of an unbeliever. Unbelievers are described in the Qur'ān as arrogant, misguided, straying in mind, false to themselves, deluded, ungrateful, diseased in their hearts, deaf, dumb, blind, and so on. The unbeliever, personality wise, is clearly a psychotic in every sense of the word.

> *Those who reject (Truth) among the People of the Book and among the Polytheists, will be in hell fire to dwell there in (forever). They are the worst of creatures. (98:6)*

The psychopathology from which the unbeliever suffers is not identical to the mental illness caused by neurogenic disorders and psychological maladies. The atheist is described in the Qur'ān as being "*majnūn*"—mad or possessed. Yet, the unbeliever regards himself as being quite normal and sane, and often accuses those who are guided in *al-fiṭrah* as being "old-fashioned", "inflexible" or "too dependent" on religion. Similarly, no apostle came to the people before them, but they said (about him) in this manner:

> *"A sorcerer or a mad man!" Is this the repeated accusation they have handed down one to another? No, they are themselves transgressing beyond bounds (51:52 -53).*

The last word in the above verse, "*tāghūna*", includes conditions of oppression and cruelty toward one's self as well as others. Even external oppression is no excuse in the final analysis for the failure to seek the Truth and strive towards *tatmīm al-nafs* (self-realization) in submission to Allah.

> *When angels take the souls of those who die in sin against their souls,
> they say: "In what (condition) were you?" They reply: "Weak and
> oppressed were we in the earth." They (angels) say: "Was not Allah's
> earth spacious enough for you to remove yourselves away (from evil)?"
> Such people will find their abode in Hell— what an evil refuge. (4:97)*

All aspects considered, most non-productive attitudes and behavior of
individuals who have reached the age of discretion are self-imposed and
reflect a lack of the proper sense of reality and the responsibilities that
accompany it. William Glassor, author of Reality Therapy, draws similar
conclusions from his experiences as a psychiatrist:

> It [orthodox psychiatry] avoids dealing with the issue of right and wrong.
> Deviant behavior is considered a product of mental illness and the patient
> is often felt not morally responsible because he is considered helpless to
> do anything about it. The basic premise of Reality Therapy is the exact
> opposite, that the patient's problem is the result of his inability (or
> unwillingness) to comprehend and apply values and moral principles in
> his daily life.[24]

Thus, individuals with emotional problems differ to the extent that they
are: (1) unable or unwilling to seek proper moral solutions to their
difficulties, and (2) to what degree proper counsel is needed from others.
In regard to what constitutes proper counsel, Allah (SWT) says:

> *O mankind! There has come to you a direction from your Lord and a
> healing for the (diseases) in the hearts, and a Guidance and a Mercy for
> the Believers. (10:57)*

In regard to life-tests, we are told:

> *So, surely, with every difficulty there is relief; surely, with every difficulty
> there is relief. (94:5-6)*

THE ISLAMIC PERSONALITY

Being a Muslim does not make an individual immune to the emotional and
psychological vicissitudes that characterize human lives. Yet, in the midst
of this mosaic of life conditions, the sincere Muslim, in heart as well as
outer behavior, experiences a sense of purpose, soundness of mind, and
spiritual rootedness unparalleled to other inner stages of being. As repeated
throughout this paper, the Islamic personality is recognized by the
distinctive characteristics that emerge in the individual who submits to

Allah and obeys Him. The characteristics may be synthesised in one verse in the Qur'ān:

Those who have faith and do righteous deeds—they are the best of creatures. (98:7)

True faith and righteous deeds encompass more than what meets the eye of another person. It is reflected in the following verse of al-Fātihah, the opening chapter of the Qur'ān.

Thee (alone) do we worship, and Thee (alone) do we ask for help. Show us the straight path, the way of those on whom Thou has bestowed Thy grace; those whose (portion) is not wrath, and who do not go astray. (1:5-7)

The believer repeats this divine formula daily. His or her psycho-spiritual growth could not take place without reaffirming the basic purpose for which he or she was created and without seeking to fulfill that purpose. When repeated with sincerity, the essence of this divine formula soon becomes, by the Grace of Allah, a part of the personality and eventually shapes and transforms the whole character into an Islamic personality. No matter what the person is doing, his conscious is focused on the Reality behind all things.

And to thy Lord turn (all) thy attention. (94:8)

Say: surely, my prayer and my service of sacrifice, my life and my death (all) for Allah, The Lord, (Cherisher) of the worlds (6:162)

Far from feeling "burdened or inconvenienced", the true believer is fulfilled in worshipping Allah, and realizes him- or herself through seeking Allah's pleasure.

Those who believe and whose hearts find satisfaction in the remembrance of Allah; for without doubt in the remembrance of Allah do hearts find satisfaction. For those who believe and do good deeds, for them there is bliss and a beautiful state of (final) return. (13:28-29)

An Islamic personality is not "something" which can be acquired in a course or assimilated through words. It is the fruit of true submission to Allah in deeds. The soul must love Allah, His messengers, His revelation, His truth and His guidance.

Whoever submits his whole self to Allah and does good, (he) has indeed grasped the most trustworthy handhold; and with Allah rests the End and

Decision of all affairs. (31:22)

In concluding this discussion, we should remember that psychology is a science that, in general, belongs to every soul in as much as each person should seek self-knowledge in the light of divine guidance. As student-scholars of the self, we must, by the grace of Allah, assist our fellow human beings in their efforts to understand what is best for personality development. If self-knowledge and inner growth are to be realized, both the psychologists and those he teaches and advises must heed the words and commandments of Almighty Allah, creator of all personalities. Psychology and the study of personality must undergo their own transformation to become the commendable sciences of the heart leading to its purification.

NOTES

1. Rashid Hamid, "Reflections on a balanced Islamic personality" in *From Muslim to Islamic* (Association of Muslim Social Scientists). (Maryland: International Graphics Printing Co., 1974).

2. J.S. Wiggins, K.E Renner, G.L. Clore, and R.J. Rose, *Principles of Personality*, (Reading Massachusetts: Addison-Wesley Publishing Co., 1976).

3. W. C. Schefler, Biology: *Principles and Issues.* (Reading, Massachusetts: Addison-Wesley Publishing Co.,1976).

4. G. Allport, *Becoming* (New Haven, Connecticut: Yale University Press, 1960).

5. G. S. Idris, *The Process of Islamization* (Maryland: International Graphics Printing Co., 1977), p. 4.

6. C. G. Jung, *Psychology and Religion* (New Haven: Yale University Press, 1963), p. 61.

7. Ibid., p. 7.

8. S. H. Nasr, *Science and Civilization in Islam.* New York: Plume Books, 1968), p. 223.

9. S. M. Quṭb, 'The Islamic basis of development", in *Islam and Development* (Plainfield, Indiana: Association of Muslim Social Scientists, 1977), p. 2.

10. C. Rogers, *On Becoming a Person* (Boston: Houghton Mifflin, 1961).

11. A. H. Maslow, *The Farther Reaches of Human nature* (New York: Viking Press, 1971).

12. D. Rosser-Owen, "Social change in Islam—the progressive dimension", in *The Muslim Institute Papers* (Slough Berks., United Kingdom: Open Press Ltd., 1976), p. 19.

13. *The Glorious Qur'ān*: Text, Translation and Commentary by A. Yusaf Ali. (Libya: The Call of Islam Society, 1393/1973).

14. S. Freud, *Origins of Psychoanalysis*, edited by M. Bonaparte, A. Freud, and E. Kris (New York: Basic Books, 1954).

15. C. G. Jung, *Psychology and Religion*, p. 34.

16. J. Fadiman, and R. Frager, *Personality and Personal Growth* (New York: Harper and Row Publishers, 1976), p. 340.

17. M. Valiuddin, *The Essential Features of Islam.* (Hyderabad, India: Da'iratu'l–Ma'arif Press, n.d.), p. 89.

18. *Sahih Muslim*: Translation by Abdul-Hameed Siddiqi, (Lahore, Pakistan: Sh. Muhammad Ashraf Press, 1393/1973).

19. A. Bandura, and R.H. Walters, *Social Learning Theory and Personality Development* (New York: Holt, Rinehert and Winsten, 1963); see J.J. Honigmann, Personality in Culture (New York: Harper and Row Publications 1967); see also R. Thompson, Psychology and Culture (Dubuque, Iowa: William C. Brown Publishers, 1975).

20. *Sahih Muslim*: Translation by Abdul-Hameed Siddiqi.

21. C. G. Jung, *Psychology and Religion*, p. 105.

22. K. Horney, *The Neurotic personality of our time* (New York: Norton and Company, Inc., 1964).

23. J. E. Sullivan, *Islamic Perspective on Crisis Prone People.* Unpublished manuscript (1977).

24. W. Glasser, and L.M. Zunin, "Reality therapy", in Raymond Corsini, ed., *Current Psychotherapies* (Illinois: F. E. Peacock Publisher, Inc., 1973).

14

The Islamic Personality:
A Sequential Model

SAIYAD FAREED AHMAD

This paper is mainly concerned with developing and constructing a sequential model of an Islamic personality.[1] An attempt has been made to identify and operationalize the main constituent characteristics of such a personality. Such a model is essential for an understanding and experiencing as to who and what we really are as a person. Self-introspection and self-knowledge are highly emphasized in Islam.[2] Yet, despite such emphasis, personality studies among Muslims are few and far between. This paper aims to fill the present void.

For the purposes of this study, the concept of a sequential model simply refers to the processes or stages of growth and development that a Muslim must pass through to cultivate an Islamic personality. In other words, such a model offers a picture of the transformational process involved. Our proposed model is holistic in nature and signifies not only an integrated view, but also the *unity* and *balance* that an Islamic personality epitomizes.

Developing such a model may necessitate contextualizing it in relation to several other factors such as, social structure, acculturation, socialization, identity, ethics, morality, and a host of other variables that may be involved in the causal nexus. A central thesis of this paper is that even though there are two distinct perspectives—sociological and psychological[3] —which exist for the study of personality, an adequate and appropriate analysis will remain severely limited if one were to use only one perspective to the exclusion of the other. Thus, a sociological analysis without insights from psychology and *vice versa* would provide an unreliable picture of a human personality. In any case, what is of crucial importance is to emphasize that using theory and data of personality systems is essential to understanding the stable functioning or change of social systems. There is an essential causal connection between a human personality and social systems.[4] An individual utterly cut-off and abstracted from any social context simply does not exist. Western personality psychology holds that personalities are a direct product of conscious, purposive choices, and are not a product of chance.[5]

Traditional Muslim scholars have generally devoted limited attention to the subjects which are the direct concern of modern psychology, but they have always evinced keen interest in human nature.[6] This is particularly true of those scholars who were endowed with "mystical leanings." For example, Ṣūfī scholars attached to the circle of the Brethren of Purity (*Ikhwān al-Safā*) assigned *ʿIlm al-nafsaniyyat* a place in their encyclopedia, the *Rasa'il*.[7] Muslims are in dire need of reviving such interest in personality studies. At the same time, we need to become more rigorous in our research and writing while delving more deeply into key personality-related problems. We must not only bring the depth and specificity of modern psychology to bear upon our studies but must rediscover our own profound sources of wisdom not just in the Qur'ān and Ḥadīth, but in the vast and varied corpus of works produced by Muslim scholars over the centuries. The insights provided by certain other religious traditions into human nature, the soul, and personality should not be ignored either, such as by Vedanta, Zen Buddhism, Christianity, Judaism, and Taoism, for example.[8] All of these religious traditions have contributed immense knowledge to an understanding of human personality as well as the enhancement of psycho-spiritual well-being.

MAIN OBJECTIVES

As a basic minimum, the task of constructing a sequential model analytically and conceptually will entail establishing the composition of such a personality; and then, one can understand what the real purpose of our creation is, and what is necessary for our real growth and transformation. By understanding the structures of our personality types[9] we come to know the intricacies and complexities of our respective individual personalities. The study has the following objectives:

1. To clearly establish what our personality system is made of; what are its structures, pattern, design and determinants.
2. To identify the necessary processes or sequences that are involved in the formation, real growth and transformation of an Islamic personality.
3. To assess research methodologies that were used by Muslim scholars in the past and indicate what methods could be used in the present situation to synthesize information to develop into formal concepts and theories of Islamic personality across different Muslim cultures and societies.
4. To suggest means and measures for initiating replication studies

to develop methods of narrowing differences and enhancing its similarities as well as a comprehensive theory of an Islamic personality.

AN OPERATIONAL DEFINITION OF AN ISLAMIC PERSONALITY

In order to fulfill our objectives, it is essential that we develop a definition of such a personality and point out our main assumptions that will guide the construction of our model. This definition will be developed from the review of already existing material on Muslim and non-Muslim personalities. However, one should bear in mind that all definitions are a product of a human mind, are purely arbitrary and can change over time. Western personality psychologists have differed widely in defining personality. Generally, their definitions have striven to be inclusive. However, a perfect all-inclusive definition is impossible. Despite some similarities, the Western conception of personality is different from an Islamic understanding since they both rely on different concepts and sources for their analysis and interpretation. In the Western perspective, anything which is not observable, measurable, and quantifiable is denied as knowledge. Consequently, human beings are reduced to merely being biochemical entities. The role of soul, heart, human nature, and intuition is not only reduced, but denied altogether and consciousness is interpreted in entirely materialistic terms.

Central to the definition of an Islamic personality are fundamental questions of meaning. The question of what role meaning plays in envisioning and constructing a model of an Islamic personality will be dealt with in relative detail in our note on methodology. Once one concedes that such a thing as human personality[10] exists, one cannot escape the questions of, who or what are human beings? What is their essence and nature? What is their duty and place in the universe? What are the abilities and qualities that enable them to fulfill these duties, and who assigns and endows them with these abilities and characteristics? Western psychologists are not bothered about such questions. Whereas, Islam has always maintained that whenever we sever or overlook the relationship of human beings with Allah we end up in state of turmoil and confusion.

In seeking a definition of the Islamic personality, we must, inevitably start at *the beginning*, i.e. the creation of the universe. Islam sees the whole universe as a created order according to a Divine Master plan. Nothing is created by Allah in mere sport or jest. Everything is created for some purpose. As such, the universe is viewed as being *teleological* in nature. Along with everything else, human beings are creations of Allah; yet they are much more in that they are His *master creation* accorded the highest place in the created order of things. Standing at the apex of the hierarchy of creation, human beings are seen by Islam as the vicegerent of Allah on Earth. They have been placed here to fully actualize and realize their potential according to Allah's guidance. The fundamentals of an Islamic personality are created by Allah to play a pivotal role in the actualization of the Divine master plan. As such, an Islamic personality is inextricably linked to the Divine and the Eternal and the inner self can only be properly understood in this context. Everything about such a personality—unity, holism, distinctive characteristics, identity, motivation, individuality—all emanate from or are derived from this masterly plan. All the traits and characteristics with which an Islamic personality is endowed with by the Creator, including the innate qualities are in complete agreement with this plan. Everything about this personality is totally integrated into a harmonious whole and nothing is superfluous in it.

Other qualities and traits that characterize an Islamic personality paradigm[11] is essentially that of Monotheism and Unity. It is linked with other unities that permeate this paradigm, like unity of self, knowledge, existence, and the universe. It is because of the linkages or connections that exist between these underlying unities that the Islamic personality epitomizes unity, balance, order, and holism. A major implication of the presence of these qualities and characteristics is that it culminates in a balanced human being based on inherent *fiṭrah* tendencies and inclinations. As a result of this it can develop only by a balanced development of all the faculties—natural, physical, moral, spiritual, and biological. Only by satisfying all the dimensions of the human self can it develop into an Islamic personality. If any part or segment is allowed to remain underdeveloped or experiences a kind of entropic degradation, the whole personality is influenced. Conversely, basic to this notion is that every constituent element is subject to decay if these are not nourished and sustained. This means that, at any moment of time, the Islamicity of this personality cannot be taken for granted. Any decay or decline will lead to a subsequent decline in psycho-spiritual health.

Personality in Islam is not bound by flimsy, ephemeral notions of a person like charisma, beauty, status, and sartorial refinement. It is not so much the importance of one part over the other of a personality that is critically important in Islam, but the whole person. It is the sum total of what we are as well as the permanent, stable and resilient characteristics which can also be referred to as universal factors which contribute to the unique character of any person and are shared by all human beings. Only by recognizing the universal factors one can comprehend not only an Islamic personality, but also the underlying laws of personality development. Some of these laws and special permanent features of this personality are discussed in earlier articles in this volume. We will return to these universal, permanent factors as part of our sequential model in the final section.

The meaning,[12] purpose and the essence for which human beings are created form an essential ingredient of this personality. All these combined together give to the processual formation, growth and development the necessary activism and dynamism. It is like moving from being and existence to becoming. The final goal is to attain an Islamic personality.

Mainly because this personality is a system, Allah has provided unique characteristics and attributes and a distinctive human nature; we have mind, will, determination, volition, motivation, and consciousness. In addition, we have the distinct ability to think, make decisions and choices. We are endowed with animality,[13] but at the same time we have been given the ability to channel, control, restrain, and subdue it. We can express it in a humane, cultured, and civilized manner. We are unique and different from animals and angels. We share with them some characteristics; because of their distinctive *fiṭrah*, or nature, human beings alone are human, and "human" alone is the appropriate[14] characteristic and description of Man.

In short, the ideal Islamic personality can now be summarized in the form of an operational definition by listing all the parts that form the whole definition. All the following ingredients play an important part in completing the wholeness and unity of this personality:

1. The Islamic personality is a unique human being, a special creation linked to the Divine and the Eternal; and on this foundation rests all subsequent approaches of the study of this personality. To deny the origin and purpose of humanity is to deny the fundamental, distinctive characteristics of humanity.

2. Islamic personality is an ethical and moral personality. It is an embodiment of the Islamic teachings as revealed in the Holy Qur'ān and as exemplified up to the perfection of al-Insān al-Kamil by the Prophet Muhammad (*ṣallah Allahu 'alayhi wa Alihi wa sallam*). In him we have the best example, who looks toward Allah and remembers Him much. If we ignore the infinite spiritual qualities[15] and potentialities within human beings, we are left with a concept of personality devoid of a soul,[16] absolved of spiritual faith and aspiration.

3. The Islamic personality ideally represents an integrated, systematic, balanced, and unified human being. This personality thrives on integrated and balanced growth of all the faculties with which human beings are created and by satisfying all of the dimensions of the human self.

4. Unlike what is erroneously presumed, human beings are endowed with a *limited free will* which they may use to their advantage or

detriment. If their volitional acts are in conformity with their true nature, they achieve psycho-spiritual progress. When they intentionally violate or deviate from the Divine law, human beings retard their own inner growth and motivational processes which are the internal springs of human actions.

5. Higher faculties and moral conscience are an inalienable part of this personality. Human beings have been granted additional faculties which enable them to gain knowledge of the natural laws of creation, to distinguish between right and wrong and to exercise their free will. By their intelligence and their capacity for speech and language, they can create meaning and share their thoughts and discoveries with their contemporaries and their future generations. These higher faculties and qualities in human beings point to a higher purpose and destiny for them, provided they chose to aspire towards them. On the other hand, if they foolishly ignore the guidance of Allah, they regress to the lowest of levels.

6. The original human nature is simply defined as "an inborn natural predisposition which cannot change, and which exists at birth in all human beings."[17] The most important point is that it does not change and the *fiṭrah*, the natural predisposition, is inclined towards right action; the Qur'ān reveals that human beings are born in a state of obedience and submission to Divine law. In brief, Islam is the religion of human nature and a correct perception and understanding of it can pave the way for the development of a theory of human behavior which is more accurate and truer to human nature. It is the most crucial element and plays a central role in the formation of an Islamic personality.

7. It is important that rather than using a single word while clarifying about the inner psychic reality of man, the Qur'ān uses words like *rūḥ, nafs,* and *qalb.* This *rūḥ* was breathed into Adam by Allah. Being the recipient of the Divine *rūḥ* is what has enhanced human beings from their humble origins and enabled them to overcome the baser part of their nature and made them worthy of being the vicegerent of Allah.

8. These are several particular individual characteristics that are part and parcel of each person, and which clearly differentiate individuals. One sign of the uniqueness of every individual is the fingerprint, but also the uniqueness of the temperament of each individual indicates that each microcosm is a world of its own, not identical with any other person. The inner growth of each person varies and develops according to their own spiritual effort and willingness and is not the same for each person. This also explains the individual differences and variations.

9. Personality development and growth are an extremely important

part of it. Proper individual development takes place only in the light of divinely ordained paradigms of life for mankind. In the absence of this paradigm, there is no real character development and self-knowledge. Personality development requires *fasl* which means "to separate, to wean, or to evolve towards a completion." Another term in the Qur'ān is *atwara* which indicates that such evolution or development takes place in lawful stages or phases (71:13-14). The development of personality in Islam is essentially regarded as the development of a human being's higher nature as a psycho-spiritual being. Analogous to but not identical to physical development, psycho-spiritual growth also takes place in ordered stages. Shaykh Muhammad Quṭb observes that the Islamic concept of personality development is also reflected in the word *tazkiyyah*,[18] which means development of the good side of human beings. It also signifies growth and disciplining of the self (*nafs*) which has the capability to do evil.

10. There are certain other things which need to be pointed out to complete this discussion on an operational definition. In Islam a personality is judged basically based on traits and characteristics that a person cultivates as part of one's ethical and moral character. Character and personality are inseparable in Islam. Also, it is the total lifestyle that is the hallmark of such a personality. Acculturation and socialization are highly emphasized as processes to transmit this lifestyle and therefore Muslims are highly encouraged to seek the company of pious people.

Summarily, then we can say that an Islamic personality is an ordered system based on the unique, individually different characteristics and traits which remain stable throughout the entire span of life. Even though these traits and characteristics remain to be fixed and are responsible for ethical and moral character, some change and adjustment is possible in it through learning and constant cultivation. The relative causes which shape and mould a personality are as numerous as the multifaceted nature of human experiences, but the essential core of a personality remains the same.[19] The universal features contributing to the unique personality of any person are shared by all human beings. If these universal features are ignored as in the case of modern theories of personality, we cannot achieve an adequate, authentic understanding of personality. Whenever these universal factors are considered, we can become aware of the laws of personality development as it is in the Islamic paradigm of personality. We are referring to those universal characteristics of human beings that make them a special creation, their essence is spiritual as they are created with a soul, they have a limited free will, an original human nature, higher faculties, and moral conscience. It is out of these constituent elements that an Islamic personality is created. It would even be impossible to imagine a human being if any of these elements were missing. Our sequential model, which will be discussed later, is built around these necessary and sufficient systemic conditions and factors.[20] These are critically associated with human behavior. In this sense, the concept of personality is not merely a descriptive category but involves processes in the person that are responsible for this behavior. People behave as they do, at least in part, because of their personalities. Hence, if an Islamic personality displays an excellent moral character, it could be because there are internal and external characteristics that cause them to behave like this. This is really the main reason for developing such a model to show that Islamic personalities will behave Islamically and will become instrumental in spreading the Islamic way of life.

A NOTE ON METHODOLOGY

Methodology is a critical aspect of the study of Islamic personalities and in the development of a comprehensive theory of such personality. I strongly believe that personality studies are long overdue in Muslim societies because most of our problems are rooted in our personalities. Problematic situations beg the questions as to who we are, and what we are, and which distinctive pattern of thoughts, feelings, and actions we display. As Muslim social scientists, we should not only study the behavior of many Muslims, but also be able to identify and classify both similarities and differences. We should attempt to recognize the complexity and individuality among people and strive to explain the relationship between the individuals and the social and biological constraints that affect their behavior.

Examining the many facets of a methodological approach suited to the reality of an Islamic personality involves considering a whole range of issues starting with philosophical debates about the nature of methodology, qualitative versus quantitative "soft" versus "hard" methodology and now the emerging debate between the "Islamic" and the "Western" methodology. It is not our intention to delve too deeply into these issues. Almost all the social sciences, such as sociology, anthropology, and psychology, are replete with conceptual, theoretical, and methodological problems. However, because of some uncertainty about the meaning of the term itself, it would not be out of place to briefly indicate the meaning and the sense in which I am using it here. The term methodology generally, is used both for a certain discipline and for its subject matter. I mean by methodology the study, the description, the explanation, and the justification of methods. One should not be obsessed with a certain method as an end in itself. Our obsession with experiment as a method par excellence to the exclusion of other methods is quite well known. As a result, any finding arrived at by experimental means is regarded as knowledge, and findings by any other method are rejected. Methodology is used in several other senses like techniques, or the specific procedures used in a certain science, or as an honorific epithet to bestow prestige on some project, or as used by philosophers, where methodology is indistinguishable from epistemology or philosophy of science. All I am urging is that Muslim researchers use a method that is appropriate to their area of investigation. The value of highly complex measuring devices used by their protagonists is the social sciences is a case in point where they have become an end in themselves rather than being intermediary tools. Its users seemingly purport to measure everything and demonstrate poor understanding of the phenomena studied. Such is the case with inner subjective aspects of human personality. It is inexcusable to force the research problem into an *a priori* scheme of technical paraphernalia rather than observing it in the context of the empirical being investigated. Mainly because the use of any methodology involves some techniques, its supporters have emphasized the other end of the spectrum in which techniques become everything. For example, there are certain techniques related with the use of the Rorschach or inkblot test, or with a mass opinion or attitudinal survey; there are statistical techniques, like those involved in regression and factor analysis; techniques for conducting an interview or for running a rat through a maze; techniques of carbon dating and deciphering unknown inscriptions. In each of these instances, techniques are only an aid to the overall objectives of research and these techniques contribute to the context of the reality being investigated. There is a right way and an incorrect way to do everything, in science and in any other work; or at any rate there are better ways of doing it. The techniques of a science are the acceptable and recognized ways of doing research and inquiry. In fact, scientific training for a Muslim social scientist is commitment and dedication to seeking truth, honesty and integrity and being ethical and moral. Not to a set of techniques on an *a priori* basis. It is for this reason that Islamic methodology advocates the notion of flexibility.[21]

Summarily then, in what follows I mean by methodology a broad, flexible range of concern with a set of techniques, principles which are grounded in certain premises and assumptions embedded in the Islamic conception of human beings and their nature. In my opinion all serious political and moral philosophy and thus, as a corollary, any social and psychological inquiry must begin and be grounded in an authentic understanding of human nature. Ignoring of this aspect will lead to erroneous conclusions and theorizing. Anything fulfilling these conditions shall correspondingly be designated as method. This concern does not predicate utterly excluding and disregarding other methods and procedures that include forming concepts and hypotheses, making observations and measurements, performing experiments, building models and theories, providing explanations, and making predictions. The main aim of methodology, as I see it, is to describe and analyze these methods, shedding light on their limitations and resources, clarifying their presuppositions and consequences, relating their potentialities, and extending the horizons of Islamic knowledge. Briefly, the aim of methodology is to extend our awareness and understanding, in the broadest possible terms, not so much of the products of scientific inquiry but of the process itself.

Having defined the meaning of the "methodology of methodology," and clarified its aims. I come specifically to suggest measures that we ought to use in studying and understanding the Islamic personality across Muslim lands. This will only be selective and far from exhaustive. It is mainly premised on the assumption that an alternative approach to studying an Islamic personality is not only a plausible idea but scientifically valid as well.

ELEMENTS OF THE METHODOLOGY

Firstly, it is imperative that Islamic personality studies should be conducted within an Islamic perspective and worldview. Islamic research has been proliferating over the years and has brought to light some of the main characteristics of this worldview.[22] Undeniably, the main sources of information on Islamic personality should be the Qur'ān and the Ḥadīth.[23] Using anything else for such a study would be superficial and misleading. The main reason for advocating such an alternative paradigm is that serious irreconcilable differences exist between each metaphysical system and worldview it adheres to. One finds considerable differences between the worldviews of many civilizations. Concepts, theories, research methods emanate because of these worldviews. Due to its wholly secular character, contemporary Western civilization and its global manifestations have transformed the concepts of knowledge, reality, and truth. Everything is relative and devoid of revealed truth. All knowledge is considered a product of the human mind, so that mechanistic, materialistic explanations predominate.[24] What is beyond sensory sources and consciousness is totally rejected. This kind of interpretation banishes any role for the soul or any spiritual explanation in the understanding of human personalities.

Secondly, we alluded to the concept of meaning earlier and the proposition that the full import of what it means to be human is at the center of all the problems in psychology. Belatedly, a group of humanistically oriented sociologists and psychologists are rejecting the extreme form of behaviorism where the concern is solely with human behavior (stimulus–response) and the factors responsible for producing them. The same is true of the cognitivist orientation which emerged as a reaction to behaviorism with the obvious notion that one cannot have behavior without cognitive ability. Yet this school can be faulted for denying the proposition that human beings are at the center of the creation of the universe, and who are to be its vicegerents.

Huq, in his paper,[25] makes a plea that if we want to understand the human self and human behavior, the dimension of meaning cannot be ignored or sidetracked because the problem of meaning is unique to the human species. Accordingly, an authentic understanding of the human personality must include the will and drive for meaning. Without understanding the implications of the concept of meaning in the context of human life, one cannot decipher the Islamic personality. Western psychologists have tended to emphasize feelings of fulfillment and significance, integration and relatedness.[26] The presence of these feelings in the human personality is undeniable, but faith and commitment provide the central core and unifying factor that bestows the experience of meaningful existence in life.[27] The most promising work on the concept of meaning has emerged with the point of view of symbolic interactionism and the topic of methodology in the discipline of sociology/social psychology. Blumer has stated that the concept of symbolic interactionism in its final analysis rests on three basic premises: that human beings act toward things on the basis of the meanings the things have for them; that the meanings of such things derives from the social interaction one has with other human beings; and that these meanings are constructed, handled in, and modified through an interpretative process.[28] As a corollary of these premises certain logical questions which have a bearing on the study of personality, such as: who am I; what does it mean to be human; what does it mean to have an Islamic personality; why are we in this universe; are there any goals and objectives of our existence—these are given short shrift in science and considered rather embarrassing. But the heart of the matter is that an appropriate answer must be found to resolve our existential dilemma.

Apart from not addressing these questions, there is an explanatory and methodological dilemma that should be addressed. For instance, few scholars would have a problem accepting the first premise that human beings act toward things based on the meanings which these things have for them. Yet, oddly enough, when it comes to explaining human behavior in sociology and psychology, the tendency is to treat human behavior as the product of multifarious factors that play upon human beings. The overpowering concern is focused on the behavior and factors which are presumed to be producing them. Both disciplines overly rely on the proverbial "variables" which are supposed to cause everything. This situation has given rise to simplistic and unrealistic explanations which do not really explain. A case in point in sociology is the overly socialized conception of human beings, and in psychology we have the learning theory. Nearly every human behavior is attributed to the human ability to learn. Psychologists turn to such familiar factors as stimuli, attitudes, conscious or unconscious motives, drives, various kinds of psychological inputs and outputs, perception, and cognition. In a similar fashion, sociologists have traditionally relied on such factors as social class, position and status pressures, cultural prescriptions, norms and values, and group affiliation to provide such explanations. In most of these instances, where actors are regarded as producing them, meanings are usually subsumed in the initiating or culminating factors, or as a neutral link between these two factors. Thus, what these factors mean to human beings is either ignored or bypassed from the resulting explanation which indicates a departure from the meanings that things have for human beings. To ignore the meaning of the things toward which people act results in reification and falsification of the behavior under study. What is being suggested here is to restore the centrality of the role meaning plays in influencing human behavior. The meaning dimension is extremely important. To bypass meaning in favor of factors alleged to produce behavior is a serious error in the neglect of the role of meaning in the formation of behavior and personality. It can seriously hamper personality studies.

Thirdly, the most important thing that we can do methodologically is to take the Qur'ān, *Ḥadīth*, and contributions of Muslim scholars on psychological themes, especially personality psychology, as the main sources.[29] In our methodological stance, we should benefit from four modes of approaches to research. Singly, or in combination, one could use the merits of these modes for analysis and verification, and deduction and induction in Islamic research. These are empirical, rational, intuitional, and revelational. However, one needs to understand some erroneous notions that are commonly prevalent about some of these. For instance, empirical methods are decried and condemned in some quarters because of their emphasis on sensory sources and materialistic explanations. However, at the same time, the reality of the empirical order cannot be denied. Allamah Iqbal, in his Reconstruction, has emphasized that Islam is empirical because it started with a concrete conceptual activity, namely the command to "read."[30] Revelation and intuition are two other approaches that are sometimes mocked and considered unscientific by their detractors, but scholars such as Allamah Iqbal, Shah Wali Allah and Mulla Ṣadrā —to name a few—have demonstrated sheer brilliance in using intuition in their works. Shah Wali Allah "regards life, with all its facets as a manifestation of Divine Unity. This thought synthesizes revelation, reason, and empirical knowledge to construct a universal paradigm that integrates man's existential concerns with the moral and spiritual purposes of life, blending these seemingly disparate elements into a meaningful whole."[31] I think it would be extremely interesting to develop a theory of Islamic personality by integrating and synthesizing the concepts and methodologies of scholars such as Allamah Iqbal, Shah Wali Allah and Mulla Ṣadrā. This is what comes closest to what I have in mind when I speak of an Islamic research methodology based on concepts from the Qur'ān, Ḥadīth, and from the rich Islamic intellectual tradition. In brief, I am suggesting that we respect the nature of the empirical world, but do not rely solely on what appears to be the sole reality and that we should adopt a methodological stance that is in consonance with this reality.

THE BASIC PARADIGM/MODEL OF AN ISLAMIC PERSONALITY

Based on the various elements presented as part of the operational definition of an Islamic personality and material included in the methodological note, it is easier now to develop the broad contours of our sequential model:

Firstly, the Islamic personality has its origins in the primordial covenant relationship described in the Qur'ān (7:172). This means that its genesis relates to the Divine and the transcendental. Human beings are Allah's vicegerent on earth and their personalities can be appropriately understood only in this context of spirituality. Under the pre-text of objectivity and pseudo-scientism, Western psychology has denied its existence. The Islamic model of personality not only recognizes it as an important element of it, but also as a basis of it. To deny this spiritual origin and purpose is to deny the fundamental, distinctive characteristics of humanity. Allamah Iqbal epitomizes the best thinking on this aspect of our life. According to him, "humanity needs, three things today—a spiritual interpretation of the universe, spiritual emancipation of the individual, and spiritual democracy."[32]

Secondly, the Islamic personality is systematic, orderly, and organized. It has stable structures inside Muslims which explain their behavior. It is generally concerned with the whole person. It derives its motivation, activism, and dynamism from belief in Allah and Prophet Muhammad (SAW). Such a personality demonstrates an inner unity of the individual spiritual life imbued with boundless potentialities and immense human possibilities. As part of its spiritual uniqueness and identity, it is generally endowed with a unique concept of individuality.[33] In sum, the Islamic personality ideally represents an integrated, systematic, balanced, and unified human being.

Thirdly, the Islamic personality is a spiritual, ethical, moral, and a personality affirmed by the Qur'ān. The ability to decipher good from bad is deeply ingrained in human nature and not relative and culturally acquired as is widely believed. Higher faculties and moral conscience are bestowed by Allah and not learned behavior. An ethical and moral character is really the sine qua non of an Islamic personality. The distinguishing feature of an Islamic personality is this ethical and moral character in every situation.

Finally, the most important components, elements, or stable characteristics and traits of an Islamic personality that complete the true inner psychic reality are a unique *fiṭrah* or original human nature which does not change and which exists at birth in all human beings, spirit or souls (*rūḥ*), self (*nafs*), and a heart with the cognitive ability to comprehend (*qalb*). As long as each one of these entities function in unison and harmony, psychospiritual health is ensured. The concept of an Islamic personality shall remain incomplete if we do not include normalcy and health of the personality. Muslims have been given the spiritual ideal of human perfection. Self-improvement and transformation are an integral part of healthy human development and fundamental to the integration of the soul with an Islamic personality.

Before presenting the actual sequential model, certain points need to be mentioned for clarification. While it is not denied that non-Islamic personalities also may have some of the characteristics and traits that Islamic personalities have, nevertheless the basic differences between the two types of personality are undeniable. The meanings and concepts used to describe and analyze are not only drastically different, but totally denied. What has been described here is an ideal model of an Islamic personality; the reality however, in many cases leaves much to be desired. The constituent elements of this model are not distinct but overlapping. Not only this, but it is extremely difficult to pinpoint where one element stops and the other begins. For instance, human beings are born with soul and Allah created them in His own image,[34] hence all the Divine attributes are inherently present in human beings from the very beginning of their life. It is these potentialities and propensities which human beings strive to actualize in the form of a personality during their lifetime. One cannot have a personality or develop one without the working of the soul at all stages of life. The same can be said about human nature, consciousness, will power and motivation, which have a synergistic relationship. Hence, the efficacy of the model really lies in its ability to be analytical and heuristic. The model, in its final analysis, is developmental and conducive to growth for personal perfection. It is difficult, if not impossible, to develop a succinct definition and a sequential model of an Islamic personality simply because there is more to the latter than the sum of its various parts or sequences of development. Nevertheless, in what follows we have tried.

SEQUENCE I: THE ORIGINAL SPIRITUAL ESSENCE, THE NATURAL, THE PRIMORAL, THE TRANSCENDENTAL

This phase refers to the act of Divine creation (*khalq*). The very first Qur'ānic revelation alludes to the humble biological origin of human beings, as well as to their consciousness and intellect.[35] This is an unequivocal declaration by the Qur'ān of the basic spiritual nature and boundless potentialities of a human personality. It also signifies all the judicious combinations of natural inclinations or created tendencies. Human beings who care to reflect seriously on their origin undoubtedly will realize that they did not exist at some initial point, nor did they have any foreknowledge about their present existence. The form of primordial existence at the dawn of creation which we are concerned with here relates to the metaphorical "question" and "answer" that took place in the spiritual realm when God asked the children of Adam, " Am I not your Sustainer?"—to which they responded, "Yea, indeed we do bear witness thereto!"[36] What the exact nature and form of this existence was is not known definitively to anybody. Yet, it nevertheless establishes the rudimentary, original, spiritual nature of the human personality. Beyond any shadow of doubt, this also establishes, among humans, the ability to perceive the existence of the Supreme Power as inborn and inscribed, as it were, in human nature (*fiṭrah*). It is none other than this instinctive, intuitive cognition which in later life subsequently is blurred in some persons by self-indulgence, or adverse environmental influences, or alternatively, kept alive and heightened by those who are pious and God-fearing (*muttaqun*). Atheists, secularists, and materialists deny that any such "event" took place. Western psychologists of all shades and variety, deny the authenticity and veracity of any such occurrence or spiritual origin. This certainly suggests that the roots of an Islamic personality are much deeper. Its study and analysis should, likewise, start much earlier than the mainstream psychological study.

SEQUENCE II: THE DIVINE SPARK OF THE SPIRIT OR SOUL (RŪḤ)

It appears from the Qur'ānic description that the spiritual event of recognizing God as our Lord and Sustainer is preceded by the actual creation of mortal Man and after fashioning, as well as full forming him, Allah breathed into him of His spirit (*wa nafakhtu fihi min rūḥi*).[37] With this act, Allah's own omnipotent Will set the process of creation into motion and introduced the Divine spark, by which we mean the *rūḥ*, into Man which is the basis for everything that makes the human personality possible. It not only indicates that the whole process of creation is conscious and purposive, but that Man's creation is a onetime act and not prone to gradual, processual vagaries of evolution. Since the human soul is invisible, it is subjective and part of the realm of inner nature; therefore, a direct understanding of its nature is not available. As a result of this, human beings have a dual nature comprised of body and soul, they are both physical and spiritual.

Little knowledge has been communicated to us by Allah regarding the soul (*rūḥ*). It is characterized as the "command" or "affair" (*amr*) of Allah.[38] Knowledge about the soul is undoubtedly scanty, but plenty of material is available about the command (*amr*) of Allah. It is also true that several interpretations have been given of the soul. These meanings of the concept of the soul are relevant for our model. Without the soul, human beings not only would not be endowed with life, but they would not be assigned the role of vicegerency in the universe. Thus, the soul endows human beings with a special capacity that belongs to the transcendental realm. It is a special source for cognition, consciousness, acquiring knowledge, intuition, powers of reasoning and rationality. It is the indestructible (except by Allah) essence of human beings connected with both the worlds of dominion (*al-Malakut*) and command (*al-Amr*).[39] In sum, the soul is basically everything needed to have a human personality. Without understanding its intricate nature and complex role in the functioning of our individuality and personhood, an understanding of an Islamic personality will remain unachievable.

SEQUENCE III: THE ORIGINAL BLUEPRINT (FIṬRAH) AS THE BASIC CONSTITUENT OF HUMAN NATURE

Thus far, what has been discussed follows a sequence, in the sense that primordial life is followed by fully grown existence with a soul or spirit in us connecting the human with the Divine. It is not being suggested that human nature is a corollary of sequences I and II, but rather that it is related to them. One cannot imagine human nature without a soul, just as one cannot imagine a human being without it. However, what can be said which is more than reasonable is that Human nature (*fiṭrah*) is crucial to understanding human behavior as well as personality. It has already been alluded to earlier that human nature (*fiṭrah*) is inherently spiritual.

As noted in a previous section, the soul is either regarded as dead and unrecognized, or modern persons are still searching for their souls. It rarely figures in the modern Western psychological explanations of human nature. Not only this, but an understanding of human nature is one of the most controversial issues in Western social sciences.[40] False erroneous, deterministic, and reified premises and assumptions about human nature predominate. As a result of this, it has led to poor concepts, theories, and explanations. A clear testimony to this fact is that progress in Western psychology appears uneven and fitful. Sanford,[41] has warned that the research of personality psychologists at any point may not accurately reflect the true nature of the main ideas in the field. Sechrest[42] is another reviewer who has noted that the field of personality psychology is especially prone to conceptual and methodological fads.

While there is no dearth of criticism of Western personality psychology and its diverse substantive areas, understanding human nature seems to be an indispensable intellectual task. This point highlights the meaning and centrality of human nature and its relationship to modern social science. Another interesting development which has changed the mainstream psychological landscape is the emergence of Islamic psychology.[43] At present, this perspective on psychology, with its uneven and erratic growth pattern, has been endeavoring to crystallize its scope and substantive areas of inquiry. At the same time, it has brought to the fore an authentic and vibrant formulation of the Islamic concept of human nature (*fiṭrah*) which is contributing to a much better comprehensive understanding of the concept.[44] Some of the concepts and assumptions that have emerged as part of this evaluation and assessment along with their relevance to our model are presented here. Secular concepts have proved to be an utter failure in providing explanations for Islamic personalities. Human nature, for our purposes, is defined as those natural, innate, inclinations or tendencies which are unchangeable and present at birth in all human beings. The key feature is its preexisting and unchangeable character. Perhaps most important among these inclinations or tendencies is its inclination towards the right action and the willingness to submit to Allah. This is why human nature in Islam is not regarded as merely being the superficial manifestation of outward human behavior. On the contrary, Islam recognizes its inner reality, at the core of which is the spirit or soul (*rūḥ*), along with the heart (*qalb*), which is a cognitive instrument of the self (*nafs*), which in turn refers to the very principle of life and consciousness. According to al-Ghazālī's elaboration of ethics, acts are evaluated by their consequences—an act is good if it produces, in the soul, such an effect as would produce happiness, directly or indirectly.[45] In this way, a human being's outward behavior is inextricably linked with the inward state.

Finally, human nature in Islam is integral to the *tawhidic* worldview. This fact has wider ramifications in terms of human *fiṭrah* – and thereby human behavior. These include epistemological, metaphysical, ethical, moral, legal, psychological, and social.[46] These implications set the tone and tenor of the likely outcomes of human behavior. The only snag is that human nature has a base and sordid element not in consonance with the exalted position human beings have been assigned to occupy by Allah. In any case, our basic contention is that if we are to understand Islamic personality, knowledge of *fiṭrah* is indispensable.

SEQUENCE IV: ISLAMIC SELF-AWARENESS, CONSCIOUSNESS AND SELF-CONCEPTION

Precisely at what particular age a human being acquires a self-concept is difficult to say, however, it is true that all persons have a sense of who they are. This relationship of self-conception is all pervasive: self-worth, self-esteem, self-recognition, self-introspection, self-determination, etc. are all a manifestation of what has been called "the cosmology of the self."[47] To try to know oneself is really like the beginning of the journey to arrive at the inner landscape of the human self.

Allah says in the Qur'ān that he does not change the condition of a people unless they change what is within themselves. This applies to each individual and society. For every serious seeker of Allah, the way to this transcendent knowledge has been made contingent upon self-knowledge. This is indicated by the Prophet (SAW): Whoever knows himself knows his Lord." It is significant that the Qur'ān, while clarifying the inner psychic nature of human beings, uses three major concepts like soul (*rūḥ*), self or selfhood (*nafs*) and the heart (*qalb*). These Qur'ānic concepts make sense only if they are analyzed and interpreted in the context of the Qur'ān. While emphasizing the locus point or the reservoir of knowledge in human beings, Islam teaches that this locus is a spiritual substance, and it is variously described in the Qur'ān as "heart" (*qalb*), or "soul" (*nafs*), or "intellect" (*'aql*), or spirit (*rūḥ*). The Qur'ān describes the three most well-known forms that the *nafs* takes. The first is the "commanding self" (*al-nafs al-ammārah*). This *nafs* is completely wayward, out of touch with its *fiṭrah*, totally selfish, most egotistical, and as the Qur'ān states, "commands to evil."[48] The second is called the "blaming self" (*al-nafs al-lawwāmmah*). It generally gives rise to the pricking of the conscience and blame for bad behavior. As a result, it apportions blame for being extreme and maybe spurred into positive action to do something about its dismal condition. The third is referred to as the "contented self" (*al-nafs al-mutma'innah*). This is the self-brought under control. The goal of the personality which is striving to achieve nearness to Allah is to progress from *al-nafs al-ammarah* to *al-nafs al-mu−tma'innah*.

What is really needed to unravel the mysteries of the self is to analyze the fundamental elements and insights into the make-up of the individual selves and how the various elements of spirituality and humanity interact in us. Furthermore, even though the self is constituted of a unified substance, it is made up of three basic systems in terms of psychology: the affective, the behavioral, and the cognitive. It has multiple functions in relation to God, nature, as well as between other selves. Its role is so critical in our model that one cannot have an Islamic personality without an Islamic self. Thus, a radical self-transformation, if you will, is an integral part of healthy personality development and fundamental to the integration of the soul with the Islamic personality.

The self is intimately related to consciousness. Consciousness makes us what we are. It is everything that we see, say, feel, think, or do. Our life would be meaningless without it. Countless opinions and controversies abound regarding consciousness.[49] Consciousness has been envisioned in many ways: as mind, brain, gray matter, as awareness, as intentionality and meaning, and as the unity that synthesizes nominal and phenomenal realms. The fact that consciousness cannot be reduced by modern science to merely measurable interactions of matter and energy, unlike so many other natural phenomena, makes it the riddle of our time.[50]

The notion of consciousness which is used as a basis in the formulation of our model is spiritual and not materialistic. It is concerned with the higher life of human beings, the realms of meaning and values. This consciousness is the manifestation of the presence of the soul within human beings. It is intimately connected to Allah and imbued with a kind of "God- consciousness." The Islamic personality thrives on spiritual activities. It is imbued with a sense of responsibility and fully aware of the higher spiritual dimensions of human life. Such a personality is dedicated to the cause of Allah through frequent remembrance of Him.

SEQUENCE V: THE CONUNDRUM OF NATURE VERSUS NURTURE, HEREDITY VERSUS ENVIRONMENT, AND THE PATTERN OF SOCIALIZATION AND ACCULTURATION

This is perhaps the longest surviving controversy in the Western social sciences. It is also variously referred to as the genotype versus phenotype debate, or the heredity versus environment debate. The crux of the matter centers around a simple question: "Why are we the way we are?" However, the nature of the arguments offered, and the positions taken have not been so simple. The scientific, the rigid, and the dogmatic are all mixed up in the positions taken by supporters and detractors. Anyone familiar with the present writings on mind and behavior is familiar with the popular middle ground—that both genes and environment contribute to the eventual outcome of human behavior and personality. In other words, environment such as the things that children experience while growing is just as important as their genes. Even when a certain behavior is inheritable, an individual is still a product of development, and thus this behavior has a caused component. What is clear from the available literature in the field is that there is an extreme "nurture" position and an extreme "nature" position, with the truth—I contend—lying somewhere in between.

Yet controversies of the either/or kind are conspicuously absent among Muslim's scholarship. It is also surprising that most Muslim scholars have devoted an inordinate amount of time to human nature, except for al-Ghazālī's contribution to personality theory. He emphasized the spiritual nature and goodness of human beings and at the same time assigned an important role to environment in preserving or spoiling the purity of soul. In his view, there are consequences for human behavior in the soul. Islam has taken great care in emphasizing social interaction and *mu'amalat.* Hence, Muslim scholars have not undermined social influences but have largely taken them for granted. This is the main reason why Islamic socialization and acculturation is still the most important means for the transmission of Islamic norms and values. The present crisis in many a Muslim land is cultural and civilizational mainly because of the impact and predominance of Western culture in its various manifestations.[51]

CONCLUSION

In the preceding pages, a preliminary outline of a sequential model of an Islamic personality was presented. It is far from comprehensive and will need further refinement in future. It is preliminary because all the pieces of the puzzle are not there, and someone can easily add new sequences or further refine those already suggested. These sequences are broad and general, and it is possible to break them down further into innumerable variables. Without a doubt, in the primordial stage, there is the first concrete proof of some form of existence in that all souls acknowledged Allah as their Lord, and then the second sequence is in the act and process of creation. It is hinted at in the revelation of the plan by Allah to the angels that He is going to appoint a vicegerent on Earth, and it is only then that the actual act of creation takes place. They are created out of "sounding clay, out of dark slime transmuted."[52] After this, an act of great significance took place when Allah breathed into human beings his own spirit. Judging from the sequence of the revelation of the Qur'ānic verses, this is definitely a later event, and in reality, no lapse of time is required for Allah's creation because "when he wills a thing to be, He but says to it 'Be' and it becomes (it is)." These two events without doubt have established the first two sequences.

Now, the presence of Allah's spirit in us can be interpreted in any number of ways as an act, as a sequence of events, as a process, as an endowment of life and consciousness, as an ability to name things and to classify and organize knowledge. In other words, this event is the harbinger of all human possibilities potentialities. Within it are also encompassed the human soul—the blueprint of innate human nature (*fiṭrah*). The reason all these events are presented in my article in some detail is to bring out our main theoretical difficulty of not being able to separate these acts into discrete activities. How does one separate the spirit or soul from innate human nature? Perhaps, for analytical purposes it may be better to call it a dimension or a continuum. In any case, it can also be taken as critical elements which constitute basic material for an Islamic personality.

Such an attempt at model building is essential if we want to better understand our problems that are rooted in our personalities. Most of our knowledge base and intellectual legacy is either in the form of low-level conceptualization or it is analytical and descriptive. Model building is also low-level theorizing, but it is relatively more rigorous and organized. If we want to develop scientific explanations and theories of Islamic personality, we must make a beginning by changing all of the descriptive material into refined concepts, models, typologies, and paradigms. For instance, we can develop typologies of Islamically committed and uncommitted personalities. The Qur'ān is full of such material which can be presented in the form of heuristic devices for a better understanding of ourselves and societies. This article is one such attempt.

NOTES

1. See also an earlier version of our paper on a similar topic, Jamil Farooqui and Saiyad Fareed Ahmad, "The Islamic Personality: Definition, Dimension, Psycho-Spiritual Growth and Well-Being," unpublished paper presented at the International Seminar on Counseling and Psychotherapy in an Islamic Perspective, Department of Psychology, International Islamic University Malaysia, held on August 15–17, 1997, p.26. "Islam" and "Muslim" have gained wide currency in terms of usage especially during the last two and a half decades. This era is especially characterized by the spread of biased and prejudicial information by the Western media. Under the aegis of "objectivity", all kinds of half-truths and misunderstandings have been created by them to spread feelings of "Islamophobia" and Islam and Muslim bashing. Because of the erroneous understanding created by them these terms are used interchangeably. Confusion persists in its usage even among Muslims. In any case, it is our contention that these two terms connote differing and distinct senses and meanings. Islam refers to the Arabic word dīn which means a complete and total way of life and not just mere religion. It is because of this reason that Islam is not a religion in the sense of other religions. Islam is generally used for the name of religion and ideology which is based on voluntary or willful submission to Allah and Muslim is used for those who believe and adhere to this ideology and worldview. Islamic is used and preferred in this article because all Muslims are expected to transform their personalities into Islamic ones. This article is an attempt to depict this progression and transformation which eventually manifests itself into an Islamic personality. See *From Muslim to Islamic*, Proceedings of the Fourth Annual Convention of the Association of Muslim Social Scientists, vol. 1, Indianapolis: 1975, p. 70.

2. For Ibn al- 'Arabī, the foundation of all knowledge—no matter how objective or impersonal some forms of knowledge seem to be—has its grounds in self-knowledge. See Peter Coates, *Ibn Arabi, and Modern Thought: The History of Taking Metaphysics Seriously* (Oxford: ANQA Publishing, 2002), 4.

3. Even though both the disciplines are differently defined, each is defined

in terms of a discrete, central analytic focus or problem. The general distinction made between the two is that sociology studies the social and group level variables and psychology concentrates on the individual level of human behavior. The purpose of sociology is to discover the basic structure of society. It studies society scientifically, looking for order, relations, patterns, and structure in social life. Thus, a sociologist examines social relationships, groups, organizations, social structures, and whole societies. Studying society involves investigating all social phenomena that emerge through social interaction. The sociological perspective means that sociology concentrates on what happens to aggregate rather than to a single individual. Psychology, on the other hand, is defined as the scientific study of the behavior of organisms or human behavior. The primary intent here is not to discuss definitional issues but to bring out the difference in approaches of study and to indicate the existence of two schools of thought or perspectives. For a classic example of the former see a pioneer anthology of essays revealing what anthropologists, biologists, psychiatrists, and sociologists have discovered about the formation and social development of personality. See Clyde Kluckhohn and Henry A. Murray, (Eds.). *Personality in Nature, Society and Culture* (New York: Alfred A. Knopf, 1950), 561; Alex Inkles, "Personality and Social Structure," in Robert Merton, Robert K. Broon, Leonard and Cottrell, *Sociology Today: Problems and Prospects* (New York: Harper and Row, 1959), 249-276; John J. Hanigmann, *Culture and Personality* (New York: Harper and Row, 1954); S.S. Sargent and M.W. Smith (Eds.) *Culture and Personality* (The Viking Fund, 1949); B. Kaplan, "Personality and Social Structure" in J. Gittler (Ed.), *Review of Sociology* (New York: John Wiley, forthcoming); A.L. Hallowell, "Culture, Personality and Society" in A.L. Kroeber (Ed.), *Anthropology Today* (Chicago: University of Chicago Press, 1953); A.R. Lindesmith and A.L. Strauss, "A Critique of Culture-Personality Writings," *American Sociological Review* 15(1950): 587-600; R. Linton, *The Cultural Background of Personality* (Appleton-Century, 1945); T.W. Adorno, Else Frenkel-Brunswik, D.J. Levinson, and R.N Sanford, *The Authoritarian Personality,* (New York: Harper and Row, 1950);B. Kaplan and T. Plaut, *Personality in Communal Society* (Kansas: University of Kansas Publications, 1956); G.G. Stern, M.I. Stein and B.S. Bloom, *Method in Personality Assessment: Human Behavior in Complex Social Situations* (New York: Free Press, 1956); J. W. Whiting and I.L. Child, *Child Training and Personality: A Cross Cultural Study*, (New Haven: Yale University Press, 1955).

4.   In most Muslim societies, the issue of personality formation, growth, development and its assessment is given a short shrift. Both the process and the product in personality development is generally neglected while the personality and the social system rarely, if ever, are thought to influence each other. People generally do not play any critical role in shaping these entities but rely on its mushroom-like quality. Children are

born, grow up, go through a certain schooling process, get their degree and work. People are exposed to a sort of generalized cultural matrix and learn to become somebody. At no stage is the process considered dynamic and activist in its thrust, and that a certain kind of an individual can consciously and purposely be produced. One does not have to be at the mercy of socio-cultural forces which leads to a hodge-podge of an individual personality lacking meaning and direction. Exposure to the Western model of schooling, values and culture further plays havoc with the process of Islamic personality formation. The personality that grows out of these complex processes, therefore, is neither of the East nor that of the West. Present day youth in most of the so-called Muslim societies bear ample testimony to this fact as they are facing a very serious identity crisis.

5. For this point, see especially Robert Hogan, et. al. (Eds.) *Handbook of Personality Psychology* (San Diego: Academic Press, 1997), 987; Robert Frager and James Fadiman, *Personality and Personal Growth*, 4th ed., (New York: Addison Wesley Longman, 1998), 602; Naumana Umar, "Psyche: A Traditional Perspective," *Iqbal Review* 27 (1986): 135.

6. See for both traditional and modern treatment of *Fiṭrah*, Yasien Mohamed, *Human Nature in Islam* (Kuala Lumpur: A. S. Nordeen, 1998), 207.

7. See J. M. S. Baljon, *Religion and Thought of Shah Waliullah Dihlawi 1703-1762* (Leiden: E. J. Brill, 1986), 64; Reynold A. Nicholson, *The Idea of Personality in Ṣūfīsm* (Cambridge: Cambridge University Press, 1923), 77.

8. See for example the writings of Toshihiko Izutsu, *Creation and the Timeless Order of Things. Essays in Islamic Mystical Philosophy* (Ashland, Oregon: Whitecloud Press, 1994); *Toward A Philosophy of Zen Buddhism* (Boulder, Colorado: Prajna Press, 1982); Ṣūfīsm and Taosim: *A Comparison of Key Philosophical Concepts* (Berkeley: University of California Press, 1984), Syed Muhammad Naquib Al-Attas, Prolegomena to the Metaphysics of Islam (Kula Lumpur: ISTAC, 1995), 358; Robert Frager and James Fadiman, *Personality and Personal Growth*, 4th ed., New York: Longman, 1997), Chapters. 15, 16, and 17.

9. Since the appearance of the first edition of *Understanding the Enneagram* in 1990, a tradition of studying personality types has grown. The concept of the enneagram has ancient roots. Elements of the system, especially the symbol itself, go back to the ancient Greeks. To date, more than 75 books have appeared in English on the enneagram. The key characteristics of this approach to personality is its reliance on Ṣūfīsm as well as other traditions. It represents a remarkable approach in which several strands are synthesized to produce an understanding about personality types. See Don Riso and Russ Thudson, *Understanding the Enneagram: The Practical Guide to Personality Types*, revised edition (New York: Houghton and Mifflin, 2000), 400.

10. The word personality is roughly translated into Arabic as *shakhsiyah* and does not occur in the Qur'ān. This term is a relatively recent neologism. The common thread in numerous definitions of personality is the distinctive characteristics of individuals that make them unique from others. The word *shakhsiyah* refers to the distinctive character, identity, and lifestyle of a person. The derived term *mushakhkhisat* stands for the influence or causes of such unique personality characteristics of human beings. There are numerous studies which shed light on the concept and articulation of Islamic personality which are presented here, but they are largely segmental and elementary. See for instance Mahmoud Rashdan, "The Islamic Personality: Dimensions and Development," *Al-Ittihad* 18 (1981): 31-39; Abdullah R. Hamid, *Self-Knowledge and Spiritual Yearning* (Indianapolis: American Trust Publications, 1982), 46–71; Rasheed Hamid, "Reflections on a Balanced Islamic Personality" in *From Muslim to Islamic*, Proceedings of the Fourth Annual Convention of the Association of Muslim Social Scientists (Indianapolis: 1975), 51; Zafar Afaq Ansari (Ed.), *The Qur'ānic Concepts of Human Psyche*," (Islamabad: International Institute of Islamic Thought and Institute of Islamic Culture, 1992); Muhammad Malik Ata, *Ap ki shakhsiyat aur uska Irtiqa* [Urdu: Your Personality and its Development] (New Delhi: Markazi Maktaba-i-Islami, 1988); Shaikh Alee Hasan Alee Abdul Hameed, *Forty Hadeeth on the Islamic Personality* (Birmingham, UK: Al-Hidayah Publishing and Distribution, 1995); Abbas Husein Ali, "The Nature of Human Disposition: Al-Ghazali's Contribution to an Islamic Concept of Personality," *Intellectual Discourse* 3 (1995): 51–64; Manzurl Haq, "In Quest of a Meaningful Model of Human Self and Behavior," *Intellectual Discourse* 2 (1994): 1–18; Shaykh Fadlalla Haeri, *Cosmology of the Self* (South Africa [city not given]: Hidden Treasure Press in association with Zahra Press, 1997); Malik Badri, Contemplation: *An Islamic Psych-spiritual Study* (Kuala Lumpur: Madeena Books, 2000). See also the whole issue of *The American Journal of Islamic Social Sciences* 15 (1998) which was devoted to psychology.

11. For a definition and detailed discussion of an Islamic personality paradigm see Laleh Bakhtiyar, *God's Will be Done: Traditional Psychoethics and Personality Paradigm* (Chicago: Kazi Publications, 1993), 160.

12. "There is a growing awareness among many modern psychologists that the will to meaning is a highly distinctive feature of man, distinguishing him from the animals. Accordingly, for a behavioral model of man to be truly representative it must include the drive for meaning as a significant dimension of human personality. See Manzurul Haq, "In Quest of a Meaningful Model of Human Self and Behavior," *Intellectual Discourse* 2 (1994): 1–18 and Abbas Husein Ali, "The Nature of Human Disposition: Al-Ghazali's Contribution to an Islamic Concept of Personality," *Intellectual Discourse* 3 (1995): 51–65

13. On this point see A.J. Halepota, *Philosophy of Shah Wali Allah* (Lahore:

Sind Sagar Academy), 25-32.

14. "Answering the question of what it means to be human lies at the heart of modern psychology. Many things depend on the way this question is answered; prominent among which are issues pertaining to the study of personality, meaning of life and purpose of creation," Abbas Husein Ali, "The Nature of Human Disposition: Al-Ghazali's Contribution to an Islamic Concept of Personality," *Intellectual Discourse* 3 (1995): 51–65.

15. Most of the recent and not so recent texts published in psychology and anthropology allege that humanity has descended from apes. These ideas are further reinforced by the Darwinian theory of evolution. These claims ignore the truth of the Divine origination of human revealed in authentic religious scriptures. For instance, see W.C. Shefler, Biology: Principles and Issues (Reading, MA: Addison Wesley, 1976), 15, and J.S. Wiggins, K.E. Renner, G.L. Clore and R.J. Rose, *Principles of Personality* (Reading, MA: Addison Wesley, 1976), 15–16.

16. Questions about the spiritual reality of the soul figure ever so faintly in the minds of modern scientists and today's technocratic individuals. The idea of the special creation of human beings by a supernatural power is outside the realm of science because the validity of its propositions and facts cannot be verified. The scientist, on the other hand, must seek a rational explanation that will be consistent with what is known about natural forces and with recognized scientific principles. See especially William Barrett, *Death of the Soul: From Descartes to the Computer* (New York: Anchor-Doubleday, 1987), 173.

17. Yasien Mohamed, *Human Nature in Islam,* 13.

18. Muhammad Quṭb, "The Islamic Basis of Development" in *Islam and Development* (Plainfield: Association of Muslim Social Scientists, 1977), 2. Also for this point see Abdul-Fattah R. Hamid, *Self-Knowledge and Spiritual Yearning* (Indianapolis: American Trust Publications, n.d.),

19. The point that I am trying to clarify is suggested in a *Ḥadīth*: "If you hear of a mountain having moved from its place believe it, but if you hear of a person's natural disposition having changed, do not believe it—for indeed they will return to that for which they have a natural propensity." This proves that an Islamic personality is made up of both changeable and non-changeable parts which form the universal, essential core and is commonly referred to as human nature.

20. See Talcott Parsons and Edward Shils (Eds.), *Toward a General Theory of Action: Theoretical Foundations for the Social Sciences*, part 2, chapter 2, "Personality as a System of Action," New York: Harper and Row, 1951, p. 110.

21. Muhammad Saud, *The Scientific Method of Ibn al-Haytham* (New Delhi Adam Publishers, 1995),

22. Fazlur Rahman, *Islamic Methodology in History* (New Delhi: Adam Publishers, 1994); Mohammad Mumtaz Ali, *Conceptual and Methodological Issues in Islamic Research: A Few Milestones* (Kuala

Lumpur: Dewan Bahasa, 1995); Mohammad Muqim (ed.), *Research Methodology in Islamic Perspective* (New Delhi: Institute of Objective Studies, 1994).

23. Shahid Sayyid Muhammad Bāqir al-Sadr, *al-Shakhsiyyat al-Islāmiyyah*, Translated by Dr P. Heseltine in *Nuradeen* 3 (1983): 21–29; Shaykh Abdul Qādir al-Jailāni, "Men of Allah," Translated by Shaykh Fattah, *Nuradeen* 3 (1983): 30–31.

24. Syed Muhammad Naquib Al-Attas, *Prolegomena to the Metaphysics of Islam* (Kuala Lumpur: ISTAC, 1995), ix.

25. Manzurl Huq, "In Quest of a Meaningful Model of the Human Self," *Intellectual Discourse* 2 (1994): 1–18.

26. See A. Maslow, *Toward a Psychology of Being* (New York: Van Nostrand, 1953); Edith Weiskopf-Joelson, "Meaning as an Integration Factor" in C. Bucher and F. Massarik (eds.), *The Course of Human Life* (New York: Springer, 1968).

27. See Joseph Fabry, *The Pursuit of Meaning* (Boston: Beacon Press, 1968); Archibald Macleish, "The Promise of Meaning," *American Scholar* (1972): 357; Viktor Frankl, *Man's Search for Meaning: An Introduction to Logotherapy* (New York: Simon and Schuster, 1969).

28. See Herbert Blumer, *Symbolic Interactionism: Perspective and Methods* (Berkeley: University of California Press, 1969); Sheldon Stryker, *Symbolic Interactionism: A Social Structural Version* (California: The Benjamin Cummings Publishing Company, 1980).

29. Some modest beginnings have been made in the form of Qur'ānic concepts and information. For instance, see: Muhammad 'Uthmān Najāti and 'Abd al-Halim Mahmud al-Sayyid, (Eds.), *'Ilm al-nafs fi al-turath al-Islami* (Cairo: IIIT, 1417/1996); Muhammad Quṭb, *Dirasat fi al-nafs al-insaniyah* (Kuwait: Minsitry of Islamic Affairs and Endowments, n. d.).

30. According to Iqbal, "Knowledge is sense perception elaborated by understanding." He goes on to add that "the character of man's knowledge is conceptual, it is with the weapon of this conceptual knowledge that man approaches the observable aspects of reality," see his *The Reconstruction of Religious Thought in Islam* (Lahore: Sh. Muhammad Ashraf, 1977), 12–13.

31. J. M. S. Baljon, *Religion and Thought of Shah Wali Allah Dihlawi* 1703–1782 (Leiden: E. J. Brill, 1986), PAGE; Muhammad al-Ghazali, *The Sociopolitical Thought of Shah Wali Allah* (Islamabad: International Institute of Islamic Though and Islamic Research Institute, 2001), PAGE; Fazlur Rahman, *The Philosophy of Mulla Ṣadrā* (Albany: State University of New York Press, 1975), 4–6.

32. Hussain Muzzaffar, "The Key point in Iqbal's Educational Philosophy" in *Selections from the Iqbal Review* (Lahore: Iqbal Academy of Pakistan, 1995), 371.

33. There is no better treatment of the Islamic concept of individuality than that of Allamah Iqbal. His concept of "ego" or individuality is at the center

of his philosophy and the rest of his thought rests on this. To him, *khudi* (literally "self-hood" or "individuality") is a real and pre-eminently significant entity which is the center of and basis of the entire organization of human life. See K. G. Saiyidain, *Iqbal's Educational Philosophy* (Lahore: Shaikh Muhammad Ashraf, 1992), 6–43, chaps. 1 and 2.

34. Qur'ān 32:9.

35. Qur'ān 96:1, 23:12–14.

36. Qur'ān 7:172.

37. Qur'ān 15:28–29.

38. Qur'ān 17:85. See also the Urdu treatise of Nasir al-Din Nasir Hunzai, *Rūḥ kya hay? Saw sawal awr jawab* [What is the *Rūḥ*? One hundred questions and answers] (Karachi: Khana-e Hikmat, 1987).

39. For a minimal level understanding of the concept of soul one must study the works of Sadr al-Dīn al-Shrārāzī, known as Mulla Ṣadrā. For a useful survey refer to Fazlur Rahman, *The Philosophy of Mulla Ṣadrā* (Albany: State University of New York Press, 1975), part iii, chap. 1, cf. Syed Muhammad Naquib al-Attas, *The Nature of Man and the Psychology of the Human Soul* (Kuala Lumpur: ISTAC, 1993).

40. Concerning issues involved in the debate on human nature, see, for instance, Alfred Adler, *Understanding Human Nature* (Connecticut: Fawcett Publications, 1954); Steven Pinker, *The Blank Slate: The Modern Denial of Human Nature* (London: Penguin, 2002); Edward O. Wilson, *On Human Nature* (Cambridge, MA: Harvard University Press, 1978); L. L. Betzig, *Human Nature: A Critical Reader* (New York: Oxford University Press, 1997); C. N. Degler, *In Search of Human Nature: The Decline and Revival of Darwinism in American Social Thought* (New York: Oxford University Press, 1991) and Brian Goodwin, *How the Leopard Changed its Spots: The Evolution of Complexity* (London: Phoenix Paperbacks, 1994)

41. R. N. Sanford, "Personality: Its Place in Psychology" in S. Kich (ed.), *Psychology: A Study of a Science* (New York: McGraw-Hill, 1963), vol. 5, 488–592.

42. L. Sechrest, "Personality," *Annual Review of Psychology* 27: 1–27.

43. Abdul Hamid al-Hashimi, "On Islamizing the Discipline" in I. R. al-Faruqi and A. O. Naseef, *Social and Natural Sciences*. Islamic Educational Series (London and Jeddah: Hodder and Stoughton/King Abdul Aziz University Press, 1981).

44. See Yasien Mohamed, *Human Nature in Islam* (Kuala Lumpur: A. S. Noordeen, 1998); Muhiuddin Haeri Shirazi, *Man's Dual Inclinations: An Islamic Approach* (Tehran: International Publishing, 1997).

45. Muhammad Abul Quasem, *The Ethics of al-Ghazali: A Composite Ethics in Islam* (Selangor: University Kebangsan Malysia, 1976), 230.

46. For a detailed discussion of the various implications of human nature or *fiṭrah*, see Yasien Mohamed, *Human Nature in Islam* (Kuala Lumpur: A. S. Noordeen, 1998).

47. Shaykh Fadlallah Haeri, *Cosmology of the Self* (Gatesville: International Book Service, 1997).

48. Qur'ān 12:53

49. For a detailed discussion of the concept of consciousness, see Ralph D Ellis and Natika Newton (eds.), *The Cauldron of Consciousness: Motivation, Affect and Self Organization—An Anthology* (Amsterdam/Philadelphia: John Benjamins Publishing, 2000); Ronald S. Valle and Rolf von Eckartsberg (eds.), *The Metaphors of Consciousness* (New York: Plenum Press, 1981).

50. Jeffery Foss, *Science and the Riddle of Consciousness: A Solution* (Boston: Kluwer Academic Publishers, 2000) and Daniel C. Dennett, *Consciousness Explained* (London: Penguin Books, 1991). Dennett outlines an alternative view of consciousness drawn partly from computers and neuroscience.

51. Abbas Husein Ali, "Al-Ghazali's Contribution to Personality Theory," *Intellectual Discourse* 3 (1995).